Imperialism and Internationalism in the Discipline of International Relations

Edited By
David Long and Brian C. Schmidt

State University of New York Press

Published by

State University of New York Press, Albany

© 2005 State University of New York
All rights reserved

Printed in the United States of America

For information, address State University of New York Press,
90 State Street, Suite 700, Albany, NY 12207

Production by Michael Haggett
Marketing by Susan M. Petrie

Library of Congress Cataloging-in-Publication Data

Imperialism and internationalism in the discipline of
international relations / edited by David Long and
Brian C. Schmidt.
    p. cm. — (SUNY series in global politics)
    Includes bibliographical references and index.
    ISBN 0-7914-6323-0 (hardcover : alk. paper)
    1. Internationalism. 2. Imperialism—Philosophy.
3. International relations—History—20th century.
I. Long, David, 1962– II. Schmidt, Brian C., 1966– III. Series.

JZ1308.I46   2005
325'.32—dc22   2004029289

10 9 8 7 6 5 4 3 2 1

This book is dedicated to our children,
Amanda and Sara & Katy and Chris,
who keep us focused on the future
even as we delve into the past.

Contents

Preface   ix

Introduction   1
David Long and Brian C. Schmidt

Chapter 1   Francis Lieber, Imperialism, and Internationalism   23
             David Clinton

Chapter 2   Paul S. Reinsch and the Study of Imperialism and
             Internationalism   43
             Brian C. Schmidt

Chapter 3   Paternalism and the Internationalization of
             Imperialism: J. A. Hobson on the International
             Government of the "Lower Races"   71
             David Long

Chapter 4   "A Liberal in a Muddle": Alfred Zimmern on
             Nationality, Internationality, and Commonwealth   93
             Jeanne Morefield

Chapter 5   Fabian Paternalism and Radical Dissent: Leonard
             Woolf's Theory of Economic Imperialism   117
             Peter Wilson

Chapter 6   Internationalism and the Promise of Science   141
             Jan-Stefan Fritz

Chapter 7   Birth of a Discipline   159
             Robert Vitalis

References   183

Contributors   203

SUNY Series in Global Politics   205

Index   209

Preface

This book reflects our common scholarly interest in the disciplinary history of International Relations (IR). As a result of the work that we have previously completed on the history of the field, we both share the sense that IR as an academic enterprise seriously undervalues the study of its own history. At one level, this is not surprising given the construction of the discipline as a social science wherein disciplinary history becomes little more than a catalogue of past errors and omissions. There is certainly an abundant literature that chronicles the history of the field with the explicit aim of either noting particular failures or advancing one agenda or another. Yet we believe that many of these accounts fail to reconstruct the actual disciplinary history of International Relations. The aim of this volume is to reconstruct in detail some of the formative episodes of the early disciplinary history of the field. Within much of the so-called historical literature, there often appears to be more emphasis placed on the present contours of the field than on recovering its institutional history. Perhaps this is one of the reasons why the same set of assumptions about how the field has developed are repeated over and over again.

As a result of the recent upsurge of interest in the history of IR, we are learning that many of the commonly held assumptions about the development of the field are actually incorrect. A number of articles and books have been written that collectively challenge the conventional wisdom regarding the history of the field. This volume is a contribution to what we consider to be a growing and increasingly sophisticated scholarly conversation not only about the origins of IR but the character of theory and theoretical development. Concomitant with the latest interest in various dimensions of the field's past has been a growing sophistication in the manner in which international relations scholars have approached the task of writing disciplinary history. Greater attention to historiographical issues on the part of the newest cohort of disciplinary historians has helped to enrich our understanding of the history of the field. At the same time, recent work has helped to legitimate disciplinary history as an important area of research activity.

This book is most directly a product of the collective effort on the part of the authors and editors who have each played an important role in what Duncan Bell has described as the "dawn of a historiographical turn." We are particularly grateful to our contributors—David Clinton, Jan-Stefan Fritz, Jeanne Morefield, Robert Vitalis, and Peter Wilson—for the quality of their essays, their professionalism, and their dedication to this project. The book has benefited from the input of a number of other scholars working in the area of disciplinary history and we are grateful to all of you. Many of the chapters in this book were first presented at the Annual Convention of the International Studies Association held in Los Angeles, California, in March 2000. We would like to thank those who asked questions and provided comments at the panel on Imperialism and Internationalism in the Discipline of International Relations. We also thank two anonymous referees who gave us constructive commentary and important suggestions for improvements in the text.

We would like to thank the editorial staff at the State University of New York Press. Michael Rinella expressed strong interest in the project from the beginning and we thank him for his assistance and patience throughout the process of completing the book. We are very pleased that this book appears in the Global Politics series and we are grateful to James N. Rosenau, Series Editor, for his support and encouragement. We would each like to acknowledge and thank our respective families for their help and support during the time we were working on this book.

Material from David Clinton's chapter is reprinted with permission of Palgrave Macmillan.

Introduction

David Long and Brian C. Schmidt

This volume is a contribution to the growing body of literature on the disciplinary history of International Relations (IR).[1] The underlying goal of disciplinary history is to reconstruct in detail the formative episodes of IR as an academic discipline. The chapters that follow examine the work of a number of the seminal, though now largely unread, individuals on either side of the Atlantic who were responsible for helping to carve out a discrete academic field of inquiry devoted to the study of international politics. The aim of this volume is not simply to recover some aspects of the official origins of IR. Rather, it is to identify and discuss the central themes of the early conversation about international relations that were incorporated into the field when it, like many of the other social sciences, began to take an institutionalized form in the late nineteenth and early twentieth century. The critical purpose of investigating this period of disciplinary history is to challenge some of the commonly held assumptions about the early history of IR that continue to inform the present identity of the field. By rereading the work of the field's forgotten predecessors and reconstructing the key themes that emerge from this work, this book provides a revisionist account of the emergence of IR.

On the basis of our collective research, we argue that the dual themes of imperialism and internationalism were paramount when the field began to take a recognizable form at the beginning of the twentieth century. In particular, it was dynamic interaction between imperialism and internationalism and not the much discussed realist-idealist debate that initially drove international theory. In this introduction, we first consider the recent developments in the historiography of IR. Then we set out the centrality and significance of imperialism and internationalism in international politics, and specifically the place of these dual concepts in the early IR scholarship. Finally, we provide an overview of the chapters that follow, and draw some conclusions for contemporary scholarship.

In this book, we argue that the dual themes of imperialism and internationalism provide a better framework for understanding the discursive evolution of the field than does the host of alternative ones. Most importantly, imperialism and internationalism are not retrospective categories that we have invented for interpreting the history of the field in order to make some presentist claim about the current contours of IR. Rather, on the basis of our research, imperialism and internationalism were determined to be two of the constituent issues in terms of which the field of IR originally took form. This means we should once and for all dispense with the outdated, anachronistic, and ideological artifice of the debate between idealists and realists as the dominant framework for viewing and understanding the history of the field.

It is an especially appropriate time to recover the themes of imperialism and internationalism since these themes are once again prominent in the discourse and practice of international relations. In particular, the discourse of empire, regarding the global status and policies of the United States as the world's sole superpower, has regained salience in the popular conversations of the media as well as in the more critical view of the neo-Marxist literature inspired by Hardt and Negri's *Empire* (2000). Unlike the retrospective analytical categories of idealism and realism that cut off the interwar scholarship from the postwar study of international relations, the discourse about imperialism and internationalism has the potential to reconnect the development of IR theory with issues of contemporary concern and saliency. Critically and theoretically in the extension of postcolonial discourse and most recently and spectacularly in Hardt and Negri's *Empire*, empire—and thus its relationship to imperialism and internationalism—is back on the academic agenda. In a more popular vein, imperialism and internationalism are being reinvented, often uncritically, in American and other Western musings about the benefits and/or necessity for the reestablishment of empire, such as recreating trust territories or the need for an American imperial role. The discourse of empire is on the rise. We submit that it is important for those involved in this conversation not to neglect and forget the insights that an earlier generation of IR scholars had on the twin phenomena of imperialism and internationalism. Forgetting would not only contribute to the general propensity to reinvent the wheel, but possibly lead to the same embarrassing mistakes that some of our ancestors unknowingly made.

DISCIPLINARY HISTORY

There has been a notable increase in both the quantity and quality of literature on the intellectual history of the social sciences in the last decade or so (Bender and Schorske 1998; Ross 1991). After years of neglect, IR scholars have finally begun to follow this trend and are examining the intellectual history of their scholarly enterprise in a more systematic fashion (Schmidt 2002b). This is not to suggest that the field has previously been immune to disciplinary introspection. Indeed, when scholars have periodically focused on the "state of the discipline," they have unavoidably felt compelled to comment on its historical development. We intentionally say "unavoidably" because as John Dryzek and Stephen Leonard have argued, in the social sciences generally, and political science specifically, there is "an essential link between disciplinary history and the actual practice of inquiry" (1988: 1246). This means that very often both challengers and defenders of the status quo seek to write the history of the field in a manner that is necessarily linked to agendas for disciplinary identity. While such a link may have gone unnoticed in the past, the recent plethora of work on the history of political science clearly recognizes the connection between establishing the identity of the field and presenting an image of its history (Dryzek and Leonard 1988; Farr, Dryzek, and Leonard 1995; Gunnell 1991).

One possible explanation for why there has been such a paucity of literature devoted specifically to the history of IR and the root of much of the skepticism that continues to be cast on the research agenda this volume advances derives from a presumption that we already know the history. This is represented in a conventional wisdom that chronicles the history of the field as a series of phases—idealist, realist, behavioralist, neorealist, rationalist, constructivist—that are punctuated by a series of "great debates" such as that between idealists and realists, and traditionalists and scientists (Banks 1986; Katzenstein et al. 1999; Lijphart 1974; Maghroori 1982). With respect to the orthodox story of the field's so-called "great debates," Ole Waever acknowledges that "there is no other established means of telling the history of the discipline" (1998: 715). Both Steve Smith (1995) and Kjell Goldman (1996) recognize that the story of the great debates provides the most dominant self-image of the field. Yet as well as providing new insights and information regarding the disciplinary history of IR, the most recent literature has cast doubt on the conventional images of the development of the field (Kahler 1997; Oren 2000; Schmidt 1998a, 1998b, 2002b; Smith 1995; Vitalis 2000; Waever 1998; Wilson 1998).

This has especially been the case with respect to the interwar period of the field's history. While the conventional accounts of the history of IR have been fairly consistent in establishing an essential link between the interwar period on the one hand and an "idealist" or "utopian" paradigm on the other, the newest cohort of disciplinary historians have systematically challenged such an interpretation. In an earlier contribution that helped to spark an interest in the history of the field in general, and the interwar period in particular, David Long and Peter Wilson explained that the impetus for their book *Thinkers of the Twenty Years' Crisis* was the feeling "that the 'idealists' were not as naïve in their assumptions, as simplistic in their analysis, nor as uniform in their outlook, as the received wisdom suggests" (1995: vii). Long and Wilson's suspicion that the scholars of the interwar period had been grossly misrepresented has been widely confirmed by the most recent research on the disciplinary history of IR (Ashworth 1999, 2002; Baldwin 1995; Kahler 1997; Osiander 1998;

Schmidt 1998a, 1998b, 2002a; Thies 2002; Wilson 1998). Many of those who have been dubbed "idealists" turn out, upon closer inspection, to be more sophisticated, complex, and hold positions at odds with the caricatures in IR's secondary literature. By carefully reconstructing the early disciplinary history of IR as a subfield of American political science, Schmidt's influential book *The Political Discourse of Anarchy* (1998) revealed that not only does the idealist or utopian label misrepresent the nature of the conversation that was taking place after World War I, but that there was also a much greater degree of continuity between the pre- and post–World War II study of international politics than has been conventionally thought to be the case.

Schmidt's work as well as that of a number of other revisionist disciplinary historians has resulted in a serious challenge to what Miles Kahler (1997) has termed the "foundational myth of the field"; that is, the notion that a "great debate" took place in the 1930s and 1940s between the rival paradigms of idealism and realism. According to this "foundational myth," World War II represented a glaring anomaly to the interwar idealists' vision of a peaceful world order that eventually resulted in its replacement by the realist paradigm, which was superior in its ability to explain the persistent struggle for power among nations (Hollis and Smith 1990; Vasquez 1998). Kahler, however, argues that the ideas of the interwar scholars have been seriously misrepresented, and he concludes that "international relations was not marked by a clear Kuhnian paradigm shift after 1945; the field remained heterogeneous and continued to include a liberal (or at least nonrealist) corps of practitioners" (1997: 29). Peter Wilson claims that "in the sense of a series of exchanges between interlocutors holding opposing 'idealist' and 'realist' points of view, the first great debate never actually occurred" (1998: 1). Lucian Ashworth concurs with Kahler and Wilson, arguing, "although well known and often quoted as a watershed event in IR, there seems little evidence that the realist-idealist debate ever occurred at all in the form in which modern IR writers suppose" (2002: 35).

These new findings about the interwar period and the alleged great debate between "idealists" and "realists" are a source of inspiration to the work undertaken in this book. The first point to stress is that the latest discoveries about the history of the field are based on detailed historical research. For too long disciplinary history has been regarded as something akin to an intellectual hobby; as something to do after the more serious and important research is completed. This is yet another reason for the poor state of our knowledge about the history of the field. In order to understand the history of IR and to correct the erroneous assumptions that have become regarded as essential truths, detailed research, like that done in any other area of IR, is necessary. The contributors to this volume have engaged in extensive historical research and have gotten their hands dirty by reading texts, journals, memoirs, and other sources that have been standing dormant on library shelves.

The most recent historiographical literature has emphasized the point that the manner in which the history of the field is constructed matters greatly. Disciplinary history is rarely a neutral or impartial undertaking. Rather, it is often closely tied to intellectual struggles to determine and legitimate the contemporary identity of the field. This insight helps to account for why the story of interwar idealism and the first great debate continues to be so essential to the present identity of the field (Thies 2002). The field derives a good deal of its contemporary identity from the notion that steady scientific progress has been made ever since it shed its idealistic yearnings and embraced realism and science. Yet by establishing that interwar idealism and the first great debate are simply retrospectively constructed myths, new possibilities for understanding the identity of the field become available.

A critical history of IR is also a method for recovering numerous theoretical insights and ideas that have been forgotten in the institutional memory of the IR community. The tendency to "reinvent the wheel" time and time again and to proclaim something new that is actually deeply embedded in the discursive history of the field is a consequence of the less than adequate understanding that most students have of the disciplinary history of IR. When the prevailing framework for interpreting the history of IR is informed by the erroneous view that a great transformation took place in the 1930s that resulted in realism eclipsing idealism, many of the ideas and issues that were of great concern to the scholars discussed in this book are either unfairly discredited or assumed to belong to the dustbin of history. Ashworth, for example, remarks that "the construction of a realist-idealist debate is important because it justifies the marginalization of liberal internationalism" (2002: 34). Not only has liberal internationalism been marginalized, but so have other antecedent conversations; most importantly, the discourse on imperialism. By investigating various elements of the field's history that preceded World War II, conversations about topics such as internationalism, pluralism, public international unions (regimes), security, race, international cooperation, functionalism, interdependence, and a host of others have recently been discovered (Baldwin 1995; Wilde 1991; Kahler 1997; Little 1996; Long 1991; Murphy 1994; Navari 1989; Osiander 1998; Schmidt 1998a, 1998b, 2002a; Vitalis 2000; Wilson 1998).

The primary justification for this volume of essays on the early history of IR is simply that we do not know this period very well. This is evident, for example, by lingering controversies over the extent to which there is a well-defined field or discipline of IR that has a distinct identity (Olson and Onuf 1985; Palmer 1980; Wright 1955); the degree to which the field is an exclusively American invention and characterized by American parochialism (Crawford and Jarvis 2001; Hoffmann 1977; Smith 2000); and even about the exact date when the field or discipline can be said to have formally come into existence. The underlying explanation for why these types of controversies continue to persist is that very little research has been done on the actual institutional history of the field. This, in turn, helps to account for the fact that almost everyone believes that the field did not come into existence until at least 1919. The standard story of the birth of the field, often associated with the founding of the world's first Chair for the study of international politics, in 1919 at the Department of International Politics at the University College of Wales, Aberystwyth, is characteristically described in terms of a reaction to the horror of World War I. This was the view E. H. Carr put forward in his influential work *The Twenty Years' Crisis, 1919–1939* ([1939] 1964). As Carr explained, the science of international politics "took its rise from a great and disastrous war; and the overwhelming purpose which dominated and inspired the pioneers of the new science was to obviate a recurrence of this disease of the international body politic" (1964: 8). This widely accepted account of the field's origins has been repeated so many times in countless textbooks and "state of the field" articles that a clear link exists in most people's minds between World War I and the genesis of the field or discipline of IR.

The basic problem with the story that Carr helped to popularize is that it is not entirely accurate. In fact, like the pervasive notion that a prevailing idealist paradigm dominated the interwar study of international politics, it is simply a myth that a full-blown field or discipline of IR came into existence in 1919 and that nothing of the kind had previously existed. Carr, however, was not engaging in the task of writing a history of the field, and difficulties are created when his work is mistaken as an actual historical description of the development of IR.[2] As the considerations of the work of Lieber, Hobson, DuBois, Reinsch, and the others in this volume demonstrate, systematic international relations scholarship predates World War I, even if institutionally separate Departments or Chairs of International Relations or Politics such as were founded at the London School of Economics, Aberystwyth, and Oxford did not. Furthermore, as Robert Vitalis explains in his chapter, the field's first journal—*Journal of Race Development*—began publication in 1910.

THE HISTORIOGRAPHY OF IR

One of the most significant problems in work on the history of IR is that these histories have failed to address adequately the question of how one should write a history of the field. Much of the existing literature fails to display sufficient theoretical and methodological sophistication in approaching the task of providing an adequate account of the disciplinary history of IR (Schmidt 2002b; Waever 1998). The tendency has been to chronicle the history of IR as if a complete consensus existed on the essential dimensions of the field's evolution. In the absence of any significant controversy concerning how the field has developed, there has been little or no attention devoted to historiographical issues. Ole Waever, after reviewing the literature on the history of IR, concurs with our general assessment. He finds that the literature is "usually not based on systematic research or clear methods" and that it amounts to little more than "elegant restatements of 'common knowledge' of our past, implicitly assuming that any good practitioner can tell the history of the discipline." Waever concludes that the field as a whole suffers, because "without looking systematically at the past, we tend to reproduce myths such as the nature of the idealists in the (alleged) first debate" (1998: 692). Duncan Bell (2001) has added his voice to those who have become dissatisfied with the historiography of IR. Bell argues that mainstream IR has disregarded the essential point that "history, in its various manifestations, plays an essential, constitutive, role in shaping the present" (2001: 116). This has resulted, he argues, in "the same old story being unproblematically rehearsed and repeated." The problem, Bell claims, is that "the common understanding of the discipline's history and the actual evidence appear to be in stark contrast" (2001: 120). This is a point that all of the contributors to this volume fully endorse.

Fortunately, the most recent work on the history of the field is much more self-conscious about the theoretical and methodological issues that are involved in approaching the task of providing an adequate account of the history of IR. There is a growing recognition that the manner in which the history of the field is reconstructed is almost as significant as the substantive account itself. Bell (2001) suggests that the latest work on the history of IR denotes what he terms the "dawn of a historiographical turn." According to Bell, "[T]he study of the history of political thought, as well as the intellectual history of the discipline, is now taken far more seriously, studied more carefully and explicitly, and plays a greater role in shaping the theoretical debate, than in the past" (2001: 123). He does point out, however, that these trends so far appear to be more pronounced in Europe than in the United States.[3]

Gerard Holden (2002) endorses the view that IR is experiencing a "historiographical turn" and, following Kjell Goldmann (1995), characterizes the type of work undertaken in this book as representing a discrete subfield. According to Goldmann, it is a subfield that "reflects on the history, geography, identity, and self-legitimation of the discipline itself" (Holden 2002: 253). While there are grounds for questioning whether we have reached the point where we can establish that the historiography of IR is a full-fledged subfield, Holden is, nevertheless, absolutely correct when he states that there are "some reassuringly 'real' theoretical issues at stake in disciplinary history, not least of which are the questions of how, and to what ends, it should be pursued" (2002: 254). And to reiterate one of our main points, these "real theoretical issues" have generally not been addressed in the literature that examines the history of IR. Waever remarks, "[T]hat the way the discipline usually reflects on its own development falls embarrassingly behind standards developed in sociology of science and historiography" (1998: 689). Exactly what standard or approach should be used to examine the history of the field is certainly a contentious matter, but the important point is for those doing work in this area to begin to address these types of issues. In this volume, no one single method of writing history has been imposed on the contributors. We have simply requested that each of the authors be self-conscious about historiography and to address the issue of how they are doing disciplinary history. We believe that such an effort will likely result in a more adequate understanding of the history of the field.

The approach and focus of this book is a challenge to the general and widely held assumption that the history of the field can be explained by reference to a continuous tradition that reaches back to the writings of Thucydides and extends forward to the present (Schmidt 1994, 1998b). IR scholars have, for a variety of reasons, been more inclined to identify the progenitors of the modern field with the writings of classic political thinkers such as Thucydides, Machiavelli, and Kant, than with scholars such as Francis Lieber, Paul S. Reinsch, Alfred Zimmern, and the others discussed in this book, who, for the most part, understood themselves to be affiliated with an institutionalized field of academic inquiry. There is a widespread conviction that classical political thinkers and the traditions they supposedly embody are an integral part of the field's past and, therefore, are relevant for understanding the contemporary identity of the field. One could argue that this conviction has become institutionalized in many of the leading undergraduate texts. John Gunnell (1991) has suggested that one explanation for this deeply embedded assumption stems from the widespread tendency to write the history of the field with the intention of conferring legitimacy on a contemporary research program. Disciplinary histories of the field are replete with references to the idea that there are epic traditions of international thought that are relevant for understanding the contemporary identity of the field (Bartelson 1996; Dunne 1993; Schmidt 1994). These histories that attempt to explain the development of the field by postulating the existence of a "historical" tradition transmitted from the ancient past to the present are legitimating mechanisms that are often employed to validate present claims to knowledge. While we do not wish to convey the impression that the field is devoid of any authentic traditions, or want to suggest that scholars should not study the classic texts of international relations theory, we do, however, want to insist that the widespread practice of treating an analytically constructed tradition as an actual historical tradition has inhibited our ability to understand the disciplinary history of IR.

Although discussions of a tradition of IR are widespread and, as Rob Walker (1993) has noted, far from monolithic, they tend to refer less to actual historical traditions, that is, self-constituted patterns of conventional practice through which ideas are conveyed within a recognizably established discursive framework, than to an analytical retrospective construction that largely is defined by present criteria and concerns. IR specialists have generally shown less interest in the actual tradition of academic inquiry that they are a part of than in the myriad of retrospectively created traditions that animate the discourse in the field. Worse yet, these retrospectively constructed traditions are presented as if they represented a self-constituted tradition in the field, and serious problems in understanding the history of IR result when the former is mistaken for, or presented as, the latter. Perhaps the greatest difficulty is that such epic renditions of the past divert attention from the actual academic practices and individuals who have contributed to the development and current identity of the field. Many scholars appear to have a better knowledge of alleged "founding fathers" such as Thucydides or Machiavelli, than of the work by a host of individuals who directly contributed to the creation of an institutionalized academic field of international politics. Our intention in this book is to direct attention toward those scholars who can legitimately be placed in an actual historical tradition of academic inquiry that continues to the present day. This is, after all, the most relevant tradition for tracing the development of the field.

IMPERIALISM AND INTERNATIONALISM IN INTERNATIONAL RELATIONS

As we have noted, imperialism and internationalism served as two of the pervasive themes during the early history of the field. When IR first began to assume a recognizable identity at the beginning of the twentieth century, nationalism, imperialism, colonization, and various manifestations of internationalism were all observable practices taking place in that realm of activity that was increasingly demarcated as international relations. In an important, though largely overlooked, contribution to the disciplinary history of IR, William C. Olson and A. J. R. Groom suggest "that a discipline of international relations had its real beginnings in studies of imperialism, not in world order, as has so often been suggested" (1991: 47). Most of the chapters in this book support Olson and Groom's claim that imperialism represented an endogenous dimension of the early-twentieth-century disciplinary history of IR. We develop this thesis further and argue that imperialism and internationalism, not idealism and realism, were the dominant themes when IR first began to take on the characteristics of a professional field of inquiry.

The book develops two arguments, one empirical and historical, and the second conceptual and theoretical. First, empirically, the pairing of imperialism and internationalism provides a more authentic understanding of the early history of IR than the realism/idealism dichotomy. We recognize that any such pairing of "isms" is open to attack as a misrepresentation or overgeneralization of what was actually occurring in international relations thinking at the time. Clearly, even if there were grand themes during this period, there were also many different currents in international relations theory, many of which were contradictory. Nevertheless, implicitly or explicitly these themes were front and center for many IR scholars of the time. Imperialism and internationalism oriented much of the interwar discussions of international relations. In short, imperialism and internationalism are the key concepts for reconstructing the discipline of IR during the early decades of the twentieth century, as we see in the chapters on individual authors that follow.

Second, we argue that the concepts of imperialism and internationalism were more deeply embedded in the early discourse of the field than post–World War II accounts have commonly recognized. The general understanding of the relationship of imperialism and internationalism and of both to international politics has been cast in a specific way conditioned by the growth of the IR discipline. Current IR scholarship sees imperialism and internationalism as either unconnected and marginal concepts or as conceptual opposites that constitute the upper and lower limits of relations of states in the international system. By contrast, many of the authors considered in this volume viewed the concepts as intimately connected and as central to international politics, even for those who did view them as antinomies. This volume, then, is a direct challenge to the current "presentist" interpretation (Schmidt 1998b) of the relationship of internationalism and imperialism as conceptual opposites in IR.

The chapters in this volume present evidence for the empirical argument. We take on the second argument more explicitly in this introduction. First of all, we must consider the argument that internationalism and imperialism are either unconnected or are conceptual opposites. In this view, imperialism denotes a hierarchical, often coercive, relationship that is the antithesis of the political independence of states that marks the fundamental basis for international politics. Internationalism, by contrast, marks equality and harmonious cooperation among nations that go far beyond the estrangement of the traditional diplomacy and power politics of interstate relations. Considered in this way, imperialism and internationalism are not merely opposites but can be seen as the upper and lower discursive limits of the practices of sovereign states traditionally understood to constitute the focus for the IR discipline, within which one finds the theoretical scope of the schools of realism, various forms of institutionalism, and the early authors of the English School.

As the conceptual outer limits circumscribing international relations, the terms imperialism and internationalism have progressively disappeared from mainstream IR discourse in the later decades of the twentieth century. While imperialism and internationalism were subjects for discussion by such IR luminaries as Carr, Morgenthau, and Waltz, they became increasingly marginalized and dropped from IR textbooks. What accounts for the disappearance of imperialism and internationalism in IR? Certainly, the end of the era of formal empire in the course of the process of decolonization and the success of national self-determination movements shifted the discourse of imperialism. On the one hand, then, the anti-imperialists seemed to have won. On the other, neo-Marxist critiques of the capitalist world system, studies of neo-imperialism, and more recently postcolonialism, suggested that imperialism had not ended with the end of empire but rather had simply been transformed or simply transposed. Neo-Marxist and other critical analysts proliferated a bewildering range of terms to reflect the changed character of imperialism. While the term *imperialism* went out of fashion in academic IR, so did the theorizing on imperialism. Most Marxist and critical analyses of imperialism and its subsequent incarnations have thus been conducted outside the disciplinary boundaries of IR.[4]

In the same period, the cold war context was hardly fertile ground for internationalism. The nuclear-tipped standoff between the United States and the USSR prevented the operation of the internationalist aspects of the United Nations and paralyzed the Security Council. More generally, internationalist causes were buffeted by the competition of the rival universalist ideologies and the attempts by each side to co-opt internationalist rhetoric and proposals. At the same time, both the United States and USSR identified themselves as anti-imperialist powers while accusing the other of being imperialist. If internationalism suffered from cynicism about its prospects, imperialism was an overused piece of rhetorical hyperbole. Given the international context, it is hardly surprising that cold war international relations theory barely mentions either imperialism or internationalism by name except in a historical reference.

While the international context meant that the terms *imperialism* and *internationalism* were consigned to the dustbin of IR theory, this was little more than a terminological disappearing trick. The discipline of IR relied upon the concepts because the world was not simply the interaction of functionally similar sovereign states, as cold war vintage realism suggested. Though both imperialism and internationalism suffered rhetorical setbacks in political and academic discourse, the concepts themselves and the limits they expressed, could not simply be omitted. With the terms out of fashion, a constellation of pseudonyms and related concepts emerged to replace them. Thus, while reference to imperialism declined, structuralism and structural violence, neocolonialism, dependency, or hegemony rose to prominence in IR scholarship.[5] While internationalism lay largely dormant, international regimes, global governance, world order/society/economy, cosmopolitanism, and lately globalization in their different ways proposed alternatives to the traditional conception of IR as nothing more than interstate relations.

Thus, imperialism and internationalism are enduring themes at the marginalized borders of IR. They are concepts that cannot simply be excised from IR discourse. Their theoretical significance is instantiated by the constant appearance in contemporary issues, conversations, and debates about international politics, such as on humanitarian intervention and the role of the United States in global politics (Ignatieff 2002; Mallaby 2002). And imperialism and empire are both back on the post–cold war agenda, specifically in the form of calls for the reinvention of United Nations Trusteeships for failed states, as well as in mainstream international relations journals such as the *Review of International Studies* (2001).[6] The idea of a U.S. empire is back in vogue and being openly contemplated in scholarly and popular publications. In the academic context, the ethics of internationalism has also been given a new lease on life in Andrew Linklater's exposition on global dialogic communities as well as the many works by David Held and Daniele Archibugi. Linklater's *Transformation of Political Community* (1998) is a bold renovation of internationalist thought that attempts to embrace difference in order to get past the homogenizing tendencies of cosmopolitanism and the exclusionary models of political community associated with the Westphalian state.

Despite their continued relevance, there has been little sustained analysis or theoretical advances on the relationship of imperialism and international-ism. Fortunately, this now seems to be changing. Part of this has to do with changes in world politics. Internationalism was briefly revived during the "neo-idealist moment" after the end of the cold war (Kegley 1993) only for imperi-alism to raise its ugly head once more in the shape of postimperial ethnic conflict and even genocide. At the same time, the postcolonial studies that have followed Said's pioneering analysis of *Orientalism* are beginning to make their way onto the agenda of IR. More significantly, work inspired by Hardt and Negri's *Empire* (2000) add to postcolonialism's rereading of imperialism and colonialism in IR. For Hardt and Negri, empire is a nonterritorial system of hegemonic, hierarchical rule that at once encompasses and surpasses both imperialism and internationalism, both of which they take to be founded on the sovereign territorial state to some extent. The concept of empire articulated by Hardt and Negri is deliberately a modernized version of that associated with the Holy Roman Empire. As such, this modernized classical view of empire as a synthesis of imperialism and internationalism is one that would be familiar to a number of the authors discussed in this volume, such as Zimmern, Hobson, and Woolf. The current reworking of the meaning of empire adds another chapter to the story of imperialism as a term of political discourse, so ably told by Richard Koebner. Koebner and others have shown how our contemporary understanding of the meaning of imperialism and empire owe a lot to the meanings ascribed to them by the early generation of IR scholars considered in this volume (Koebner and Schmidt 1961).

These developments suggest that a reconsideration of imperialism and internationalism in international politics is required. Combining postcolonial sensibilities with a deep reading of the history of political thought, Uday Singh Mehta (2000) and Barry Hindess (2001) delve into and challenge liberal understandings of empire. They both point out that, far from being an anom-aly for liberalism, empire was central to the interests of liberal political thinkers and integral to the liberal intellectual project. In this volume, Jeanne Morefield (chapter 4) provides a compelling case that this was particularly true with respect to Alfred Zimmern, just as it was for J. A. Hobson, as demonstrated by David Long (chapter 3).

Neither Mehta nor Hindess considers liberal international thought in the twentieth century, however, or for that matter deals in any serious way with internationalist thought more generally. They are concerned with the rule of, and impacts on, subject populations themselves rather than with the wider implications for thinking about international order. We believe that it is important for IR to engage imperialism and internationalism directly and critically, and this book is one attempt to bridge the gap between critical studies of postcolonialism and the disciplinary history of IR. Reading imperialism and internationalism through the prism of empire, as presented, among others, by Hardt and Negri, Mehta, and Hindess, suggests that an internationalism of order and peace may be premised on an imperialism of hierarchy, violence, and suppression. What is missing are insights from IR, yet current scholarship in the field has, as we have seen, until very recently ignored imperialism and internationalism. Failure to build this bridge is tantamount to an abdication of responsibility and a resignation of self-marginalization for IR not unlike that criticised by Craig Murphy (1996) with regard to the relationship of IR to issues of gender. The attention paid to imperialism and internationalism in the interwar period is therefore not only of historical interest but the starting point for a reconstruction of a critical view of international politics and can be the basis for a critique of the contemporary revived discourse of empire.

By specifying, challenging, and presenting an alternative to the assumptions of this implicit framework we intend to both recover some of the forgotten figures and discourse of the field, and to reconstruct the emergence of IR as a scholarly discipline. Simply considering the logical relation of the two concepts we have just outlined suggests a complex theoretical history. And the theoretical history of imperialism and internationalism is telling not only for the historical emergence of the discipline of IR but for our contemporary understanding of international politics. In the last section of the introduction, we briefly comment on the contemporary implications of this analysis. Looking to the period up to the middle of the twentieth century, when the formal empires of the European great powers still existed and the League of Nations, though in dire difficulty, had yet to be utterly compromised, imperialism and internationalism were the major preoccupation of IR scholarship across the ideological, theoretical, and disciplinary spectrum.

Indeed, prior to the twentieth century, the history of peace proposals is littered with internationalist schemes that are little more than dressed up apologias for extending or dividing up imperial rule by the great powers (Hinsley 1963). Given this context, it is not surprising that the first few decades of the institutionalized study of international politics should reinforce the association of imperialism and internationalism within IR. In addition, the first years of the twentieth century see simultaneously the apotheosis and catastrophic consequences of imperial rivalry as well as the emergence of IR as an academic field both within and beyond departments of political science. In this new field, very often imperialism was a driving force of the relations of states and particularly the great powers, and internationalism was commonly a proposed solution for the overt conflict that was so prevalent as a result (see the chapters on Reinsch, Lieber, and Zimmern that follow).

Imperialism and internationalism are at the very foundation, then, both conceptually and historically, of the discipline of IR. Many of the early texts reflect a common preoccupation with imperialism and the administration of empire. Among the most important examples are Parker T. Moon, *Imperialism and World Politics* (1926), J. A. Hobson, *Imperialism: A Study* (1902), and Leonard Woolf, *Empire and Commerce in Africa* (1919). Yet as the chapters in this book make apparent, there also are a number of equally important yet forgotten authors who identified with the emerging field of IR and contributed to the discourse about imperialism and empire. Some of the prominent examples that are discussed in the chapters that follow include Paul S. Reinsch, *World Politics* (1900), W. E. B. DuBois, "The African Roots of War" (1915), Raymond Leslie Buell, *International Relations* (1925), and Alfred Zimmern, *Nationality and Government* (1918). Moreover, during the period from 1904 when the American Political Science Association (APSA) was formed to the outbreak of World War I, the study of colonial administration occupied a large portion of the discourse within the field of IR (see the chapter on Reinsch and Robert Vitalis's chapter dealing with race). And a further measure of the interest in imperial and colonial matters can be found in the reports from the Geneva Institute of International Affairs and the focus of discussions at the International Studies conferences held during the 1930s under the auspices of the International Institute for Intellectual Cooperation (the forerunner of UNESCO). The formal agenda of these conferences concerned classically internationalist topics such as collective security and peaceful change. But the substance of discussion was more often about demographic change and the allocation of colonial dependencies—a war of words among the so-called have and have-not great powers shortly to descend into the violence of World War II.

Today, internationalist concerns are often associated with or related to interwar "idealism." This does a great disservice to the internationalist writing of the period and conceals discussions of imperialism altogether. To begin with, the period was much more diverse than the idealist label suggests (Long and Wilson 1995; Wilson 1998; Thies 2002). There was a good deal of ideological tension in internationalist proposals, and the approach taken was more likely to be institutionalist or materialist analysis than wishful thinking prescription, the prejudice regarding this writing today. As Fritz shows in his chapter, more recent IR scholarship on international regimes and epistemic communities highlights the importance of science and technology in international cooperation in ways that parallel the concerns of interwar theorists. Current IR literature draws on many of the same notions as so-called idealist authors with the lineage from the early decades of the twentieth century through international functionalism to work on interdependence and regimes.

More pertinently, the anti-imperialist writing of the period is all but ignored in the characterization of 1919–1939 as dominated by the idealist-realist debate (Ashworth 1999). And yet, realist and idealist arguments that are drawn from this time are often arguments about imperialism. Key figures in the early development of IR, such as Leonard Woolf, Parker Moon, Paul Reinsch, J. A. Hobson, Alfred Zimmern, and Raymond Leslie Buell, invariably wrote as much about imperial/colonial concerns as they did about the now traditional IR topics such as the balance of power and diplomacy.

OVERVIEW OF THE BOOK

In each of the chapters that follow, the authors recognize that it is necessary to establish and define the relevant context of their particular object of historical investigation while acknowledging the complex interplay of the social, political, and economic milieu with more specific disciplinary and departmental contexts. Some give greater weight to institutional factors while others emphasize how developments in the day-to-day practice of international politics impacted the discourse of IR.

In this book, we consider a series of authors who, for the most part, were writing in the decades before World War II. Each of the contributors, whether focusing on a specific individual or a particular theme, addresses questions regarding how the disciplinary boundaries of IR were determined. They attempt to clarify episodes of the gradual process by which the field became demarcated and institutionalized as an academic enterprise. The question of the extent to which a specific scholar was self-conscious about being a member of, or affiliated with, an institutionalized field of IR is also addressed. By remaining flexible about the composition and definition of the field or discipline of IR, and by questioning the conventional wisdom regarding its origins, we believe that a number of interesting themes and issues quickly rise to the surface. While the chapters do not adopt a single approach to writing disciplinary history, each addresses imperialism and internationalism as either themes in the work of individual subjects or as a subtext to broader issues in IR. The first five chapters are devoted to considerations of individual authors and their writings on imperialism and internationalism. These themes arise in a number of ways but most particularly in critiques of formal empire, proposals for imperial reform, and prescriptions for colonial administration.

In the opening chapter, David Clinton reaches deep into the disciplinary history of IR and focuses on the work of Francis Lieber (1798–1872), who was one of the pioneering figures that laid the foundation for the eventual formation of the discipline of political science. Lieber, Clinton explains, did not turn his attention directly toward the study of international politics, specifically international law and organization, until relatively late in his career. Yet when he did, Clinton finds that imperialism and internationalism occupied Lieber's thoughts about international politics. In this regard, Clinton argues that although Lieber was writing well before we can discern the boundaries of a discrete subfield of IR, he should nevertheless be viewed as a precursor of the IR specialists discussed in this volume.

As with many of the early American political scientists, Lieber's ideas about international politics were largely a function of his particular organic theory of the state. Clinton devotes attention to explicating Lieber's organic theory of the national state and in the process considers his views on race and its relation to the meaning of nationhood. He then goes on to reveal how these views profoundly influenced Lieber's thoughts about both imperialism and internationalism. With respect to imperial expansion, for example, Lieber did not object to territorial adjustments that resulted in the creation of authentic national states. He was, however, sharply opposed to territorial aggrandizement that threatened the existence of legitimate national states or that over-extended the boundaries of the properly demarcated national state. A world of independent national polities, Lieber argued, ultimately led to a form of internationalism that represented the negation of imperialism. In this manner, Clinton demonstrates the way in which rather than being conceptual opposites, Lieber regarded internationalism as the culmination of a vibrant nationalism. Lieber's internationalism, Clinton explains, was one that sought to preserve the autonomy of distinct national states and that was adamantly opposed to any form of hierarchical or supranational control from above that would restrict the sovereignty of the state.

In chapter 2, Brian Schmidt finds that imperialism and internationalism were paramount in the work of Paul S. Reinsch, a prominent political scientist at the University of Wisconsin and a founding member of the APSA. Reinsch's first book, *World Politics at the End of the Nineteenth Century* (1900), was devoted chiefly to an analysis of the phenomenon of national imperialism that he viewed as the fundamental factor shaping international politics at the dawn of the twentieth century. Unlike the older form of nationalism that Reinsch believed had contributed to a healthful vitality in the relations among states, the transition to national imperialism threatened the very existence of the states system. In the age of imperialism, Reinsch argued that the use of force and the ability to impose one's will on other peoples had become the conspicuous feature of international politics.

Schmidt reveals that the study of colonial government and administration within political science comprised a sizable portion of the early discourse about international politics. He carefully reconstructs the contours of this conversation and documents Reinsch's specific contribution to the task of creating a science of colonial administration. Before Reinsch left the University of Wisconsin to accept the position of minister to China in the Wilson administration, he began to detect change in the landscape of international politics pointing in the direction of a robust internationalism. The best evidence of this, for Reinsch, was the existence of numerous public international unions that were being formed by states. Schmidt argues that Reinsch's *Public International Unions Their Work and Organization* (1911) was a seminal contribution to the early literature on international organization, even though it has largely gone unnoticed by contemporary students. Schmidt's chapter leaves little doubt that Reinsch was an important figure in the early development of IR and that his work was located at the intersection of the study of imperialism and internationalism.

David Long argues in chapter 3 that J. A. Hobson's famous anti-imperialism is tempered by a paternalistic attitude. Hobson's proposal for an international arrangement to supersede colonial possessions has been described as a precursor to the League of Nations system of mandated territories. Engaging in a close reading of a number of Hobson's writings on imperialism, especially the later chapters in the classic, *Imperialism: A Study*, Long concludes that Hobson does not manage to rid himself of imperialist assumptions and as a result, his reformist proposal for the international government of subject peoples is little more than an internationalized version of imperialism.

Long emphasises the moral and political aspects of Hobson's critique over the more notorious economic theory with which his name is usually associated. Despite the critique of imperialism, Hobson does not advocate the end of imperialism but rather its transformation. Hobson's qualified defence of imperialism is mounted on certain conditions, that imperial control must contribute to global order and security, that it must make for improvement in the living conditions and standards of the subject people, and that the determination of these first two conditions is to be made by an international body rather than the imperialist nation itself. This third condition is the basis for Hobson's argument for an international government to oversee imperialism. However, these arguments for an international government are tempered in several ways and remain in any case generalities. Long scrutinizes Hobson's paternalist terminology and assumptions in which the peoples of the developing world are seen as "lower races" for whom the analogy to a child could be applied. Hobson's assumptions regarding "lower races" color his proposals, driving a reformist agenda that arguably would legitimize exactly the sort of internationalized imperialism that Hobson elsewhere condemns.

In chapter 4, Jeanne Morefield investigates the relationship between nationalism and internationalism. She explores this relationship by focusing on the work of Sir Alfred Zimmern (1879–1970), the first Woodrow Wilson Chair of International Politics at the University of Wales, Aberystwyth, whom Hans Morgenthau once described as the most influential representative of the field during the interwar period. Morefield argues that Zimmern's approach to

nationalism and internationalism was framed by his liberalism, a liberalism
that was both explicitly communitarian and, ultimately, paternalistic in its politics. To understand this approach, Morefield begins her chapter by reconstructing the liberal intellectual context when Zimmern was a student at
Oxford in the late 1800s. She explains that many liberal thinkers at Oxford
were searching for a more intimate and authentic sense of community to overcome the excessive individualism that they associated with orthodox liberalism.
Like other liberals, Zimmern was profoundly influenced by the ideas associated with German idealism, especially the spiritual and organic notion of
society found in the writings of Hegel.

Morefield goes on to reveal how Zimmern's particular version of liberalism
strongly influenced his own attempt to achieve a synthesis between the dual
forces of nationalism and internationalism. Like many other liberal thinkers, she
finds that Zimmern's ideas about international politics were a logical extension of
his views of domestic society. According to Zimmern, the fundamental problem
of international politics was similar to the problem faced by individuals in
domestic society; namely, finding a way to overcome the narrow pursuit of self-
interest so that a more authentic community that embraced the collective good
could be realized. This did not entail the dissolution of national states—
Zimmern was sharply opposed to cosmopolitanism on the grounds that every
individual needed their own national home—but instead required a degree of
spiritual harmonization among all of them. Internationalism was a natural outgrowth of the spiritual development that took place among the individuals living
inside particular "national families." As to the question of what to do about those
living in dependent territories, Zimmern endorsed a paternalistic type of politics
grounded in a conservative approach to empire. In expounding Zimmern's views
regarding the composition of his proposed international commonwealth, Morefield points to some of the glaring inconsistencies and problems that flow out of
his peculiar brand of imperial liberalism. And yet, despite the theoretical and practical shortcomings, Morefield concludes that certain aspects of Zimmern's
thinking remain relevant to contemporary IR scholars who are seeking a solution to nationalist violence by moving away from the sovereign state model, but
who nevertheless continue to value distinct national cultures.

In chapter 5, Peter Wilson considers Leonard Woolf's theory of economic
imperialism and his place in IR scholarship. Woolf was a significant figure in
IR for much of the twentieth century. Along with Hobson and others, Woolf
was integral to creating the climate of opinion that undermined the legitimacy
of imperialism and colonialism. Wilson outlines Woolf's theory and dissects
it in terms of theoretical and methodological consistency. He also provides an
insight into the contemporary reception of Woolf's arguments by examining
reviews of his books. Wilson concludes that Woolf is best portrayed as a radical dissenter and Fabian paternalist in his critical attacks on empire.

Woolf has gone down in IR historiography as an idealist, but this label distorts more than it reveals. Woolf's writings on imperialism, while they may be open to criticism on various counts, are not especially marked by their idealism. Certainly Woolf had ideals, but he recognized the need to be realistic in pursuit of them. Thus, a careful study of Woolf's thought on imperialism adds another nail in the coffin of the idealist-realist dichotomy, a dichotomy that has had a baleful influence on IR as a serious social science. The dichotomy implies that to have ideals is impractical. Wilson shows that this putative idealist certainly did not ignore facts and "reality" when it came to that most important of twentieth-century questions: imperialism.

The last two chapters shift the focus from specific individual authors to themes that relate closely to imperialism or internationalism or both, that is, the internationalist perspective on the implications of science, and the imperialist dimensions of the missing race factor in IR.

In chapter 6, Jan-Stefan Fritz analyzes the role a scientific analogy played in shaping thinking about cooperative internationalism in international relations. The chapter considers a cross-section of writers who contributed to the study of internationalism during the first half of the twentieth century. At that time there was a surge of interest in ways of making IR more about cooperation than of competition, conflict, and conquest. The question facing these early-twentieth-century writers was how best to make cooperation work systematically and durably. Fritz argues that science was their answer as it provided an alternative basis for internationalism from the imperialist and state interest–driven international relations of the nineteenth century. In particular, scientific knowledge was seen as an invaluable means toward better understanding and tackling increasingly important economic and social concerns.

Fritz compares the work of Paul Reinsch, John Hobson, Leonard Woolf, and David Mitrany, who were among the most influential in the development of IR, and especially in the study and practice of cooperative internationalism. A comparative analysis shows that despite conflicting views over what cooperation and internationalism meant, these and many other writers looked to the sciences as a basis for their analysis of the trends in international politics. Fritz argues that the study of cooperative internationalism as reflected in international institutions was shaped from its beginnings by the expectation that scientific knowledge and technological innovation held out the promise of both deeper and broader cooperation. Assumptions about the link of science and international cooperation seminally influenced and/or are rehearsed in later theories, including neo-functionalist regional integration theory, as well as various approaches to complex interdependence theory, regime theory, and the study of global governance. This chapter systematically assesses what promises were expected from the sciences and how these influenced the study of IR, and in particular the study of cooperative internationalism.

Robert Vitalis's chapter, "Birth of a Discipline," provides additional support to the claim that imperialism and empire were central themes when the field was initially launched in the early 1900s. The main thrust of his chapter is on the role that race, racism, and white supremacy had and continues to have on the evolution of IR discourse. Utilizing critical methods borrowed from African American studies, Vitalis asks, What strategies and anodyne versions of history have had to be employed in order to make race invisible to mainstream international relations theory? He provides a wealth of answers to this provocative question.

In order to recover and reconstruct the discourse about race, Vitalis argues that two things are necessary; first, we have to clearly establish the origins of the field, and second, we have to identify properly the context in which IR emerges as a professional field of inquiry. Vitalis concurs with our view that the field's origins predate the conventional post–World War I account of IR's birth and he focuses on key developments that were taking place between 1900 and 1910. With respect to context, he argues that the context that really mattered to the individuals and institutions that comprised the field in formation was empire. According to Vitalis, it is the context of empire that helps to account for the fact that the most important pioneers in the field, such as Paul Reinsch, Raymond Leslie Buell, Parker T. Moon, W. E. B. DuBois, and others that he discusses in his chapter, were teaching and writing about nationalism and imperialism, and articulating strategies for administering colonial territories and uplifting "backward" races. Vitalis also focuses on the institutional and university context in which IR developed in the United States. Strengthening his thesis about the prominence of race, he finds, for example, that the field's first academic journal was not *Foreign Affairs*, as is commonly thought, but rather the *Journal of Race Development*, which began publication in 1910.

CONCLUSION

One of our aims in this book is to make a case for the relevance of disciplinary history for contemporary international relations theory. Instead of considering the history of the field as little more than a proving ground for contemporary categories of thought, we should read more closely and devote more attention to the historical context in which an author was writing rather than simply replaying his or her presumed place in contemporary IR. Important insights into the historical development of IR but also about our present condition can be drawn from disciplinary history. Disciplinary historians agree that there is an intimate link between the present-day identity of the field and the manner by which a field chronicles and understands its older identities. In the case of IR, we argue that many of the field's older identities have, for a variety of factors, been misrepresented. We believe that the revisionist project that the authors in this volume are engaged in does have important implications for the contemporary study of international politics.

In this introduction we have attempted to indicate that the simple logical relation of the two concepts of imperialism and internationalism as the upper and lower limits of international politics, marking selfish aggressiveness on the one hand and an altruistic morality on the other, hides a different and a more complex and subtle relationship of the concepts. This more subtle relationship is evidenced in the analysis of a number of the authors and themes that follow. We have also argued that the salience of imperialism and internationalism in the early disciplinary history of IR is more than a coincidence or a simple historical curio. Imperialism and internationalism are fundamental to our understanding of the early development of the field and a vital component of understanding the present conjuncture in international relations theory. First of all, this is because attention to imperialism, and the reliance of internationalism on imperialism, focuses our view on the continuing importance of unequal relationships and structures in international affairs. Relationships of inequality cannot be swept under the carpet by claims of legal or sovereign equality, or by asserting the natural and unchanging quality of the uneven distribution of power in the international system. In short, internationalism and imperialism are not simply limits to real international relations, but rather are integral to our understanding of international society.

NOTES

1.   Throughout this book the abbreviation IR refers to the institutionalized academic field or discipline of international relations.

2.   There recently has been an E. H. Carr revival of sorts that has shed considerable light on his professional career. See, for example, Cox (2000, 2001), Haslam (1999), and Jones (1998).

3.   On this point also see Brown (2000).

4.   See, for example, Darby and Paolini (1997) on the call for a reconciliation of IR and postcolonialism. For examples of the voluminous neo-Marxist literature, see Magdoff (1969) and Amin (1977).

5.   For example, see Gilpin (1981), Galtung (1971), and Gill (1990).

6.   Indeed, there has been a general increase in the use of the terminology of imperialism in popular discourse in the last several years. See for instance the critical view presented by Maria Misra (2002) that decries the tendency to neglect the ruthlessly repressive aspects of empire in the rush to see the potential benefits for international order in the face of failed states.

Chapter 1

Francis Lieber, Imperialism, and Internationalism

David Clinton

Francis Lieber (born Franz Lieber in Prussia in 1798) was a naturalized American citizen who found time in a life of nearly three-quarters of a century to develop fluency in French, Italian, Spanish, Latin, and ancient Greek, as well as German and English; to risk his life at the Battle of Ligny just prior to Waterloo; to participate in the Greek Revolution against Turkish control; to meet and court his future wife during a year spent teaching in London; to strike up friendships with everyone from Tocqueville to Napoleon's elder brother Joseph; and to teach history and political economy at South Carolina College (now the University of South Carolina) from 1835 to 1856, history and political science at Columbia College (now Columbia University) from 1857 to 1865, and constitutional history and public law at the Columbia School of Law from 1865 to 1872—all of which subjects he infused with elements of what today would be termed comparative politics and international relations. In his own life, then, he displayed a concern for international affairs that would make his views on international politics interesting even if, at a fairly advanced age, he had not turned his talents to international law and organization. To his long-standing advocacy of free trade, he added a comprehensive attention to the law of war, drafting a code governing the actions of the Union Army in the American Civil War in 1863, and continuing to publish on international topics for the remaining nine years of his life.[1]

Lieber died a full generation before the turn from the nineteenth to the twentieth century. Yet he can be viewed as a precursor of many of the later analysts treated in this volume, given his importance in the development of the new American discipline of political science (Gunnell 1993: 24–25; Farr 1995: 131–67; Schmidt 1998: 47–52). His works were still commonly employed in college classrooms three decades after his death, and it has been asserted to the author that at least one of them (*Civil Liberty and Self-Government*) remained a required reading in the graduate seminar on American political thought at one major university into the nineteen fifties—an admirable run for a book published in 1853.[2] As for his reputation among policymakers, one may find a suggestion, at any rate, in an account of the formal reception of Lieber's manuscripts by the Johns Hopkins University Library on March 18, 1884, an event presided over by a garlanded bust of Lieber and attended by Lieber's only surviving son. There, "Mr. Woodrow Wilson, A.B., … reported upon the manuscripts relating to the Mexican Claims Commission of 1868, in which Dr. Lieber acted as umpire." Wilson praised "the clear, concise, and altogether admirable decisions of the umpire," who "went with few words direct to the core of each case, clearing the way with rapid argument and reaching his conclusion with unhesitating judgment"—surely a rare example of Lieber's being commended for brevity (Gilman 1884: 13–14, 20–21).

It is the argument of this chapter that Lieber, despite his renown, balanced imperialism and internationalism in a manner different from that arrived at by many of those who wrote on these subjects a generation later. He was in fact a critic of imperialism, in large measure because he was an ardent nationalist and believed that imperial control inevitably came into conflict with the self-government that national states required. By contrast, he held that nationalism and internationalism not only were not in tension, but were in large measure mutually supporting. A world of national states was a world in which international society could flourish through voluntary steps of international cooperation. Large states would "lead," but this leadership would consist primarily in advancing a set of international norms that would serve the interests of all.

It is also the intention of this essay to illuminate Lieber's place in disciplinary history. The rather vain "scholar and publicist" would be gratified by the recent revival of interest in his contribution to the study of politics in the United States (as evidenced by several of the works cited below), and particularly his role in supplanting an earlier bloodless social-contract theorizing on the institutions of government, with an interpretation grounded in the concepts of "the state" and "the nation."[3] These terms were also the building blocks in his conception of international politics, so that the Prussian American professor represented the introduction of a line of continental thought into the Anglo-American world, just as the arrival of this "Stranger in America" (to take the title of one of his early autobiographical publications) marked the beginning of an ascendancy of German models and German methods in American university life. Lieber was far from systematic in separating his academic work from his other social, poetic, and personal writings, though, and thus this chapter will draw on his letters and essays as well as his longer published scholarly output. Consistent with an internal approach to disciplinary history, these sources can be construed as representing the discursive artifacts of the field's past. The aim of the chapter is to reconstruct the contribution that Lieber made to the early academic discourse about international politics.

LIEBER AND IMPERIALISM

The first thing that must be said about Lieber's attitude toward imperialism is that he lived before its apotheosis. His death in October 1872 came only four months after Disraeli's Crystal Palace speech asking British voters to declare "whether you will be a great country,—an Imperial country—a country where your sons, when they rise, rise to paramount positions, and obtain not merely the esteem of their countrymen, but command the respect of the world" (Wiener 1972: III: 2500), and preceded by twelve years the Berlin Conference that sought to regulate the final phase of the "great scramble." To be sure, the British and other European powers had undertaken a good deal of overseas conquest by the close of the third quarter of the nineteenth century, and in the United States itself numerous proposals had been heard for the acquisition of various territories, primarily in Central America and the Caribbean. Nevertheless, when Lieber used the word "imperialism" he generally did not give it the meaning imparted by the "new imperialism" of the late nineteenth century: the large-scale acquisition of territories far from Europe or North America with the intention of ruling into the foreseeable future over their non-white populations and with little prospect of considerable emigration from the metropole and settlement by Europeans or those of European descent. Rather, Lieber's usage tended to be of the midcentury variety—"Imperialism" with a capital "I," denoting a revival of Napoleonic methods and imagery in France in place of royal or republican regimes, and, more broadly, a reliance on auto-cratic government instead of the limitations imposed by the rule of law, both within and among states. "Imperialism" in this sense was a synonym for what Lieber also called "imperatorial sovereignty," or "arbitrary power or centralism" (Lieber 1853).

Of the imperialism associated with the regime of Napoleon III, Lieber was a severe critic, as he was of the idea that strong states should dictate to weak ones in an arbitrary fashion (of which more below). Nor did he evince interest in overseas territorial expansion, and in fact he vigorously opposed many American territorial acquisitions accomplished or proposed during his life-time. His test for both internal and external policies was their effect on the prospects for, or the preservation of, a free, self-governing, national state.

What allowed a state to be free and self-governing? A close connection between rulers and ruled, and among all segments of the population, was a sig-nificant element of strength for those states fortunate enough to rest on it. Lacking such support, autocratic governments were brittle; they could find the ground of public backing cut from under them at any time, and their ability to continue their foreign or domestic initiatives—and even their capacity to remain in power—would then rest solely on the physical force they could bring to bear in imposing their will on their people. Regimes characterized by the rule of law and popular representation were stronger, not because they necessarily wielded more material power (after all, both the British and the American armies were small compared with those of the continental powers) but because once a line of policy had percolated up through the slow process of widespread discussion and accommodation, it would be supported by the entire society with the necessary resources:

> How weak and fragile are the theoretically absolute governments of the East! And where is the state more powerful than in England? Where has it greater resources, where does every individual feel himself more identified with it, or rush more readily to its assistance when in danger? ... I mean that the essential attributes of the state become more distinctly understood, affect more powerfully each individual, unite men into a more closely interlinked community, that it extends protection and receives stronger support, that vast, powerful public opinion joins it—in short, that the intensity of its action in a thousand different ways increases. (Lieber 1838: I: 163–64)

This intimate sympathy among all members of the society protected by the state gave rise to Lieber's Burkean conception of the organic state. A state, or at least a proper state, was more than a contract among self-interested individuals for their protection: "The foundation of the state lies too deeply in the human soul, in man's whole nature, to be explained simply by selfishness. It is no accidental mass of atoms, it is an organism" (Lieber 1838: I: 170).

In the circumstances of the nineteenth century, Lieber held that an organic state was necessarily a national one, and a nation by definition displayed an organic connection among its members:

> The word Nation, in the fullest adaptation of the term, means, in modern times, a numerous and homogeneous population ... permanently inhabiting and cultivating a coherent territory, with a well-defined geographic outline, and a name of its own—the inhabitants speaking their own language, having their own literature and common institutions, which distinguish them clearly from other and similar groups of people; being citizens or subjects of a unitary government, however subdivided it may be, and feeling an organic unity with one another, as well as being conscious of a common destiny. Organic intellectual and political internal unity, with proportionate strength, and a distinct and obvious demarcation from similar groups, are notable elements of the idea of a modern nation in its fullest sense. (Lieber 1840: 227–28)

A nation was a unique type of organic state, not found in the ancient world, but peculiarly suited to the requirements of the modern. In particular, one might note Lieber's attribution to a nation of "a coherent territory," by which he meant a territory more extensive than was occupied, for example, by the city-states of the Hellenic states-system. Elsewhere he spoke of "a portion of the earth with a dignified geographical character" in contradistinction to "the crowns of many little kingdoms crowded on one head ... jarring and unmeaning sovereignties, that have not the strength to be sovereign" (Lieber 1860: 96).

What could bind together those living in these extensive territories into the organic union that Lieber thought the best states would possess? One force that came naturally to the mind of Lieber, a student of philology, was a common language, leading to a shared literature. Language was necessary to "the communion of mind with mind," which could unite distinct individuals in common understanding and common purpose (Lieber 1850: 443). In turn, it was a sense of common purpose that gave otherwise disassociated individuals the collective strength and determination to undertake action in concert for political and legal ends. It was therefore useless to expect a group lacking this unified resolve to protect its legal rights or to make the sacrifices necessary to establish political freedom. Through the medium of language, in Lieber's eyes, freedom and nationalism were closely connected.

By contrast, one item that did not appear on Lieber's list of defining characteristics of nations—and a highly significant omission, given the role it came to play in the imperial project—was race. His attitudes on the tortured subject of race were not always plain, in part because he felt that discretion was necessary to his professional advancement. He taught for twenty-one years at South Carolina College, and the experience of living at the center of pro-slavery sentiment seems only to have increased his existing dislike for slavery, as evidenced by the private letters he wrote to Senator Charles Sumner and other friends in the North. In a series of "public" but unsent letters to Senator John C. Calhoun, who had been helpful to Lieber on other matters and whom he respected, Lieber compared slavery with scaffolding that had been necessary to the construction of a building but now could and should be removed, and warned that every delay in its peaceful dismantling made it more of an anachronism: "It is not the *North* that is against you. It is mankind, it is the world, it is civilization, it is history, it is reason, it is God, that is against slavery" (Friedel 1947: 241; Friedel 1943). The Liebers had three sons to rear and a certain social position as a college faculty family to keep up, however; as property, slaves could be rented, and Lieber rented a succession of household servants over his two decades in Columbia, South Carolina. After his move to the North in January 1857 when he joined the faculty of Columbia College, he made his opposition to slavery public, and in 1865, "when the news arrived early one morning in January that Congress had approved the thirteenth amendment [abolishing slavery], he was so excited that he could not shave" (Friedel 1947: 357). Yet in a letter written in 1870 to Hamilton Fish, who was at the time not only the president of the Columbia board of trustees but also secretary of state, he pressed on Fish "an idea, doubtless distasteful to most men just now, which I have had for many years," that immediately after adoption of the Fifteenth Amendment guaranteeing the voting rights of all Americans regardless of race, "the U.S. ought to pass a law prohibiting the immigration of any but white people. We would have a right to do it. As the Mongolians, with their rat-like procreation, advanced in the middle ages as far as Liegnitz in Silesia, so they come now from the West and invade our country similar to the Norway rat" (Lieber to Fish, April 15, 1870).[4] In his scholarly publications, he dismissed the idea of "the pretended Latin race," but, especially in his writings in the 1860s and 1870s, he often employed one of the many terms of his own coinage, the "Cis-Caucasian race" or the "Cis-Caucasian races"—the "white Caucasian races as developed in Europe and the Western hemisphere"— which included in the parlance of the time such groups as the Slavonic, the Celtic, the Teutonic, and the "Anglican" "races" (Lieber 1838: II: 8; Lieber 1871a: 308–309; Lieber 1872: 311, 320; Farr 1995: 147–48). Because he thought the "Cis-Caucasian race" was leading the way to international understanding, he asserted, "Internationalism is part of a white man's religion" (Sears 1928: 61).

Such references, however, did not mean that Lieber accepted notions of unalterable racial superiority. Indeed, particularly in his earlier writings, he spoke of the social problems caused by a narrow exclusivity in sympathy, resulting in a tendency to read certain groups out of full membership in the human race and deny them the right to justice. "I was walking one day in the streets of Rome, when I met with a nurse who had strung a number of chafers [beetles] on a knitting-needle in order to amuse the infant she held in her arm, by the contortions of the tortured animals," he once recalled. "When I expressed my horror, the answer was, *Ma non e roba battizata* (but it is unbaptized stuff)." Lieber strongly condemned a similar inability to sympathize with and give justice to those viewed as belonging to lesser races. "Those Spanish adventurers, cruel almost without parallel ... were vindictive, bloodthirsty, and without any faith towards the Indian. ... [because] bigotry and avarice had perverted their judgment and moral feeling," he charged. "The Indian was not considered within the pale of ethic obligation." The case was the same "with Christian merchants who smuggle opium into China, though they know it leads to the destruction of the infatuated buyers." Lieber continued, "[T]hey may, in their perverted judgment, consider the Chinese out of the pale of civilization" (Lieber 1838: I: 44–45). Nor did Lieber exempt his own country from his critique. Neatly encompassing both racialist and antiracialist sentiments in one sentence, he called the slave trade "the very worst crime of the race to which we belong" (Lieber to Allibone, December 3, 1856). Referring to the purported "belief of our Indians that [George Washington] is the only white man who ever went or ever will go to heaven," he granted that the tale was

> not very complimentary to us, but [was] unfortunately only an exaggeration of that for which there is good ground. The ancient *vae victis*

must be changed in the white man's modern history into "Woe to a different color." The white man has shown little sympathy with the other races, and sympathy is the first basis of all idea of justice. (Lieber 1864: 427)

Where all this seems to have left Lieber is a belief that "races" were defined at least as much by culture and history as by blood or physical characteristics. A race was therefore largely synonymous with a nation, not a preexisting fact that defined a nation. No race was by nature superior to any other, but one racial grouping—the "Cis-Caucasian"—had been the first to discover and put into practice the principles of modern government that advanced liberty. Over time, the beneficent influence of interdependence and advancing technology would see that these insights were shared, in the latest instance of "the rule of all spreading humanity that the full amount of what has been gained by patience, blood, or fortunate combinations is transferred to other regions and distant tribes" (Lieber 1853: 291–92; Robson 1946: 57–59).[5]

More likely, in Lieber's eyes, than race to bind together an extended nation was a common sense of nationhood. Understanding one another through the medium of a common language, identifying with one another through the experience of sustaining common institutions, citizens would naturally assume "an organic unity with one another, as well as being conscious of a common destiny" (Lieber 1868: 227). Nationalism grew from long-shared historical experience, and then both informed and was strengthened by immediate political cooperation. It could elicit from Lieber, who was also a would-be poet, passages that were almost lyrical in their praise of the benefits derived from this sense of national community:

[T]he people have tasted the sweets and securities, the mutual support and mutual elevation which modern political society, enlarged as it is, yet forming one organized and united thing throughout,—the social guarantee, which the modern state alone affords, and can afford; and because this political form—a *nationalized* society, and *socialized* population—stands on an enlarged and broad foundation, is the essential form of our times. ... and the only one which can satisfy the many high, great and noble demands, which in the course of civilisation, men have come to urge in our present period—demands never made in ancient times, or the middle ages. (Lieber 1838: II: 314)

This ardent nationalism, coupled with a conviction that the bonds of sympathy could and eventually would cross racial divides, meant that Lieber was certainly prepared to countenance territorial expansion if its object was to unite areas populated by members of one nation and create one national state. Smaller political units were outmoded, for "the *patria* of us moderns ought to consist in

a wide land covered by a nation, and not in a city or a little colony," he proclaimed. "Moderns stand in need of nations … for their literatures and law,
their industry, liberty, and patriotism; we want countries to work and speak,
write and glow for, to live and to die for" (Lieber 1858: 333–34). He was
equally dismissive of multinational states. "[T]he merely agglomerated monarchy" was as unsuited to modern liberty as the weak and provincial sliver of a
state. Austria, "a monarchy which never had any but an artificial and forced
existence, and in which true greatness or simple and national development was
made impossible by its various conglomerated elements," was a particular *bête
noire* of the Prussian American professor (Lieber to Mittermaier, June 4,
1849). "But what is Austria?" he demanded. "The term is brief, compact, and
unitary; the thing, however, termed Austria is a vast, heterogeneous conglom-
eration of numberless different tribes." Resting uneasily on this unstable mass,
the Viennese elite nevertheless had the wealth to purchase the best workman-
ship that European artistry could produce. "The sight of such an article is apt
to shed a luster on the whole idea—*Austria*—as it is in our minds; [but] she
counts nearly forty millions of people, and how many of them live in deplorable
semi-barbarism, in filth, ignorance, and low bigotry?" (Lieber to the *Times*
(London), November 10, 1851). As long as it remained something other than
a national state—and by its nature it could not do otherwise—it would be hos-
tile to liberty domestically and a hindrance to international progress—"the
drag-chain to the chariot of advancing Europe" (Lieber 1851: 125–26).

Supported by ties such as language, institutions, and a sense of national
identity, "the normal type of modern government is the National Polity,"
thought Lieber. In the conditions of contemporary life in Europe and in areas
of European settlement, the national state was the only legitimate state, and
the modern era was "the period of nationalization." The rise of nationalism
could almost be said to be divinely inspired. "The instinctive social cohesion,—
the conscious longing and revealing tendency of the people to form a nation"
was the result of "the providential decree of nationalization." "Modern patriotism" lay under the injunction of "a mission imposed by Him who willed that
there should be nations. … It is sovereign to all else. It is the will of our
Maker—the Maker of history" (Lieber 1860–61: 96–97, 98, 101, 113). All of
this may not justify the description of Lieber as "a pre-Bismarckian superna-
tionalist" (Dorfman and Tugwell 1938a: 159), but it is true that in Lieber, the
anxious proponent of German unity and the determined defender of the
American Union against secession, the nationalist currents of the nineteenth
century ran deep.

Expansion that "rounded out" a state to its full national dimensions, then,
was for Lieber unquestionably justifiable. Lieber all but asserted that the purchase
of the Louisiana Territory by the United States in 1803, for example, was
unconstitutional under then-current understandings of the national charter.
"But there are reasons and circumstances which carry along states and nations.

To be securely and truly master of the western country it was necessary for the United States to possess the mouth of the Mississippi" (Lieber 1838: I: 326). If France had declined to sell its North American possession and the United States had mounted an invasion, "a war would have been the consequence where right would have been on either side," France appealing to its legal right and the United States to necessity. "This is a dangerous theory," he admitted, "but danger is not a test of truth" (Lieber to Bluntschli, March 24, 1872). Nor was this the only expansion of American territory that could be so justified. "I ask you as a fellow internationalist," he wrote to Bluntschli in 1869, "whether the annexation of Nova Scotia, not by haggling, cheating or war, but by the manly action of the people [of Nova Scotia] and the equally manly yielding of the British Government, would not be one of the choicest acts or procedures in all history. Would it not be unique and one of the crosses on the breast of the 19th century" (Lieber to Bluntschli, October 11, 1869).

In a similar vein, Lieber strongly argued that the Prussian destiny to unify the German nation was a call of necessity that overrode the legal rights of the smaller states that Berlin would be required to absorb. In the aftermath of the lightning victory of Prussia over Austria in 1866, he criticized the North German Confederation as insufficient: "Although Prussia took possession in a revolutionary way of Hannover, she has still not been bold and resolute enough" (Lieber to Bluntschli, February 12, 1867). When Baden and the other small German states endeavored to preserve their independence, he queried, "Who can blame them? But also, who can blame the friends of Unity, for wanting a powerful and revolutionary Emperor?" (Lieber to Bluntschli, October 1, 1867), and he returned to the subject in a letter at the end of 1867, voicing his dissatisfaction that "Germany remains with 'the stocking half pulled up'" (Lieber to Bluntschli, December 8, 1867). Moreover, it was not only the duchies and city-states of Germany that stood in the way of history; it was also the despised empire to the south. Upon receiving a copy of *The Right of Conquest* from his German friend Franz von Holtzendorff, Lieber questioned the absence of "the conquest of a country if required to fulfill a distinct mission" from von Holtzendorff's list of justifiable grounds for an expansionist war. If there were no other way, should Germany "never have the right to compel the ... Austrians, by conquest, to return again to her dominion ... ?" (Dorfman and Tugwell 1938b: 292; Perry 1882: 424–25).

If nationalism provided an impetus for expansion, however, it also supplied the strongest reason for self-limitation. Once the bounds of territory occupied by the national group had been reached, Lieber not only saw no reason to reach farther, he was convinced that continued growth risked great dangers, both to the state involved and to the international system as a whole. He opposed the Mexican War, because he expected it to lead to the addition of new areas favorable to the introduction of slavery (Sears 1928: 47); he was highly skeptical of "Mr. Seward's scheme" of buying Alaska and called it "silly," because he thought that such a noncontiguous and uninhabited territory had no natural connection to the Union; he feared the annexation of "that black, Catholic Spanish mass" of Cuba and Puerto Rico, because he doubted the feasibility of their cultural assimilation into American society. "I am no *extensionist*," he insisted (Lieber to Bluntschli, October 11, 1869). "[M]ere aggrandizement indicates no highly organic and intrinsical development of a nation.... mere extension, inorganic extension always weakens... mere extension and pure accumulation burthens" (Lieber to White, April 12, 1867).[6]

Such extension had been possible, even normal, before the idea of nationalism had obtained such sway. "The ancients knew of no nations, in the modern acceptation of the term," Lieber recalled.

> [T]here existed vast empires, but they were only annexations of countries over which one victorious tribe—the Mede, the Persian, the Arab—ruled, without fusing the many discordant components into one society, one organized thing, one nation which should be animated and impelled, in some respect or other, by one moral agent, one vital social principle, or impulse extending through all parts and through a series of periods. (Lieber 1838: II: 314; I: 375)

In the modern period, the forces of cultural and historical dissimilarity that limited the groups of people who could be brought to share such a sense of unity also limited the geographic reach of a state that could claim to be a legitimate national state. Empires of the ancient type were as outdated as the Austrian relic; the contemporary state perfected civil liberty through institutions established among its population unified through a common nationhood. Certainly, even in advanced states, large sections of the people could be "misled," as was the case with those "who seem to believe that the highest destiny of the United States consists in the extension of her territory—a task in which, at best, we can only be imitators, while, on the contrary, our destiny is one of its own, and of a substantive character" (Lieber 1853: 55). The substantive aim of advancing liberty and strengthening the institutions that protected liberty was an ongoing and never-ending task, unlike mere territorial increase, which had a definitive terminus.

For Lieber, then, imperialism, when understood as the growth of the state to reach its natural boundaries as established by the territories populated by its nation, was desirable and in accord with the will of Providence. Imperialism, when understood as the boundless expansion of the state with no regard for the ill-assorted collection of nations over whom it might come to exercise control solely through coercion and not in institutionalized union and liberty, on the other hand, was an outdated idea, contrary to the design of the Maker of nations. Lieber never ceased to rhapsodize about the former and fulminate against the latter, and on this centrality of nationalism he remained consistent throughout his career.

LIEBER AND INTERNATIONALISM

Internationalism was also a concern for Lieber—he did, after all, claim to have coined the very word—particularly in the later stages of his life when international issues became a prime subject for his scholarship and his political activism (Friedel 1947: 179). As was the case with nationalism, internationalism, too, was a matter of destiny, in that he believed that cooperation among states for ends defined by intrinsic justice was the end toward which the international system was inevitably tending. Internationalism was in fact the completion of nationalism and the negation of imperialism.

"Patriotism in modern times ... requires a *country*, to be deep and fruitful" (Lieber 1838: II: 210–11). Such, as we have seen, was Lieber's starting point. He was convinced that, under contemporary technological, cultural, economic, and social conditions, the state was the setting in which humans could live best, and he thought it "one of God's holiest ordinances ... that man should live in the state" (Lieber 1838: II: 288–89). The existence of the state necessarily implied a multiplicity of states, with each one ideally resting on a unified nation and a well-developed network of societal and governmental institutions. Moreover, it was fortunate that physical capacities limited the growth of states, preventing any one state from conquering all the rest:

> Mankind extend over so vast a space, the various countries have characters so different, the several portions of mankind stand in so different degrees of civilisation, their wants, physical and intellectual, their taste and genius promoted or retarded by circumstances and events uncontrollable by them, the objects they strive for by joint exertions, their dangers, desires, interests and views, languages and religions, capacities and means, are of such infinite variety—that human society does not, and according to the order of things, ought not to form one state. There exist many states; that is, mankind are divided, in consequence of countless concurring circumstances, into a number of societies, in each of which exists the absolute necessity of forming a state—a necessity without which man cannot rise higher. (Lieber 1838: I: 245)

The picture is clear and familiar: a world of many independent units, each equal in its sovereignty and legal rights, and each resting on a society defined by nationality. Anything that called into question this fundamental organizing principle of the international system by introducing a more hierarchical structure was, for Lieber, a threat to be opposed. "Universal monarchy" was, in all its manifestations, "obsolete" (Lieber 1868: 239–40). It might take the form of "a single leading nation," which overstepped its proper national limits and presumed to dictate to the rest of international society; such was the foreign policy of Napoleon, which "ended almost exclusively in conquest" (Lieber 1864: 424). It might take the form of a vestigial supranational authority claimed by the papacy, and Lieber's biographer has remarked that "[c]ertainly Lieber's anti-Catholicism was largely an outgrowth of his ardent nationalism" (Freidel 1947: 408). It might take the form of an international organization or tribunal wielding coercive sanctions against its member states. Here, he could not have been more explicit, despite his life-long advocacy of international cooperation and the spread of international law, when he wrote, "[It] is not puerile jealousy, but the necessity of autonomy, which would prevent a free nation of any magnitude joining a permanent international high court" (Lieber to Dufour, April 10, 1872). Whatever might have been the necessities of political life in earlier periods, "[u]niversal monarchy would be, in our modern civilization, universal slavery" (Lieber 1871b: 652).

This demand for autonomy was, for Lieber, both fundamental and normative. It in fact defined the state. Lieber argued that, because the state was a society among a specific group of people, it necessarily excluded dictation by those who were not participants in its scheme of social cooperation; if it did not, then the society would be governed by a force outside the society. "Since the state, then, implies a society which acknowledges no superior, the idea of self-determination applied to it means that, as a unit and opposite to other states, it be independent, not dictated to by foreign governments, nor dependent upon them any more than itself has freely assented to be, by treaty and upon the principles of common justice and morality, and that it be allowed to rule itself, or that it have what the Greeks chiefly meant by the word autonomy" (Lieber 1853: 22). The fact that any state of the American Union could be bound by a larger majority beyond that state to accept an amendment to the Constitution demonstrated that the states were not sovereign, for "[n]o minority of *sovereigns*, however small, can be made subject to a majority of sovereigns, however large" (Lieber 1868: 237). This definition of the sovereign state meant that individual liberty required national liberty, that self-determination of citizens within the polity would mean nothing if authorities beyond the polity could impose their will on it:

> It is impossible to imagine liberty in its fullness, if the people as a totality, the country, the nation—whatever name may be preferred—or its government, is not independent on [*sic*] foreign interference. ... This independence or national self-government farther implies that, the civil government of free choice or free acquiescence being established, no influence from without, besides that of freely acknowledged justice, fairness, and morality, must be admitted. (Lieber 1853: 41)

It was precisely because Lieber saw international society as a moral order that he believed that any supranational compulsion had no place in it. By definition, morality consisted in acting because the action was in itself right, not because of any threatened punishment. He made this Kantian point at the very outset of his *Political Ethics*, as applied to all spheres of human life: "Indeed, it would not be a moral world, if the necessary consequence of theft were the withering of the arm that committed it; if the tongue that lies were stricken with palsy. On the contrary it would be a non-moral world, a world of necessity and not of freedom of action. ... Fear of itself is no moral motive" (Lieber 1838: I: 25). Morality entered the world because punishment (at least in this life) did not always follow crime; and humans, whether in their personal or their social-political lives, if they were to act morally had to do so out of conviction and not out of the expectation of reward. Although he was more prone to say that moral action would serve the self-interest among states than among individuals (Beaumont and Tocqueville: xxv), he held that praiseworthy conduct among states, too, was a matter of free choice, not coercion. One of the dangers of universal monarchy on which Lieber constantly pounded was that it impaired this unfettered action, shackling it with a centralized system of dictation. Likewise, one of the evidences of humanity's progress was that international life in the ancient world had been subject to the will of "one leading state or country at any given period," an idea that in the modern world was "an anachronism, barren in everything except mischief, and always gotten up, in recent times, to subserve ambition or national conceit" (Lieber 1859: 370). Lieber strongly criticized Napoleon III on this score. "He clings to the idea of the Roman universal monarchy," Lieber told a correspondent, referring to the papacy, and if that device should prove to be "utterly impossible, to the idea of French predominance and leadership" (Lieber to Thayer, July 22, 1870). Both a state or other institution that swallowed up other states to become a universal monarchy and a leading state that laid down the law to other states, making their independence only nominal, removed the element of free will, and therefore the possibility of morality, from the world.

This centralization of authority in world politics—even more harmful, in Lieber's eyes, than the centralization of governmental power within states, which he also opposed—was destructive of the fruitful variety among peoples. Nations formed "separate communities, large enough to be, in a degree, their own world, and separated by language, history, law, views, prejudices, desires, [etc.]" (Lieber 1838: II: 664–65). Such disparity in states' mores and outlooks militated against the effective or just operation of shared institutions, which would tend to impose uniform rules on highly unlike circumstances: "A congress on the banks of the Po, or on the Bosphorus, for Asia, Europe and America, would make galling decisions for people near the Rocky Mountains. ... The difference of nations, which nevertheless is necessary, must needs lead to very different wants and views" (Lieber 1838: II: 652). This very difference would impede the working of any international institution that pretended to direct the actions of sovereign states, if indeed it did not prevent the creation of such an institution from the outset. Bereft of sustaining public opinion and sentiment, cultural ties, and institutions grounded in a national consensus, any "supposed [international] congress" would be either unavailing or tyrannical. It would, in a word, be unnatural.

It would also be unnecessary. The same providence that had ordained sep-arate states resting on organic nations was pressing these states into ever-closer voluntary cooperation based on common ideas and shared interests. "It was a peculiar feature of antiquity that law, religion, dress, the arts and customs, that everything in fact was localized," Lieber asserted. By contrast, "Modern civi-lization extends over regions, tends to make uniform, and eradicates even the physical differences of tribes and races. Thus made uniform, nations receive and give more freely" (Lieber 1853: 250). That extension of likeness was a mark of the ever-widening scope of "civilization" within which human "socialism"— the natural social urge to associate—could express itself fully. Measures, whether technological or legal, that bound peoples together more tightly, enabling them to recognize their underlying similarity, ought to be encouraged; thus his advo-cacy of mutual pledges not to take military actions that would disrupt the international telegraph cables, which linked the international community "in the great cause of intercommunion and intercommunication" (Sears 1928: 55); and his decades-long effort to secure by domestic legislation and by treaty "the mutual acknowledgment of international copyright peculiarly necessitated by our common and interwoven civilization, as well as by the most elementary principles and ideas of individual property" (Lieber 1872: 319; Lieber 1840). These were not simply desirable acts of public policy; they were duties that nature had dictated. Even war, though peace was humanity's natural state, con-tributed to this drawing together, for, as "[p]aradoxical as it may seem at first glance ... the closest contact and consequent exchange of thought and produce and enlargement of knowledge between two otherwise severed nations, is fre-quently produced by war" (Lieber 1838: II: 649).

If innate sociability drew humans toward international cooperation, self-interest prodded them in the same direction. The "all-pervading"—indeed, the "divine"—"law of interdependence" applied "to nations quite as much as to individuals," and, "like all original principles of characteristics of humanity," was increasing in both scope and power as civilization advanced (Lieber 1868: 242). Further drawing on Kant, Lieber held that, because human wants were everywhere the same, while the resources to satisfy those wants were unequally distributed across the earth, sheer necessity dictated economic exchange that would result in constantly increasing and universally profitable mutual depend-ence. "All men stand in need of coin, desire silk, are pleased with indigo blue; but very limited regions only produce them," he noted. "This is the way the Creator enforces inter-dependence. This is the law which necessitates and more and more promotes international good-will and leads to the great Commonwealth of Nations." Moreover, the beneficial consequences of such contacts went well beyond the purely economic (or the wholly lower-case): "Barter, Division of Labor and Trades, Commerce, the greater portion of the Law and the whole Law of Nations, all Politics, and the Spread of Civilization are based on this Inter-Dependence" (Lieber 1869: 393–94, 399–400). Increasing international contact was providential, both in the sense that it was furthered by transcendent forces over which humans had little control, and in the sense that it was in the long run in accord with humans' social nature and beneficial to their well-being.

Because "nations are no more destined for oyster-like seclusion and self-sufficiency than individuals, but, on the contrary, are made for inter-dependence and inter-completion," the removal of barriers to their exchange was for Lieber a vital part of the internationalist creed. His devotion to the cause of free trade was a position to which he held consistently for half a century and in unequivocal terms. "Free Trade is nothing else than the application of the gospel of good-will and love to production and exchange, or to the material intercourse of distant societies which always precedes their intellectual intercourse," he declaimed, and "he who interferes with free exchange, and consequently with free consumption, interferes with the divine law in Inter-Dependence" (Lieber 1869: 394, 410–12, 435; Friedel 1947: 132, 136, 191, 223, 344, 410). He distrusted the very introduction of terms referring to political entities into the analysis of economic questions; for him, "the words domestic and foreign have very little meaning in economy, as they have none whatever in nature," and he denied that there was any such thing as "national wealth," declaring that "this is merely a term for the aggregate wealth of a certain number of individuals." If governments would refrain from hindering the free economic exchange of individuals across state borders, they would contribute greatly to "the close of short-sighted international selfishness and unneighborly ill-will" (Lieber 1869: 402, 412; Lieber 1841: 60). In a more positive vein, they should take steps to encourage international economic activity by simplifying the mechanisms of commerce. Lieber was a determined proponent of a universal currency, decrying "the chauvinism regarding the Dollar" (Lieber to Sumner, January 26, 1872), and predicting that "Universal Coinage would be one of the greatest elements of all Internationalism" (Sears 1928: 61). Of lesser importance, but still a beneficial effect, would be the adoption of a single worldwide system of weights, measures, and time, all of them taking the logical French standards. These steps would, by easing the way to greater international contact, "hasten the advent of general peace" (Lieber 1871b). And Lieber was certain that the international community would embrace such measures, as he was confident that free trade would inevitably triumph. "Our race is now going to enter the period of International Free Trade," he wrote, adding, "—that is, of International Peace and Good-Will" (Lieber 1869: 412). (Lieber expressed this idea of inevitability more colorfully in a private letter in which he declaimed, "Free Trade is the distinct course of history. … [A] hundred years hence … protection will be looked upon as the exceptional deviation and with the same surprise as we look upon the beauty-patches of our great-great-grand-mothers" [Lieber to Allibone, June 20, 1865]).

These political expedients rested on the deeper foundation of a constantly increasing similarity of thought and appreciation of the universal standards of justice that bound all nationalities. Lieber long favored the "non-political" idea of gatherings of experts or "publicists" (another term he claimed to have coined) whose identification of just rules of conduct would carry weight simply due to the disinterested prestige their authors brought to them:

> The strength, authority and grandeur of the Law of Nations rests on, and consists in the very fact that Reason, Justice, Equity speak through men, "greater than he who takes the city"—single men, plain Grotius; and that nations, and even Congresses of Vienna cannot avoid hearing, acknowledging and quoting them. ... [I]t has ever been and is still a favorite idea of mine that there should be a congress of from five to ten acknowledged jurists, to settle a dozen or two of important yet unsettled points—a private and boldly self-appointed congress, whose whole authority should rest on the inherent truth and energy of their own *proclama*. (Lieber to Thayer, May 7, 1869)[7]

This internationalism of thought would be the product and constantly strengthening manifestation of an unforced melding of previously parochial loyalties, local ties of community, and particular standards of right conduct. The higher the level of transnational communication, the more readily would general public opinion in all countries—first the civilized states inhabited by the "Cis-Caucasian" race, but eventually all states everywhere—grant to all human beings the same rights that had previously been recognized as belonging only to a caste, a town, or a group of fellow citizens. Thus Lieber's stress on education as one of the most important public responsibilities, and his devotion to all means of the diffusion of knowledge, such as libraries. "We cannot do now-a-days without large *public* libraries, and libraries are quite as necessary as hospitals or armies," he wrote. "Libraries are the bridges over which Civilisation travels from generation to generation, and from country to country—bridges that span over the widest oceans" (Lieber to Halleck, November 16, 1865). Free trade, international protection of copyright, international congresses of private persons holding common interests—all these would advance the sharing of material and intellectual progress and more clearly reveal the universal rules of justice that would circumscribe the sovereignty of force, leavening it with laws that applied equally to strong and weak alike. The extension of sympathies and the mutual instruction of cultures was the defining trait of the modern age:

> With the ancients everything was strictly national; religion, polity, knowledge, literature, art, acknowledgment of right, all were local;

with us, the different colors on the map do not designate different districts of religion, knowledge, art, and customs. There are wires of mental telegraphs which cross all those red and blue and yellow lines. And who will say that the time cannot arrive when that broad sea of history... this commonwealth of active and polished nations, shall extend over the face of our planet? (Lieber 1845: 214–15)

For Lieber, then, no contradiction existed between the expansion of states to the fullest extent defined by the territory occupied by their nationalities or necessary to their flourishing—what some might call imperialism—and his understanding of internationalism. Indeed, constructive internationalism relied on cooperation among states constructed on a solid national basis, which could rely on domestic popular support and had the enlightenment to understand their shared interests, as well as the disinterested principles of justice that would increasingly meliorate their relations as civilization progressed. Lieber accepted that significant, and perhaps growing, inequalities among states would exist, and he saw in the special rights, privileges, and responsibilities of the great powers the means to further progress. The fact that several powers of the first rank cooperated with and restrained one another was an advance over an international system marked by the overlordship of one "universal monarchy." In one of his favorite and most frequently employed similes, he drew the contrast between the ancient world, in which "one government always swayed and led," and the modern, in which the "leading nations—the French, the English, the German, the American—" would "draw the chariot of civilization abreast, as the ancient steeds drew the car of victory" (Lieber 1868: 241–42). In this "commonwealth of nations," both unity and diversity would thrive, as "there will be no obliteration of nationalities," while free and voluntary submission to principles of justice would reduce conflict and extend the sway of law without the danger of a dictating supranational authority (Lieber 1868: 241–42). Supported by both nationalism and internationalism, Lieber's vision was one of optimism and confidence.

LIEBER AND CONTEMPORARY INTERNATIONAL RELATIONS

Writing at a time when a discipline of political science was just coming into existence in the United States and a discipline of international relations was still decades in the future, Lieber by no means saw himself as a scholar of international politics as such. In part because of his own immigrant background, in part because of his unquenchable interest in all questions of contemporary public policy, and in part because of the subjects on which his somewhat peripheral involvement in the making of policy occurred (in drawing up the "Lieber code" during the Civil War, and in serving as an umpire on the U.S.-Mexican commission settling claims arising from the Mexican War), he never excluded international politics from his analysis of politics in general, and he wrote on international questions increasingly in later life. How should he be seen in relation to the contemporary field and discourse of IR?

First, in contrast to those who seek to problematize the basic concepts that, in their view, have been privileged under the present structure of power, Lieber saw the nation, nationalism, and the state as entirely unproblematic. He was preeminently a theorist of the state and its connection with the organic people, and he saw as his great task, and the task of all students of politics in the modern era, the reconciliation of nation, state, and individual liberty. Just as the sense of nationalism derived from a providentially inspired longing in all humans for community and marks of likeness with others, so was there an inborn instinct for individuation and sense of justice that could be satisfied only under the rule of impartial law—hence Lieber's liberalism. Not only were these natural and political phenomena palpable, they were literally God-given; they were facts, and it was right that they should be facts. A conscience—a realization that certain things were right and others were wrong—was a universal facet of human character, and although particular systems of ethics differed, the area of overlap was large. The fact that they differed at all, according to their varying circumstances, did not demonstrate that such standards were only social conventions. Increasing civilization would bring all such systems into greater uniformity, reflecting the inherent validity of certain moral and political principles. Although cognizant of the force of historical contingency, Lieber had drunk deeply at the spring of German Idealism.

A more promising link between Lieber and the discipline of IR at the outset of the twenty-first century may be found in the significance he attributed to interdependence. While he never suggested that higher levels of economic interaction and mutual dependence would guarantee international peace, he did frequently assert that economic rationality based on these conditions would have the tendency to promote a higher level of peace, as well as a greater willingness by states to bring their relations under predictable and nondisruptive international law. The concept of an international "regime," with its widely accepted formal or informal rules and conventions gaining great sway over the actions of the participating actors, was one of the few terms that Lieber did not stake a claim to have invented, but it is a prism through which he would have found himself perfectly comfortable viewing the international system. Such norms and procedures were for him a mark of modern internationalism. The fact that they were frequently mediated through non-state actors—private economic, cultural, scholarly, or other contacts—for him demonstrated the limited role of the state, as one kind of society among many. His contention that free self-government could be carried on only if the domestic institutions subject to popular control were not themselves dictated to by presuming foreign authorities presaged by more than a century contemporary concerns over the "democratic deficit" in international organizations such as the WTO. (And his assiduous gathering of statistics on all political and other subjects would probably have made him sympathetic to quantitative demonstrations of the scope and effect of interdependence.)

Nevertheless, states remained the primary political actors in the international system, and their power relations continued to set the terms within which other nonpolitical activities could be carried on. Free trade, as we have seen, was a lifelong objective of Lieber, who wished governments to exercise as little control as possible over economic exchange, both domestic and international, but if, as he also hoped, belligerents were to respect the sanctity of private goods and ships on the high seas, including those belonging to citizens of enemy countries, the decision to accept such a limitation would have to be taken by states. He connected this expectation of the vitality of the state with a realistic appreciation for the inescapable influence of considerations of power. "Wherever people meet, the most powerful must sway, in politics as in every other sphere," he pronounced, "and wherever ... entire nations meet nominally on terms of parity, it is unavoidable that the most powerful must sway the less powerful" (Lieber, 1838: II: 651).

A conception of international society that lay in "spontaneous rapprochement of ideas and norms, combined with independence of nations" (Anonymous: 297), a refusal to close his eyes to the perennial competition for power among independent states, an equal belief in the increasing authority of voluntarily accepted rules embodying the common interests of these states, and an insight into the broader transnational community of civilization, at least theoretically open to all human beings, regardless of race or culture—these are terms familiar to any Grotian of a pluralist bent, to use the language of Bull (1966) and Wheeler (1992). Lieber, the unfailing exponent of "Anglican liberty," might well have been pleased to think of himself as a forerunner of the English School.

While Lieber tended to dichotomize political phenomena, his work implicitly relies on the continuum formed by all three of Martin Wight's traditions of international thought. In considering the role that war had played in the construction of the domestic and international institutions of his day, and in deriding the pretensions of international organizations because they lacked instruments of coercive power, he evidenced a realist appreciation for the ineradicableness of force and conflict from international life. In his wish that contact between Western and non-Western peoples would bring "civilization" to the latter and his firm belief that over the long run of history there were no such things as subject and master races, he flirted with a revolutionist faith in the ultimate triumph of the human community over political division. It was in the "broad middle way"—what Wight called the rationalist tradition—that Lieber would find his clearest intellectual descendants, nonetheless. His belief in the natural, unforced confluence of interests among states, his confidence in the inevitable growth of international law and institutions (properly limited), and his restricting of the use of force to just wars mark an optimistic and progressive, if perhaps naive, internationalism that would be challenged by the imperialist trends in international society in the decades after his death.

NOTES

1. The standard life of Lieber is Freidel 1947. See also the forthcoming collection of essays on Lieber's life and work, to be published by the University of South Carolina Press.

2. I am indebted for this information to my colleague William Gwyn, who was a student in the graduate program at the University of Virginia in the early 1950s.

3. Most recently, Onuf (2002) has considered Lieber's work on institutions.

4. Lieber's extensive correspondence, along with many of his other papers, may be found in the Francis Lieber Papers, Huntington Library, San Marino, California. The letters cited in this essay were addressed to the following parties: Samuel Allibone, Johann Bluntschli, G. H. Dufour, Hamilton Fish, Henry Halleck, Franz von Holtzendorff, Franz Mittermaier, Samuel Ruggles, Charles Sumner, Martin Russell Thayer, the *Times* (London), and Andrew Dickson White.

5. Lieber was even more emphatic in his article denying the existence of the "Latin Race":

> Some great and eminently leading nations—such as the Greek and the English—have been and are a mixture of varied tribes and races. There are, unquestionably, distinct characteristics belonging to different races; but it must never be forgotten that the tendency of all our civilization is to the greater and greater assimilation of these Cis-Caucasian races, and that all the noblest things—religion, truth, and science, architecture, sculpture, and civil liberty—are not restricted to races. To all these the mandate is given: Go into all the world. (Lieber 1871a: 308–309)

6. He urged Sumner in 1871 to send to European scholars copies of his "Domingo speech" opposing the purchase of Santo Domingo (Lieber to Sumner, March 29, 1871), but a generation earlier, in 1847, he had favored making the cession of California a condition of any treaty of peace with Mexico, on the grounds that California, unlike Mexico proper, had no unassimilable population, and the few existing inhabitants were making no proper use of it. Friedel 1947: 227–28, points out the contradictions in which this stand involved Lieber. See also Dorfman and Tugwell 1938a: 177.

7. This was a long-standing theme that Lieber sounded frequently. See Lieber to Sumner, January 4, 1870; Lieber to White, December 15, 1866; Lieber to Bluntschli, March 24, 1872; Lieber to G. H. Dufour, April 10, 1872.

Chapter 2

Paul S. Reinsch and the Study of Imperialism and Internationalism

Brian C. Schmidt

The two main themes of this book, imperialism and internationalism, occupied much of Paul S. Reinsch's (1869–1923) scholarly attention. In addition to studying and writing on imperialism and internationalism, Reinsch was also deeply concerned with the closely related issue of colonialism which, following the Spanish-American War of 1898, engrossed the minds of American states-men and academics alike. It is fair to say that Reinsch was one of the leading American authorities on the subject of colonialism in general and colonial administration in particular. Throughout the early 1900s, he was a central figure in carving out a distinct discourse about international politics. Reinsch pursued this discourse within the institutional context of the newly formed academic discipline of political science, a discipline that he promoted both in his capac-ity as a professor in the Department of Political Science at the University of Wisconsin and in his various administrative roles in the American Political Science Association (APSA), which was formally established in 1903. My main intention in this chapter is to reconstruct in detail the contribution that Reinsch made to the early-twentieth-century academic conversation about international politics. In reconstructing this episode of disciplinary history, my purpose is to indicate that the early conversation about international politics among American political scientists was shaped most fundamentally by a focus on the late-nineteenth and early-twentieth-century practices of imperialism and colonialism. This revisionist account of the early disciplinary history of IR runs counter to the dominant view that the early discourse was absorbed in the idealist quest to create a pacific world order.

I begin the chapter by noting the curious fact that although Reinsch played a prominent role in the early development of IR, he is, nevertheless, generally unknown to contemporary students in the field. After suggesting a couple of explanations of why this is the case, I provide a preliminary justification of Reinsch's importance to the field. The remainder of the chapter is devoted to reconstructing Reinsch's contribution to the early discourse about international politics. I first provide a brief sketch of Reinsch's professional life as an academic. Next, I turn to his seminal work, *World Politics at the End of the Nineteenth Century* (1900). This book is interesting for a number of reasons, but most important is the insightful analysis of the phenomenon of national imperialism, which Reinsch viewed as the fundamental factor shaping international politics at the dawn of the twentieth century. The discussion of national imperialism within the context of the late-nineteenth-century scramble for colonial possessions is followed by a focus on Reinsch's efforts to create a science of colonial administration that could meet the twin demands of the colonized and the colonizer. While often ignored, or only given scant attention, the study of colonial administration within political science comprised a considerable share of the early discourse about international politics. This conversation is noteworthy for revealing the limitations of the internationalist ethos that was conspicuous in the writings of those studying the so-called society of states. The prevailing view among political scientists and international lawyers at the time was that the colonized regions were not full-fledged members of international society. Consequently, a different set of political relationships was held to exist between those who were deemed to be "inside" and "outside" of international society. Martin Wight, one of the founders of the English School of international relations, who had an interest in the study of colonial administration, once remarked that "the question of relations with barbarians was a political problem forming a bridge between international relations and colonial administrations" (Wight 1992: 50). Reinsch offered a unique perspective on what the proper relationship between the "civilized" members of international society and the "other" should be, and his view, despite its paternalistic overtones, was, in many ways, consistent with the basic tenets of contemporary internationalism. In the final section of the chapter, I turn to the theme of internationalism that was most apparent in Reinsch's work on what was termed "public international unions," which today are commonly referred to as "international regimes" or "international institutions." In this manner, I aim to reveal the way in which Reinsch's academic work was very much located at the intersection of the study of imperialism and internationalism.

DISCIPLINARY HISTORY AND REINSCH

Before proceeding any farther, it is worthwhile addressing the puzzle of why most contemporary political scientists entirely overlook Riensch's contribution to the field of IR, despite his long list of impressive academic achievements. Part of the explanation is that while political scientists have begun to devote much more systematic attention to recovering the history of the discipline, the historiography of IR continues to remain in an essentially impoverished condition (Waever 1998). The situation, as noted in the introduction, is certainly improving; especially with respect to correcting a number of erroneous assumptions about the interwar period of the field's history (Kahler 1997; Osiander 1998; Schmidt 1998a, 1998b; Wilson 1998). Yet the period before World War I, which might be termed the "prehistory" of the field, has received hardly any attention at all. Perhaps the most telling explanation of why the overwhelming majority of orthodox histories of IR have overlooked the contributions of Reinsch is rooted in the deeply entrenched belief that the field did not come into existence until after World War I. By unreflectively assuming that the institutional origins of IR emanate directly from World War I, earlier periods of disciplinary history, such as that when Reinsch and his political science colleagues were writing, are almost completely ignored.

Reinsch's work is a testimony to a thriving conversation about international politics that was taking place well before the outbreak of World War I. The sheer volume of academic literature and variety of course offerings in international relations that appeared in the 1920s and 1930s would not have been possible without the foundations that had been provided by an earlier generation of IR scholars.[1] The existence of this conversation, which I reconstruct in the main body of this chapter, raises a number of critical issues about the manner in which scholars have approached the task of chronicling the history of the field. I argue that existing histories have tended to exaggerate the significance of *external* influences, such as wars or major international crises, on the development of the field and underemphasized the importance of *internal*, institutional factors. There is a deeply ingrained assumption that what is happening in the field can be directly accounted for in terms of the external context provided by "real world" political events. While I certainly do not want to suggest that a great divide exists, or should exist, between the field and the "real world," I do want to argue that the relationship between the two is not as direct as many have tended to assume. From the point of view of disciplinary history, the focus should be on describing how the field has perceived and responded to external factors rather than on how these factors can account for the dynamics inside the field.

I adopt an approach that can be described as a critical internal discursive history.[2] The intention of such an approach is to reconstruct the internal developments and transformations that have occurred in the field of IR by following and describing a relatively coherent conversation among participants in this professional field of inquiry. The term *conversation* is not employed metaphorically, for what is being reconstructed is an actual conversation among academic scholars and others who self-consciously participated in an institutional setting devoted to the study of international politics. This approach in no way discounts the significance of exogenous factors, but it does give greater weight to endogenous factors in accounting for the specific character of the academic conversation about international politics. I argue, at least with respect to the situation in the United States, that the university context from which IR arose as a distinct field of study is the most immediate and relevant milieu for under-standing its historical development.

Besides failing to recognize that the intellectual and institutional origins of the field predate World War I, there are additional reasons why the work of Reinsch and his colleagues has been generally ignored. One reason is that most people today would be either embarrassed or offended by the perceptions as well as the language of our political science ancestors. In describing the relations between the "developed" countries and their colonized regions, they referred to the "dark," "uncivilized," "backward," and "barbaric" areas of the world. A num-ber of racial and prejudicial assumptions were never far from the surface of what at the time were considered intellectually justifiable depictions of inter-national politics. John Burgess, for example, who played a major role in estab-lishing the Columbia School of Political Science in 1880, maintained that "the Teutonic nations—the English, French, Lombards, Scandinavians, Germans, and North Americans—as the great modern nation builders" were justified in their "temporary imposition of Teutonic order on unorganized, disorganized, or savage people for the sake of their own civilization and their incorporation in the world of society" (Burgess 1934: 254–55). While Burgess's views might fall on the extreme side of the spectrum, they were not atypical of the period during which Reinsch was writing. In our present day commitment to a sani-tized and politically correct social science vernacular, it is perhaps not surpris-ing that many might want to forget the early history of American political science. Yet, I submit, we ignore this history at the peril of failing to understand the pedigree of our field.

There are a number of reasons why it is important for contemporary stu-dents of IR to be familiar with the contribution that Reinsch made to the early study of international politics. Part of Reinsch's significance stems from his role in helping to institutionalize the study of international politics within the dis-ciplinary matrix of American political science. If, as I argue, institutional con-text is an important variable for understanding the disciplinary history of an academic field, then Reinsch's role in helping to demarcate the discursive boundaries of what was, at the beginning of the twentieth century, considered to be the subject matter of international politics is crucial. The fact, for example, that the subject matter of the field has come to be largely understood in terms of the interaction of states, in which war is regarded as the central dynamic, is a function of the disciplinary origins of IR. In his positions both within the APSA and as professor of political science at the University of Wisconsin, Reinsch was instrumental in creating the institutional infrastructure that not only helped to launch the fledgling field of IR but created the conditions for its subsequent development. Of crucial importance here is the "Politics" section of the APSA that Reinsch chaired from its inception. As I indicate in this chap-ter, the core of what eventually became the subfield of IR was carved from the substantive content of the Politics section.

In addition to calling into question the link that has been assumed to exist between the origins of the field and the occurrence of World War I, an analysis of Reinsch's writings problematizes the dichotomy that has been constructed between the poles of idealism and realism. The idealist-realist antinomy is widely regarded as one of the foundational truths about the history of IR and it continues to structure the terms of debate in the field (Booth 1996). According to the conventional wisdom, World War II represented a glaring anomaly in the prevailing "idealist paradigm" that was the subject of the first "great debate" which took place between the interwar scholars and a new group of scholars who began to enter the field in the late 1930s and early 1940s under the label of "realists."[3] Most accounts of the history of the field make it appear as if the approach of the realists, with their claim to focus on what "is" rather than what "ought" to be, was far superior to previously existing approaches in the field. This judgment has contributed to the prevalent view that realism won the first "great debate" and that, consequently, the ideas of the interwar scholars have become irrelevant.

Even if it is the case that the self-identified realists were responsible for changing the focus of the field, this does not entail that those writing before 1945 were necessarily idealists or utopians. It was, after all, the post–World War II realists who invented and employed the label of "idealism" to describe the character of the scholarship between the two world wars. There were those who early on recognized the dubious nature of the dichotomy between idealism and realism. Quincy Wright, who was at the University of Chicago when Hans J. Morgenthau joined the department in 1943, wrote that "the distinction between 'realism' and 'idealism' is of doubtful value in either political analysis or political philosophy." He added that they "have functioned as propaganda terms according to which everyone sought to commend whatever policy he favored by calling it 'realistic'" (Wright 1952: 119–20).

Reinsch's work is intriguing in that it incorporates elements of both what is taken to be "idealism" and "realism" and thereby reveals the difficulties of understanding the intellectual history of IR when it is cast in terms of an opposition between idealism and realism. Reinsch clearly recognized the fundamentally important role of power in the political relations among nation-states, which many realists have argued defines the essence of international politics. Carr's indictment of the interwar "utopians" rested on his claim that they had ignored the role of power, and like Morgenthau, he proclaimed that "politics, are, then, in one sense always power politics" (1964: 102). Reinsch was fully cognizant of the role that power played in politics. His analysis of what he perceived to be the unrestrained power struggle occurring at the end of the nineteenth century led him to be deeply concerned about the possibility that certain states would rekindle the atavistic ambition to establish a world empire. Reinsch made specific reference to Machiavelli, who is almost always portrayed as a hard-nosed realist, and declared him to be the spokesman for the age of national imperialism. According to Reinsch, as well as for "realists" such as Carr,

Machiavelli's significance stemmed from the Florentine diplomat's recognition that "morality is the product of power."

Machiavelli's ideas, Reinsch argued, were particularly relevant in the context of hyper-nationalism that characterized national imperialism, which was the primary focus of *World Politics at the End of the Nineteenth Century*. Reinsch declared that "in the birth struggle of national imperialism, just as centuries ago in the birth struggle of nationalism, Machiavellian thought and Machiavellian means are characteristic of political action" (1900: 16). This illustrates the significance of Reinsch in particular, and disciplinary history in general, namely, that ideas from the past can shed light on our present situation. Contrary to a recent claim made by Jan Jindy Pettman (1998) that IR has, until recently, paid remarkably little attention to nationalism, Reinsch's work, as well as that of a host of other figures in the history of the field, was directly focused on the phenomenon of nationalism.[4] The fact that Pettman can declare that "nationalism has been so peripheral a concern to International Relations" illustrates the dismal state of our knowledge about the history of the field (1998: 149). As nationalism has once again become a divisive force in the world, it is appropriate to tap the wisdom of those who addressed this phenomenon in the past.

While it is possible to recognize a number of what may be termed "realist themes" in Reinsch's work, it is also the case that several themes and issues generally associated with liberalism can also be found. The liberal belief in progress is unmistakably present in Reinsch's work. He was convinced of the possibility that the international system could be gradually reformed, and provided empirical evidence to indicate that change pointing toward a robust internationalism was indeed taking place. The best evidence of this, for Reinsch, was in the realm of international organization. Reinsch argued that "the idea of cosmopolitanism is no longer a castle in the air, but it has become incorporated in numerous associations and unions world-wide in their operation" (1911: 4). His detailed analysis of the increasing number of international public unions, which he argued coincided with the growing ties of interdependence among nations, is strikingly similar to the attempt of contemporary neoliberal institutionalists to explain the role that international regimes and institutions perform in facilitating interstate cooperation. The contemporary literature, however, for the most part, fails to acknowledge the significant contribution that Reinsch made to the early study of international organization.[5]

Finally, Reinsch's work raises a number of interesting issues for those in the field who recently have begun to emphasize the constitutive role of international relations theory, and who are interested in how certain identities are constructed and represented. Steve Smith has argued that one of the main lines of contention in the field today is "between those theories that seek to offer explanatory accounts of international relations, and those that see theory as constitutive of that reality" (Smith 1995: 26). The argument being made by those who accentuate the constitutive role of theory is not that "reality" does not exist, but rather that our cognitive understanding of what is taken to be "reality" is unavoidably mediated through theory and, even more fundamentally, through language.

These theoretical insights have begun to be employed by those who are interested in understanding the representational practices that have enabled the "West" both to discover and know the "other" beginning within the so-called age of discovery and continuing to the present day.[6] A recent example is provided by Roxanne Lynn Doty in her provocative book *Imperial Encounters* (1996). Doty's basic argument is that the identities of individuals and places are not simply given, but rather are constructed on the basis of some theoretical and epistemological claim to know the world that has served the power interests of the center over the periphery. With respect to the categories of "North" and "South," Doty explains that "thinking in terms of representational practices highlights the arbitrary, constructed, and political nature of these and many other oppositions through which we have come to 'know' the world and its inhabitants and that have enabled and justified certain practices and policies" (1996: 3). She describes the process through which the "North" has discursively constructed the identity of the "South" as one of "imperial encounters." According to Doty, "Imperial encounters is meant to convey the idea of asymmetrical encounters in which one entity has been able to construct 'realities' that were taken seriously and acted upon and the other entity has been denied equal degrees or kinds of agency" (1996: 3). In her own attempt to provide a critical genealogy of North-South relations, Doty uncovers a number of representational practices that have served to provide an authoritative account of that region of the world that has been subsumed under the heading "third world."

Reinsch's writings on colonial administration provide an especially good case through which to explore the representational practices that were at work in the field of IR. A number of peculiar identities were constructed by IR scholars in order to create a sharp disjuncture between the "civilized" members of international society and the "other." The point of examining these representational practices, however, is not to condemn Reinsch and his colleagues for using categories and terminology that are unacceptable by today's intellectual standards. Rather, the point is to illustrate the manner in which the discourse of colonial administration constructed a particular representation of the "other" that, in turn, created the problematic of what the proper relationship should be between the "developed" states and their colonies. This was the central problematic that the scientific study of colonial government attempted to solve.

BIOGRAPHICAL BACKGROUND

Reinsch was born on June 10, 1869, in Milwaukee, Wisconsin, to parents of German descent (Pugach 1970). He attended the University of Wisconsin, where his education consisted of a broad liberal arts curriculum culminating in an introduction to history and the social sciences. He graduated in 1892 with a BA and was elected Phi Beta Kappa. Noel Pugach, Reinsch's principle biographer, describes how Reinsch's desire to pursue graduate work in Germany, which was common among aspiring American intellectuals in the late 1800s and early 1900s, was thwarted by his family's limited financial means. Reinsch consequently decided to pursue a career in law and graduated in 1894 from the University of Wisconsin law school with an LLB. He was admitted to the Wisconsin bar and began a private practice in Milwaukee. According to Pugach, however, Reinsch increasingly became unhappy and disillusioned with his law career.

Meanwhile, exciting developments were taking place at the University of Wisconsin that would convince Reinsch to discontinue his law practice and pursue a PhD in history and political science.[7] In 1892, the School of Economics, Political Science, and History was established under the directorship of Richard Ely, a prominent American economist who before his arrival at Wisconsin was teaching at Johns Hopkins University. The creation of this school made the University of Wisconsin one of the leading institutions for the study of the social sciences. The reputation of the school rested on the prestigious faculty that, in addition to Ely, included Frederick Jackson Turner, Charles Homer Haskins, William Scott, Charles Bullock, Albert Shaw, Jerome H. Raymond, and a number of other leading figures in the fields of economics, history, and sociology. After being offered a position as instructor in the Department of History, Reinsch enrolled in the fall of 1895 as a doctoral candidate in history and political science. Having previously completed courses taught by Turner on American history, Reinsch selected him as his dissertation advisor. Reinsch's dissertation, *English Common Law in the Early American Colonies*, bridged his interests in law and American history, and the thesis, according to Pugach, "mirrored the Turnerian influence" (Pugach 1979: 9). Turner, in a famous essay titled "The Significance of the Frontier in American History," attributed American exceptionalism, the peculiarity of American institutions, and its experiment with democracy to the existence of the western frontier. Yet by the end of the 1800s, Turner claimed that the frontier was all but closed, which he argued represented a crisis to the health of American democracy and liberal individualism.

After completing his PhD, Reinsch left for Europe where he spent a year reading, writing, and attending lectures in Bonn, Leipzig, Berlin, Rome, and Paris. It was during his year abroad, from 1898 to 1899, that Reinsch wrote most of what would become *World Politics at the End of the Nineteenth Century*. The manuscript helped him to secure a newly created full-time position, in 1899, at the University of Wisconsin, as assistant professor of political science. This marked the beginning of his illustrious career as a political scientist.

At the University of Wisconsin, Reinsch was essentially synonymous with the study of political science. He was the chair of the Department of Political

Science from its formal creation in 1901 until he left Wisconsin in 1913 after President Woodrow Wilson appointed him minister to China. Beginning in 1899, Reinsch regularly taught a course titled "Contemporary Politics." In 1906, the title of the course was changed to "Contemporary International Politics," which several intellectual historians have claimed was the first course in the United States to concentrate specifically on the subject matter of international politics (Haddow 1969: 211; Curti and Carstensen 1949: 630–38). Reinsch was a popular teacher and taught a wide range of subjects, and regularly offered courses on political theory, law, comparative legislation, diplomacy, and a specialized course, titled Oriental Politics, that reflected his interest in China.

In recognition of his stature as one of the leading American political scientists, Reinsch was appointed to a committee, headed by Jeremiah Jenks, that was assigned the task of canvassing the level of support among other like-minded scholars for forming an independent political science association. Other disciplines, such as history and economics, already had formed their own associations: the American Historical Association (AHA) was established in 1884, and the American Economic Association (AEA) in 1885. Sufficient interest in forming a political science association resulted in the Jenks Committee issuing an official announcement for an organizational meeting to take place on December 30, 1903, in New Orleans, in conjunction with the AHA and AEA meetings. As one of the founding members of the APSA, Reinsch participated in the drafting of the association's constitution. According to the constitution, the objective of the APSA was "the encouragement of the scientific study of Politics, Public Law, Administration, and Diplomacy" (Reinsch 1904). To carry out the work of the APSA, seven sections were created, and a committee headed by a chairperson was selected for each one.[8]

In addition to serving as second vice-president of the APSA, Reinsch was appointed chair of the "Politics" section, which, compared to the other sections, appeared to lack a clearly defined focus. Yet Reinsch's scholarly interest in imperialism and colonial administration were inevitably carried over to the Politics section. The panel topics from the early annual meetings of the APSA indicate that the general subject of colonialism formed the nucleus of the Politics section. A review of the APSA's original journal, *Proceedings of the American Political Science Association*, later changed to the *American Political Science Review*, indicates that a fairly significant percentage of the published articles were written on the topics of imperialism and colonial administration. Moreover, the index of recently published literature in the earliest volumes of the *American Political Science Review* included a separate section entitled "colonies." This helps to establish the point that the early generation of American political scientists, especially those who identified with the international field, were deeply interested in the issues of imperialism and colonial administration. These interests, which originally were pursued and discussed in the Politics section, would later form the nucleus of what became the subfield of IR.

WORLD POLITICS

From the point of view of reconstructing the early disciplinary history of IR, Reinsch's first book, *World Politics at the End of the Nineteenth Century* (1900), is of great importance insofar as it helped to establish a discursive framework for an ensuing conversation centering on the topics of imperialism and colonialism. Many of the core features that are most often associated with the study of international politics—the interaction of states, the ubiquity of power, the dynamics of war and peace, the mechanism of the balance of power—all can be found in Reinsch's text. William Olson and A. J. R. Groom suggest that "the first glimmerings of international relations as a discipline had appeared with the publication of Reinsch's *World Politics at the End of the Nineteenth Century*" (1991: 47). Although the immediate focus of the book was on the events taking place in China, Reinsch did not in anyway restrict his attention to the "Chinese question." He began the book with a broad overview of the major economic, political, and intellectual forces that were currently influencing international politics. In the preface, Reinsch announced that his intention was "to gather into a harmonious picture the multitude of facts and considerations that go to make up international politics at the present time" (1900: v). After providing a perspicuous account of the forces shaping contemporary international politics, Reinsch turned his attention to the political situation in China and concluded with an analysis of German imperialism and American expansionism.

The major force that Reinsch argued was shaping world politics at the end of the nineteenth century was nationalism. Like many of the founding figures of political science, such as Francis Lieber (1798–1872) and John Burgess (1844–1931), Reinsch described the closing decades of the nineteenth century as the age of nationalism. Lieber, who in 1857 was named America's first professor of history and political science at Columbia College, had described the era in which he lived as the "National Period," which he argued was distinguished by the existence of numerous independent national polities. Lieber regarded the national polity, as opposed to all other types of political arrangements, to be the only one sufficient "for the demands of advanced civilization" (Lieber 1885: 228). Reinsch maintained that ever since the lingering aspiration for a universal world order had come to an end during the course of the Renaissance, the existence of independent nation-states, each striving to attain and assert its own national identity in an environment consisting of actors with similar goals, had become the most prevalent feature of world politics. This particular ontology of world politics is one that subsequent generations of IR students have endorsed. Reinsch argued that the power struggle that was characteristic of this early form of nationalism contributed to a productive vitality in world politics that would otherwise be expunged "from the dead uniformity of a world empire" (1900: 6).

By the beginning of the twentieth century, however, it was evident to Reinsch that a qualitatively different and much more dangerous form of nationalism had arisen. Unlike the older form of nationalism that had been able to coexist within a community of independent nation-states, an exaggerated and expansionistic form of nationalism was making itself felt by the fact that states now desired "to control as large a portion of the earth's surface as their energy and opportunities will permit" (1900: 14). National identity, Reinsch claimed, was no longer derived endogenously, but now was determined exogenously by juxtaposing the superiority of one's own civilization to the inferiority of others. This, he argued, was what contributed to the desire to extend and spread one's own civilization upon "barbaric" and "decadent" peoples. This new form of nationalism, which Reinsch termed "national imperialism," first made its appearance at the dawn of the twentieth century. National imperialism was defined by Reinsch as the endeavor "to increase the resources of the national state through the absorption or exploitation of undeveloped regions and inferior races, but does not attempt to impose political control upon highly civilized nations" (1900: 14). Reinsch pointed to the situation unfolding in China, with each of the great powers seeking to carve out their own exclusive sphere of interest, as a highly representative example of the phenomenon of national imperialism.

According to Reinsch, each of the two types of nationalism, the earlier nineteenth-century version and the newer national imperialist variety, held radically different prospects for world order. With respect to the former, not only was the energy associated with nationalism primarily directed inwardly, but a number of safeguards existed that contributed to a rough equilibrium between the dual forces of nationalism and internationalism. Reinsch argued that some of these safeguards, such as the balance of power and the role of international law, were institutional and resulted in a "balance between states by preventing any of the stronger members from unjustly oppressing the smaller civilized nations" (1900: 6). Other safeguards were largely ideational and worked to foster a reasonable degree of international harmony. Foremost among these ideas was the notion that individual nation-states could coexist within the larger family of nations. In this manner, Reinsch, like Lieber, thought that the earlier form of nationalism was not inimical to the basic tenets of internationalism.

Imperialism, Reinsch argued, negated the beneficial aspects of nationalism. Not only did imperialism rupture the compatibility between nationalism and internationalism, but rendered the two forces mutually antagonistic. Reinsch believed that twentieth-century nationalism was an "exaggerated" form of nationalism that led to a dichotomized view of the world in terms of friend and foe, civilized and barbaric, and self and other. Reinsch wrote, "[T]he older ideas of solidarity of humanity, of universal brotherhood, have largely lost their force, and have been replaced by a narrow patriotism" (1900: 20). The spokesmen of the age no longer embraced Kant and Grotius, but instead, Hegel, Nietzsche, and especially Machiavelli. Reinsch concluded that a dangerous precedent was being set in which considerations of power and allegiance to the state trumped all other concerns.

Reinsch maintained that in the age of national imperialism, force had come to be "regarded as the index or measure of fitness: as the strongest, the most resourceful, survive, these must be the true agents of civilization—through them the human spirit realizes itself" (1900: 7). He judged that world politics was being turned into a Nietzschean contest of imposing one's will on the "other"; especially on the "backward" and "uncivilized" regions of the world, a contest that Walter Lippmann would later describe as the "stakes of diplomacy" (Lippmann 1915). The great powers, according to Reinsch, were "straining every nerve to gain as large a share as possible of the unappropriated portions of the earth's surface," and they employed every possible means to achieve this end (1900: 66). Once again, Reinsch pointed to the situation in China as exemplifying the pattern of behavior whereby each of the great powers was striving to carve out an exclusive sphere of interest over extended tracts of territory. Reinsch noted that the irony of this competitive form of expansionistic nationalism was that it was actually rekindling dreams of world empire, which if fulfilled, would result in the dissolution of independent nation states. In dismay, Reinsch wrote "the phantom of world empire is again beginning to fill men's minds with vague fears and imaginings, and is everywhere a most potent agency for the creation of international animosities" (1900: 68).

While the possibility that a successful policy of national imperialism could eventually lead to the absorption of separate nation-states into a world state was something that could not be ignored, the most immediate concern was that it would eventually lead to a major international conflict. Lippmann would later express Reinsch's concerns as he attributed the cause of World War I to the failure to find a solution to the struggle between the "strong" developed states and the "weak," "backward" regions (Lippmann 1915). Reinsch had, in part, written *World Politics* as an attempt to warn of the dangers that national imperialism posed to world peace and to dissuade those who believed that economic gains could be realized through acquiring exclusive control of the earth's surface. Like other liberal thinkers such as Norman Angell, Reinsch thought that greater economic benefits could be achieved through trade than by territorial conquest. He emphasized that there was more than enough work to be done in "developing and civilizing the primitive regions" and that it was not necessary for the great powers to fight amongst themselves in the process of spreading "civilization." The liberal strand of Reinsch's political philosophy led him to the conclusion that "each of the leading nationalities can fully develop its own character and impress its best elements on the civilization of the world, without desiring the downfall and ruin of other powers" (1900: 70). In other words, economic expansion did not necessarily entail militarism and territorial conquest. This belief would lead Reinsch to be one of the chief supporters of the United States Open Door Policy in China. In order to appreciate his advocacy of the Open Door, we first have to consider the underlying motives that Reinsch attributed to imperial expansion.

In his search for an explanation for the rise of national imperialism, Reinsch granted a modicum of legitimacy to sentimental motivations for increasing national prestige by extending the flag to distant lands as well as to the moral motivation of spreading Western civilization to the far corners of the globe, but he argued that the most fundamental factor prompting states to expand was economic. Reinsch subscribed to the view that capitalist development had reached a stage that required that foreign outlets be found to absorb the surplus goods and capital being produced within the more economically developed nations. In his second book, *Colonial Government* (1902), Reinsch wrote, "to-day the primary object is the search for markets, and the chief purpose of commercial expansion has come to be the desire to dispose of the surplus product of European industry" (1902: 60). Yet while Reinsch recognized that capitalist development in a number of economically advanced states, including the United States, had reached a point where foreign outlets of capital investment were necessary, this did not settle the question of the most appropriate means to achieve this end. Although Reinsch was generally sympathetic to the analysis that John Hobson offered in *Imperialism: A Study* (1902), he questioned whether it really was the case, as Hobson submitted, that "better social service could be obtained by distinctly improving the income of the working classes than by using capital for the acquisition of tropical products" (Reinsch 1903: 532). While Reinsch agreed with Hobson that at the present time "the highly civilized countries of Europe and America offer far better markets to each other than could ever be expected of the colonies," he still thought that expansion to the far reaches of the world was not only necessary, but both inevitable and justifiable (1900: 37).

While he unequivocally rejected national imperialism on the grounds that it jeopardized world peace, unjustly established colonial rule over indigenous populations, and tended to undermine efforts to achieve domestic reform by diverting attention to external crusades, Reinsch was, nevertheless, an avowed expansionist who often couched his justification in terms of the "white man's burden." Reinsch wrote, "[I]t is well, then, to look the facts clearly in the face and to recognize that it is a serious and sad duty which the white race is performing in making way for its own further expansion" (1900: 43). He claimed the "civilized" states, by dint of their mastery over the forces of nature, had come to represent a reserve of restless energy that could not be contained within national boundaries. It was thus inevitable, according to Reinsch, that this energy would be directed outwardly to regions that, for various reasons, lacked the dynamism found in the "civilized" states. Reinsch was convinced that expansionism, if pursued correctly, could produce positive benefits for humanity at large. This, for Reinsch, was the crux of the justification issue; expansionism not only had to reap economic gains for the "civilized" powers, it also had to bring tangible benefits to the people living in the undeveloped areas of the world. Optimistically, Reinsch declared, "[H]umanity is one, and the members of the brotherhood who through barbarous customs and irrational institutions are kept in a state of backwardness are to be led out into the light of freedom and reason and endowed with the multiform blessings of civilization" (1906: 399).

While not everyone shared Reinsch's view that the fruits of expansion should be beneficial to all parties concerned, which we will see was a central pillar of his ideas about the appropriate ends of colonial administration policy, the thought that expansion was inevitable was widely shared by those participating in the early American discourse about international politics. Bernard Moses, for example, a professor of political science at the University of California who created one of the first formal courses in the subject of political theory, argued that in light of the interdependent character of contemporary international politics, which made "every country contiguous to every other country," it was utopian to believe "that a rude people should be permitted to develop its own life without foreign interference." Moses concluded that "the spirit of contemporary civilization is intolerant of barbarian isolation" (Moses 1906: 388). Moses argued that a principal justification for external intervention into the tropical regions was to reap the material benefits, for the world at large, of the resources that remained unused by the local inhabitants.

While the prevailing view may have been that some form of expansion on the part of the developed states was inevitable, the relationship between imperialist expansion and colonization was a much more contentious issue. Reinsch believed that although there was a close association between colonization, which he defined as "the exertion of influence by a higher civilization upon one of a lower one, or the creation of civilized life where none had existed before," and imperialism, the two phenomena, in his view, were in no way identical (1902: 14). Since Reinsch believed that it was primarily economic factors that were the driving force behind the latest wave of expansionism, he remained unconvinced about the alleged necessity of installing formal political rule over the inhabitants living in these territories. He felt that in many instances, especially in the case of China where the great powers were carving out exclusive spheres of interest in areas where they had not yet established any commercial or industrial enterprises, the imposition of political control contradicted economic logic. Reinsch argued that there often was an economic loss involved in extending formal political rule over distant territories. He recognized that the investment of large sums of capital by individual entrepreneurs and the increasing movement of citizens to distant lands was typically accompanied by the demand for political sovereignty to be extended to ever-increasing tracts of territory. Yet these arguments by themselves did not, for Reinsch, provide a solid justification for colonialism. At the very least, the supposed advantages of colonialism had to be weighed against all of the negative aspects associated with colonial policy. Moreover, he was sharply critical of individual entrepreneurs who, in the pursuit of their own economic interests, tended to exaggerate the financial gains to the nation as a whole that were to be achieved through investment in the tropical regions.

Both as an academic and in his role as a diplomat, Reinsch thought that the U.S. Open Door policy in China represented an ideal way in which the imperative of expansion could be realized without the need to impose direct colonial rule on distant lands. Reinsch was critical of the imperial method of establishing exclusive spheres of influence, which he believed to "be very dangerous to the world's peace," since "it encourages a habit of looking upon the whole world as available territory for partition among civilized powers" (1900: 61). Reinsch was a great supporter of the Open Door policy formally introduced by Secretary of State John Hay in September 1899. With respect to the situation in China, the aim of the Open Door policy was for those countries who already had established spheres of interest to adhere to the principle of free trade and to respect the territorial integrity of China. While it is beyond the scope of this chapter to deal with the complexities of Open Door diplomacy, it is significant to note that this policy was later interpreted by the members the "Wisconsin School" of historians to be the basis of the United States' imperial, anticolonial policy.[9] William Appleman Williams, the most famous member of the Wisconsin School, described Secretary of State John Hay's Open Door Notes as "a classic strategy of non-colonial imperial expansion." According to Williams, "[T]he policy of the open door was designed to clear the way and establish the conditions under which America's preponderant economic power would extend the American system throughout the world without the embarrassment and inefficiency of traditional colonialism" (1972: 50). By embracing, and actually, in his role as minister to China, implementing the Open Door policy, Reinsch can be viewed as a participant in the American foreign policy tradition of fostering economic expansion through imperialist means, but without the burden of a formal colonial empire.

In the final analysis, Reinsch was a severe critic of both national imperialism and colonialism. Together, he argued, they represented a dangerous threat to world peace, and nowhere did Reinsch think this was more apparent than in the case of China. Yet his objections to national imperialism went beyond the risks that he thought it posed to world peace. As a Progressive-reformer, Reinsch was deeply troubled by what he perceived to be the adverse impact that imperialism had on the domestic home front. Reinsch observed that there was a general tendency amongst the imperial powers to divert attention away from pressing domestic reform issues to foreign policy concerns. Imperialism, he argued, was a diversionary tactic that temporarily withdrew public attention away from domestic affairs. Reinsch wrote, "[A]s national attention is centered on the acquisition of territory and national glory abroad, less attention and energy is left for the national regulation of home affairs, and that the cause of good government must therefore suffer" (1900: 78). He concluded that imperialism represented a threat to the survival of liberal democracy. In the case of the United States, he judged that recent foreign policy developments, particularly those undertaken in the Pacific and the Caribbean, were likely to lead to an enhanced role of the executive to the detriment of the legislative branch of government. This proved to be the case during the course of the McKinley administration in which the executive branch of government finally surmounted the legislative branch (Zakaria 1998).

Finally, within the pages of *World Politics*, Reinsch provided an additional basis for opposing colonialism that would figure prominently in his work on colonial administration, namely, the harmful consequences that the practice had on indigenous populations. He was aware of the damage and destruction that usually accompanied contact between "civilized" and "barbaric" peoples, which paradoxically, for Reinsch, was brought about by the dictates of "advanced civilization." Poignantly, Reinsch wrote:

> The men who, as civilization pushes forward its outposts, come into contact with the savages, usually have no ability or desire to understand them. Cruel methods of conquest and subjection are pursued and most of these races would be happier of they had never seen their civilizers. (1900: 43)

Thus, while the argument of spreading civilization was often put forward to defend the practice of colonialism, Reinsch claimed the reality was that the "promised civilization often consists in a speedy eradication of the savages from the face of the earth" (1900: 20).

While Reinsch championed the Open Door Policy and strongly objected to the practice of colonialism, the spoils of victory that followed the Spanish American War, which Secretary of State John Hay described as a "splendid little war," presented the United States for the first time with several of its own colonial possessions: the Philippines, Puerto Rico, Cuba, Guam, and the Wake Islands. Subsequently, the question of how the United States government should administer these territories became a central component of the public and academic discourse about international politics. Reinsch would emerge as a central voice in this conversation.

COLONIAL ADMINISTRATION

Although rarely acknowledged in the orthodox histories of the field, the study of colonial government and administration within political science comprised a considerable share of the early discourse about international politics. The study of colonial government concerned itself, most broadly, with a variety of issues that arose from the political relations existing between the colonial powers and their dependent territories. A review of the programs from the early annual meetings of the APSA reveals that many panels were devoted to the topic of colonial administration. At the first annual meeting held in Chicago, it was recommended that the APSA establish a colonial section to study the problems connected with colonization and colonial policy (Morris 1904). Many of the leading political science textbooks of the time, such as those by Stephen Leacock (1906) and Raymond Gettell (1910), included a chapter on the topic of colonial government. Gettell claimed that the governmental problems involved in colonial rule "are of prime importance to the student of political science" (Gettell 1910: 348). Yet while it was obvious to most political scientists that the problems of governing and administering distant territories were indeed important, the question of the appropriate way to study these problems elicited a variety of responses.

The study of administration had originally occupied a central position within the discipline of political science. Mary Furner has suggested that it was a "common interest in comparative administration that ultimately led to the creation of a separate national association of political scientists" (1975: 287). Yet while the study of administration had achieved a measure of scientific respectability, the same could not yet be said of colonial administration. Elevating the scientific stature of colonial administration became a major desideratum of the early IR scholars. Alpheus Henry Snow, for example, who was an expert on colonial affairs at George Washington University, raised the possibility of establishing a "science of imperial relations." Snow wrote that just "as there is a recognized science of international relations and another recognized science of the internal relations of nations and states, there may yet perhaps be recognized a science of imperial relations" (1908: 590). Snow's *The Administration of Dependencies* (1902) was considered to be a major contribution to the literature devoted to the general topic of colonization. Unlike much of the existing literature, which merely provided a historical narrative of the past practices of colonial rule, Snow's work was an explicit attempt to draw lessons for the United States from the experiences of the British and French colonial systems.

Alleyne Ireland, a leading authority on colonial administration in both the United States and Great Britain, observed that while the subject of colonial administration increasingly was gaining the attention of both political scientists and the general public, there were few, if any, professional standards guiding research in this area. He sarcastically wrote that "knowledge of calligraphy is regarded as the only qualification necessary for a writer on colonial topics." Ireland argued that the "torrent of ignorant and often violently prejudiced writing" on the subject had resulted in great damage to "the cause of a scientific study of colonial administration" (1906: 210). In a paper that he delivered to the annual meeting of the APSA in 1906, Ireland sought to remedy this situation. He argued that one of the chief defects of the existing literature was the pervasive tendency to include issues about the morality of colonization in the analysis of the administration of dependencies. He felt that such concerns did not come under the proper purview of colonial administration. The morality or immorality of colonialism, Ireland maintained, was an issue that should be examined and resolved irrespective of the consequences that it might produce. Yet when it came to articulating the method that should be followed, Ireland argued that the "method of judging by results, which is false and unscientific when applied to the moral principle of colonization, is precisely the method which must be followed when the subject under investigation is an applied science of colonial administration" (1906: 214). As with much of the administration literature, he argued that efficiency should be the standard used to judge the relative merits of a specific administrative program.

In order to determine the efficiency of a colonial administration policy, Ireland argued that it was important to recognize that there were two conflicting motives or principles from which two completely different methods of colonial administration resulted: the principle of development and the principle of exploitation. With respect to the first principle, Ireland argued that the aim of colonial administration was to provide beneficent rule. The underlying assumption behind this principle was that a prosperous and content native population would, in the long term, yield the best commercial results. Conversely, when the principle of exploitation was applied to colonial administration, the aim was to extract as many resources as possible from a country in the shortest period of time. He maintained that it was important to distinguish clearly between these two fundamentally different policies of colonial administration. With this distinction in mind, the student of colonial administration could then utilize the historical-comparative method, which Ireland argued was the defining element of a science of colonial administration. The method of comparison offered the possibility of providing practical advice to government officials whose responsibility it was to administer efficiently colonial possessions. Instead of merely providing historical descriptions of how other countries had administered their colonies, Ireland encouraged the use of the comparative method in order to evaluate the strengths and weaknesses of different colonial policies. This was the method that Ireland followed in both *Tropical Colonization* (1899) and *Colonial Administration in the Far East* (1907).

REINSCH'S APPROACH TO COLONIAL ADMINISTRATION

There is little doubt that Reinsch, like Ireland, believed that a scientific study of colonial administration should have the practical effect of providing policymakers with the knowledge to devise better colonial policies. As originally conceived, political science was understood to be a scholarly enterprise devoted to acquiring the authority of knowledge over its subject so as to be in the position to reform the practice of politics. During the period that Reinsch was writing, the historical-comparative method was viewed as a scientific mode of investigation, similar in form to the natural sciences, that would eventually lead to the discovery of laws of political development. As a political scientist at Princeton University, Woodrow Wilson had argued that "nowhere in the whole field of politics, it would seem, can we make use of the historical, comparative method more safely than in this province of administration" (1887: 45). Wilson assured American political scientists that it was important to look at foreign systems of administration, because "so far as administrative functions are concerned, all governments have a strong structural likeness" (1887: 45).

On one level, Reinsch thought that now that the United States had become a colonial power, it was appropriate that students of colonial administration make use of the comparative method in order to derive lessons from those powers that had a longer historical experience of colonial rule. In *Colonial Government*, which was written as a textbook for Richard Ely's Citizen's Library of Economics, Politics, and Sociology series, Reinsch explained that with the United States' unexpected possession of an extensive colonial domain, "it is the natural, and the only wise, course to turn to the experience of other nations who have had similar problems to face, and by whose failures and successes we may instruct ourselves" (1902: 13). Unlike some of his colleagues, Reinsch did not believe that the United States could adopt the same methods that were used to "settle" and "subdue" the American continent and apply them to the new insular regions it had acquired. Reinsch claimed that, notwithstanding the unique character of the United States, "it is the part of wisdom at this juncture to review modes of action and institutions by which other nations have been for a long time attempting, with varying results, to solve similar problems" (1902: vi).

On another level, however, Reinsch had reservations concerning the extent to which the United States could derive meaningful lessons about colonial policy from the European powers. When he turned his attention to articulating the sort of colonial policy that the United States should follow toward the insular regions, no one was more critical of the methods of the European powers than Reinsch. Partly as a consequence of the United States' late entry as a colonial power, as well as his belief in the idea of "American exceptionalism," Reinsch concluded that American policymakers could embark on a different path and achieve a truly "enlightened" colonial policy.

At no time, however, did Reinsch suggest that the United States simply grant formal political independence to the territories that Spain had ceded. It was sympathy for Cuban independence from Spanish rule that had provided one of the key justifications for President McKinley's decision to declare war on Spain, but Cuban independence, and for that matter, Philippine independence, proved to be just as illusionary under the tutelage of the United States as it had under Spain.[10] While Reinsch argued that economic motives were the root cause of the most recent wave of colonial expansion, he nevertheless argued that "it was a political motive,—the desire to weaken the prestige of Spain,—that led the American government to make an attack upon Spanish dominion in the Philippine Islands, at a time when the American nation had as yet no economic interests in the archipelago" (1904a: 116). Reinsch felt that the United States had legitimate national interests in the Pacific region, and he personally supported the annexation of the Philippines. He argued that since the United States was in possession of several overseas territories, it would be improper to abdicate responsibility for governing them. In this manner, Reinsch failed to overcome the prejudicial stereotype of his day that held that certain groups of people were simply unfit for self-rule.

Although there were inconsistencies and contradictions in Reinsch's views on expansionism and colonialism, he attempted to resolve many of them by advocating what he considered to be an enlightened and altruistic administrative policy toward the overseas territories. Reinsch devoted considerable effort to devising the most appropriate institutional mechanism for reconciling the indigenous interests of those who inhabited the undeveloped regions with the need for economic expansionism on the part of the "developed" states. After much deliberation and careful thought, Reinsch believed that he had found the proper formula for a successful colonial administration policy: "To foster the cohesion and self-realization of native societies, while at the same time providing the economic basis for a higher form of organization,—that should be the substructure of an enlightened colonial policy" (1906: 412).

The bulk of Reinsch's ideas concerning the appropriate means and ends of colonial administration policy were outlined in his third book *Colonial Administration* (1905), which was a companion volume to *Colonial Government*. Reinsch stated that the purpose of the book was "to furnish a statement of the various problems confronting colonial governments; and to indicate the main lines of solution that have been attempted; selecting from the vast amount of material the most striking illustrations" (1905: v). The historical comparative method was once again invoked as Reinsch surveyed the various methods of colonial administration utilized by the Dutch, English, French, Germans, and Spanish. Individual chapters were devoted to issues such as education and social improvement, colonial finance, colonial commerce, land policy, and the labor question. In the process of formulating colonial administration policy, Reinsch argued that it was necessary to take two different points of view into consideration: the needs of "advanced civilization" and those of the indigenous inhabitants. The needs of the former, according to Reinsch, rested on the fact that the modernization process had resulted in such a successful mastery over the forces of nature that there really was no option but to direct this energy to the far corners of the globe. Confidently, Reinsch declared

> No other society has achieved so complete a mastery over the productive and impellent powers of nature. Out of these characteristics the expansionist movement has naturally developed. It was impossible to restrict the mobility of social forces to national boundaries. (1905: 9–10)

It was on this basis, and no other, that the needs of "advanced civilization" should be considered when developing colonial administration policy.

The needs and interests of the inhabitants in the "backward" regions were the second matter to consider when devising colonial policy. Reinsch took this concern very seriously, and much of *Colonial Administration* was actually written with this in mind. In his review of Reinsch's book, Frank J. Goodnow claimed that the title was somewhat misleading, because it was "devoted to a consideration, largely from the view-point of the dependency, of the policy which should be followed by the mother country towards its colonial possessions" (1906: 135). Reinsch was well aware of many of the ill consequences that often accompanied contact between "advanced" and "backward" peoples. He was genuinely concerned about the negative impact that modernization often had on traditional societies. He believed that colonial administration policy should, to the extent that it was possible, respect local customs and ways of life. At the same time, Reinsch also felt that colonial administration policy had a responsibility to improve the basic living conditions and economic opportunities of the local inhabitants. Possessing superior scientific knowledge made it incumbent on the colonial powers to foster improvements in the areas of health, education, sanitation, communication, transportation, and general infrastructure. "A civilizing colonial policy," Reinsch argued, is one that "improves the general conditions of life" (1905: 30).

Experience has shown that there is often a sharp tension between, on the one hand, respecting local conditions and customs and, on the other hand, working to "improve" and "modernize" a different people's way of life. Quite often, as evidenced by the theory and practice of the modernization school that was dominant throughout the late 1950s and 1960s, of which W. W. Rostow's *The Stages of Economic Growth* (1960) serves as an exemplar, it was the former that frequently was sacrificed to the latter. Reinsch was aware of this tension, and it was on the basis of his view that colonial policy should satisfactorily reconcile the needs of both modern and traditional societies that he emerged as one of the leading critics of the colonial policies that the United States adopted toward the Philippines. In the case of the Philippines, Reinsch observed that the United States was attempting to combine two different and antithetical colonial policies. He argued that the United States was pursuing a policy of assimilation whereby its own institutions were systematically being introduced and adapted to a completely foreign setting. He maintained that no attention whatsoever had been directed toward ascertaining the local conditions of the island or the characteristics of the people living there. Instead, the naïve belief prevailed that what was right for the United States must certainly be right for other people. Assimilation policy, Reinsch argued, "rests upon the old rationalist doctrine of the universality of human reason" (1905: 20). Accordingly, all institutions judged to be rational must also be universal. But this doctrine, according to Reinsch, was fallacious: "Experience seems to show that even those institutions which are by us considered the very foundation of good government may have harmful results when introduced into another society" (1905: 15). Reinsch felt that the defense of assimilation policy on the basis of rationalism was really nothing more than an ideology masquerading as a scientific truth. The historical evidence proved to Reinsch that the policy of assimilation was not only unsuccessful, but often disastrous. Yet Reinsch noted that the second facet of U.S. colonial policy was geared toward the achievement of self-government and autonomy for the people of the Philippines. This was actually the policy that Reinsch preferred, but he objected to the fact that it was being pursued concurrently with a policy of assimilation. Reinsch argued that a policy of autonomy was the exact opposite of a policy of assimilation, because the aim of the former was self-determination. Yet it was self-evident that there were limitations to the United States assimilation policy in that it was never the intention to grant American citizenship to the people of the Philippines. Reinsch suggested that the United States move away from its two-track antagonistic policy and embrace those principles of colonial administration that fostered autonomy and that would, consequently, serve the best interests of humanity.

Reinsch claimed that he had found the answer—one that granted the colonial territories the greatest amount of autonomy—in the form of the protectorate. According to Reinsch, the protectorate embraced the flexibility, insight, and imagination that were necessary for a colonial administration policy dedicated to fostering autonomy. The protectorate, Reinsch explained, "presupposes two separate states, the weaker of which places itself, by treaty, under the protection of the stronger, retaining its internal autonomy, but permitting the protecting state to exert a guiding influence in its foreign affairs" (1902: 109). Influence could still be exerted, but rather than by imposing one's own institutions and seeking to modify directly the social institutions and psychology of "alien races," it would be done indirectly by modifying the economic structure of the dependency. There was a delicate balance to be struck between letting the dependency develop autonomously and exerting just the right amount of indirect influence to ensure that the blessings of modernity were enjoyed by everyone. This required a new type of colonial administrator; one who not only possessed a thorough understanding of the local people and territory, but who had the insight and imagination to construct a colonial policy that could "modify their social evolution in accordance with our experience and thus to obtain for them gradually a higher degree of social well-being and efficiency" (1905, 24). To be able to achieve these ends without simultaneously destroying the society and the people living in the dependent territories was the ultimate task of colonial administration policy.

INTERNATIONALISM

We come full circle when we consider Reinsch's work in the area of international cooperation and his pursuit of a pacific world order. While he had

argued in *World Politics* that the end of the nineteenth century was characterized by an extreme version of nationalism that manifested itself in the form of
national imperialism, he later concluded that the beginning of the twentieth
century was marked by a profound sense of internationalism. Reinsch wrote:

> [N]otwithstanding the definiteness and energy with which the action
> of nationalism asserted itself in nineteenth century politics, the force
> of its current was all the time being diminished and its direction
> modified by that other great principle of social and political combin-
> ation which we may call internationalism, and which comprises
> those cultural and economic interests which are common to civilized
> humanity. (1911: 12)

The national state, Reinsch argued, continued to be the focal point of international politics, but fundamental changes in the relations among states was con-
tributing to a vibrant internationalism. He thought that the best evidence of
this was to be found in the growing ties of interdependence that increasingly
made it difficult for statesmen to achieve their objectives without acting in
concert with others. Certain ends such as economic prosperity and a healthy
population were now desired by all states. Yet Reinsch claimed that these ends
were only achievable if states mutually cooperated with one another. He argued
that the underlying foundations for internationalism were to be found in the
recent convergence of cultural, economic, and scientific interests that were common to all of humanity. Reinsch declared, "[I]n our age such bonds of union
have been powerfully supplemented by the growing solidarity of economic life
throughout the world, as well as by the need in experimental and applied science to utilize the experience and knowledge of all countries" (1907: 579).

Here we can appreciate how Reinsch's ideas about the proper elements of
a colonial administration policy were logically consistent with the manner in
which he viewed the world. Growing ties of interdependence meant that no
state or territory was an isolated island. The well-being of humanity increasingly depended on everyone achieving greater levels of social and economic
efficiency. "Our destiny is a common one," Reinsch asserted, and "whatever
may happen to the nations of Africa and Asia affects *our* life" (1911: 3). The
fruits of modernization could not, therefore, be restricted to the privileged few,
but instead had to be extended to everyone. These arguments are essentially the
same as those made by contemporary advocates of interdependence who insist
that the fate of the developed world is closely tied to that of the impoverished
masses. The condition of interdependence requires that attention be directed
toward the problems plaguing the poorest states in the world; for nothing less
than the very survival of the planet and the human race is at stake.

Given the pervasive view that the writings of the earliest IR scholars were
idealist or utopian in character, it is important to accentuate the fact that

Reinsch did not consider interdependence and solidarity among states to be an abstract or lofty ideal. Rather, he argued that, empirically, they were the defining characteristics of international politics in the early decades of the twentieth century. Reinsch judged his age to be "realistic and practical," and its concepts "positive and concrete." He stated that "the temper of the age is positive and constructive rather than given to idealism and speculation" (1911: 141). Reinsch claimed that more than anything else it was economic factors that were uniting people and fostering an interdependent world. The underlying unity of the world, especially in the areas of economics, science, and technology, made it absolutely necessary for states to coordinate their specific national activities and to establish formal mechanisms for achieving international cooperation. Greater cooperation, Reinsch argued, was to be achieved by the formal creation of international institutions.

Although Reinsch's pioneering work in the area of international organization has gone almost completely unnoticed, his position was nearly the same as those currently working under the heading of neoliberal institutionalism.[11] Like contemporary students of international organization, Reinsch argued that it was the traditional conception of sovereignty that proved to be the greatest obstacle to states realizing their common collective interests. He recognized that independence of action, the ability to act unilaterally, unfettered by commitments to other states or multilateral organizations, was erroneously considered to be the hallmark of state sovereignty. Yet, in language that appears to be strikingly similar to contemporary arguments, Reinsch found it to be "evident that the old abstract view of sovereignty is no longer applicable to the conditions in a world where states are becoming more democratic and where the organization of interests is taking on an international aspect" (1909: 10). What was needed, Reinsch believed, was a conceptual shift in the traditional meaning of sovereignty that could incorporate the view that acting jointly with others to achieve collective aims and interests did not represent a violation of state sovereignty. Reinsch felt that because of the circumstances of modern life, states were "compelled to international cooperation." This meant that the notion of "political sovereignty as enabling a nation to do exactly what it pleases to others" was simply no longer tenable (1911: 5).

The best practical example of a slowly evolving change in the theory and practice of sovereignty was indicated by the development of the more than forty or so public international unions that were the focus of Reinsch's landmark book *Public International Unions Their Work and Organization* (1911). In this work, Reinsch examined the formation, composition, activities, and functions of the numerous public international unions that had arisen in the late 1800s and early 1900s in areas such as trade, health, communications, agriculture, and crime. Public international unions were defined as associations of states that had common interests in coordinating and regulating specific areas of international politics. In this sense, public international unions were nearly identical to what are now termed international regimes or institutions. Examples of public international unions included the International Telegraph Union (one of the earliest examples of a public union formed in 1865), the International Labor Office, the Metric Union, the International Institute of Agriculture, and the Universal Radiotelegraph Union. Once formed, public international unions attempted to fulfill three of the core functions typically associated with governance: legislative, executive, and judicial (1909: 1). In describing how public international unions arose from the expressed need to fulfill vital functions common to all people, and how, once formed, they fulfilled a crucial welfare-maximizing function, Reinsch's work was a precursor of the theory of functionalism later developed by David Mitrany.

Reinsch argued that the desire of states to enter formal associations with other states provided tangible proof of the extent to which their interests and activities were transnational in nature. In each case he examined, Reinsch attempted to demonstrate how common interests among states in specific issue-areas led to the necessity of forming international public unions. The existence of these unions, many of which possessed executive bureaus, arbitration tribunals, and legislative assemblies, proved to Reinsch that true internationalism was taking hold. For those states who were formally members of a particular public international union, Reinsch wrote, "it is not so much the case that nations have given up certain parts of their sovereign powers to international administrative unions, as they have, while fully reserving their independence, actually found it desirable, and in fact necessary, regularly and permanently to co-operate with other nations in the matter of administering certain economic and cultural interests" (1907: 581). These ideas are entirely consistent with the modern functional approach to international politics (Mitrany 1966, 1975). Reinsch viewed the development of international public unions in the most favorable light, believing that a true sense of internationalism had taken hold and confirming that international organization was now an accomplished fact.

Most importantly, Reinsch thought that these developments were advantageous to world peace. Like almost every liberal proponent of interdependence, he reasoned that as states depended ever more on one another, their incentive to engage in war would dramatically decrease. In an age of interdependence, particularly economic interdependence, war would prove to be disadvantageous to all states. Reinsch argued "the incentive to war will become weaker and weaker as the bonds of community between nations increase, such as are provided by communication agencies, by economic and industrial ties, or by scientific cooperation." He added, "[H]ow intolerably painful will be the ruthless interruption of all such relations and activities!" (1911: 7). Both in his capacity as a scholar and activist in the early-twentieth-century peace movement, Reinsch attempted to redirect diplomacy in the direction of achieving greater levels of cooperation among states. After the Great War, Reinsch emerged as a strong critic of secret diplomacy, arguing that "had the decision of war or no war been laid before the peoples of Europe in 1914, with full knowledge of the facts, the terrible catastrophe would have never come about" (1922: 178). He was a strong supporter of the League of Nations and openly endorsed the Covenant's provision to make all treaties public. This was consistent with his firm belief in democracy and in making diplomacy accountable to the people. Before he embarked on his new career as a diplomat, Reinsch was confident that the progressive force of internationalism had been able to tame the destructive path that nationalism had assumed at the end of the nineteenth century. When he resigned from his position as professor of political science at the University of Wisconsin in 1913 to accept President Wilson's offer to become minister to China, Reinsch could look back on the formative role he had played in launching the subfield of IR. His writings on imperialism, colonial administration, and internationalism formed the nucleus of the early academic conversation about international politics.

The themes of imperialism and internationalism were ones that engaged the scholarly attention of Reinsch and his political science colleagues. Reinsch was an active participant in a thriving discourse about international politics that predated World War I. He played an instrumental role in institutionalizing this discourse within the academic context of the newly formed discipline of political science. In his various roles within the APSA and through his career as a prolific scholar and professor at the University of Wisconsin, Reinsch ensured that the subject matter of imperialism, colonialism, and internationalism came under the purview of political science. His important role in helping to launch the field of IR necessitates that we overcome our collective amnesia and recall the formative period of the field's history. Many of the central features that we associate with the study of international politics are a function of the disciplinary origins of the field. In this chapter, I have attempted to reconstruct the early history of IR in order to indicate the prominence that the study of imperialism, colonial administration, and internationalism received when the field was being established. Through this examination of Reinsch's writings, I have aimed to demonstrate that the early discourse cannot be construed as simply idealistic or utopian. Many of Reinsch's ideas continue to have enduring value. His ideas have been incorporated in the main body of work about international politics, and although he is seldom given credit for his significant contributions, we should not ignore Reinsch's profound contributions to the field of IR.

NOTES

Authors note: During the course of writing this chapter, I have benefited greatly from the opportunity to share my thoughts on Paul S. Reinsch and the early history of the field with colleagues at the University of Wales, Aberystwyth, where I presented an early version of the chapter at the Cambrian Seminar series in April 2000. I would like to thank the following colleagues who were in that remarkable Department of International Politics: Ken Booth, Ian Clark, Michael Cox, Tim Dunne, Randall Germain, Steve Smith, Colin Wight, Nicholas Wheeler, Howard Williams, and Mike Williams. I would also like to thank John G. Gunnell, David Long, Ido Oren, Noel Pugach, and Robert Vitalis for their comments and assistance.

1. Symons (1931) provides a comprehensive survey of undergraduate instruction in international affairs at 465 American colleges and universities.

2. For additional clarification of this approach, see Schmidt (1994, 1998a, 1998b).

3. On the first great debate see Kahler (1997), Lijphart (1974), Schmidt (1998a), and Wilson (1998).

4. Not only was nationalism a central concern of interwar scholars such as Angell (1912) and Zimmern (1918, 1923), but also for some of the early realists such as Carr (1939, 1945) and Morgenthau (1948).

5. Murphy (1994) is the major exception to the general tendency of contemporary students of international organization to ignore Reinsch's contribution to the literature. The fiftieth anniversary issue of *International Organization*, for example, does not include a single reference to Reinsch's pioneering work in the area of international organization.

6. Said (1978) and Todorov (1984) represent two important examples of this undertaking.

7. For a historical account of the developments taking place at the University of Wisconsin during this period, see Curti and Carstensen (1949).

8. The original seven sections of the APSA included: comparative legislation, comparative jurisprudence, international law and diplomacy, administration, constitutional law, political theory, and politics.

9. Prominent work by the Wisconsin School includes LaFeber (1963, 1989), McCormick (1989) and Williams (1969, 1972).

10. For background on the Spanish-American War, see Foner (1972), Freidel (1958), LaFeber (1963), May (1961), Williams (1969) and Zinn (1980).

11. A good introduction to the work by neoliberal institutionalists can be found in Keohane (1989) and Baldwin (1993).

Chapter 3

Paternalism and the Internationalization of Imperialism

J. A. Hobson on the International Government of the "Lower Races"

David Long

In this chapter, I consider the English liberal and anti-imperialist J. A. Hobson's defense of an internationalized form of imperialism, an international government of the relations between the so-called developed and less developed world, or as Hobson called them, the "backward" peoples or "lower races." Hobson is famous for his critique of imperialism in his classic work, *Imperialism: A Study*. It is less well known that in *Imperialism* and elsewhere, Hobson proposes international government as a solution to the problem of imperialism. This chapter critically examines Hobson's attempt to soften Western imperialism through the development of global representative institutions. It concludes that Hobson is ultimately trapped in an imperialist and more particularly a paternalist mindset. Paternalist prejudices limit and skew Hobson's proposals for an equitable solution to imperialism. Far from transcending imperialism, Hobson's interventionist liberal prescriptions for international government recast imperialism in a modern form. The chapter concludes that Hobson's flawed proposals for ending imperialism are not anomalous but rather a consequence of a paternalist reflex of liberal internationalists in the face of difference.

Hobson considered international government to be not only a solution to imperialism, but a prescription for an end to international anarchy and an agent of global economic redistribution. Hobson's remedies for aggressive imperialism were interventionist both domestically and internationally. The domestic context is well known and has been criticized by among others Kenneth Waltz (1959, 1979). However, Hobson sought international rules for states and some form of international regulation of imperial activity by an international government, or what we today would call an international regime (Hobson 1917: 85–86; for an extended discussion, see Long 1996).

Recent work by Uday Singh Mehta (1999) and Barry Hindess (2001), combining postcolonial sensibilities with a close reading of the history of liberal thought, delve into and challenge our understandings of liberal rationalizations and critiques of empire. They both point out that, far from being an anomaly for liberalism, empire was central to the interests of liberal political thinkers and integral to the liberal intellectual project. Refocusing on political thought and outlook in the cosmopolitan center, Mehta and Hindess consider liberal justifications and exclusions at the peak of nineteenth-century justifications of empire. By extension they critique the contemporary rationalization of continued oppression of postcolonial peoples. In this chapter, I extend Hindess's and Mehta's analyses to an examination of the writings of a key twentieth-century liberal thinker, J. A. Hobson. Hobson's attempt to get past earlier liberal rationalizations of imperialism does not avoid the paternalist suspension of liberal principles of international conduct. Hobson's international government, though putatively a solution to international inequity and rampant nationalistic imperialism, is still premised on the construction of "backward" peoples or "lower races." Though Hobson was among the great liberal humanists and most progressive reformers of his time, his paternalism as well as his other liberal principles follow in the liberal tradition. Despite Hobson's challenge to liberal laissez-faire and to liberal defenses and rationalizations of imperialism, the way in which he suspends his liberal principles is the same and has essentially the same effect as that of earlier liberals, that is, the paternalist construction renders non-Western peoples the defenseless objects of liberal projects.[1]

The method I adopt in my analysis is a close reading of selected writings of a liberal theorist as an exemplar of a phase in the development of liberal internationalist thinking. In looking at Hobson's arguments and assumptions regarding relations of the so-called civilized and backward peoples,[2] I shall concentrate on his classic study, *Imperialism*. The critique of liberal thinking on international relations advanced in this chapter comes from within the liberal perspective itself. British liberal thinking sets the parameters for the essay. Within this context, I pay attention to ways in which the suspension of liberal principles of mutual recognition in international relations is justified in the case of relations between industrialized Western nations and the African subjects of Western imperialism.

What I mean by paternalism here is the assumption that the relationship of the developed and less developed, or in Hobson's terminology, imperial powers and backward peoples, could be simply viewed as analogous to that of a parent (father) and child (for continuing examples of this metaphor, see Doty 1996: 88–90 and Brysk, Parsons, and Sandholtz 2002). Hobson was at times explicit about this but more often deployed the terminology without explicitly noting where it came from. In my assessment of Hobson's use of the metaphor, I note George Lakoff's argument that we think on the basis of experiential metaphors (Lakoff 1987; Lakoff and Johnson 1980). Hobson had not traveled a great deal in the areas of the world he was discussing. South Africa and Canada were the full extent of his travels in the British Empire. In understanding the relationship, Hobson shortcuts the need for empirical and conceptual comprehension through the use of a then common metaphor that appealed to experience, that is, parenting.[3]

While some critics have identified a discourse of disease in Western approaches to the Other, Hobson relies for both the humanistic and authoritarian aspects of his approach to backward peoples, on a view of the relationship that suggests liberal peoples as the father and nonliberal peoples as the child. The equality so venerated by liberals in international relations dissolves into a paternalistic discourse where liberal states need to take care of backward peoples or lower races. This paternalistic discourse is double-edged. The metaphor of the child should conjure up care and responsibility as well as power and superiority such as is inspired by words such as animal, disease, or vermin. As a result paternalist discourse is more ambiguous than the discourse of disease and other biological metaphors as it applies to imperialism.[4]

From a feminist perspective, the metaphor of the parent-child relationship is in fact paternalistic in a more specific sense, that is, that the metaphor is of a stylized, masculinized father-child relationship, where a more distant and strictly hierarchical teacher-pupil relationship is implied. It might indeed be argued that the discourse of paternalism feminizes as well as infantilizes the Other in order to create a domesticated context in which the usual rules of public order and propriety in international relations can be suspended or deferred, and coercive policies justified.

The chapter begins with a discussion of some of the elements of Hobson's new liberalism, especially its interventionist contrast with laissez-faire liberalism, as well as briefly noting his critique of imperialism, emphasizing the moral and political aspects over the more notorious economic theory with which his name is usually associated. The second section considers Hobson's defense of imperialism on certain conditions, and in the third the role of international government to oversee imperialism is presented. Fourth, I scrutinize Hobson's paternalist terminology and assumptions in which the peoples of the developing world are seen as lower races for whom the analogy to a child could be applied. I conclude with a brief discussion of the implications for contemporary liberal internationalism and for proposals for international reform today.

NEW LIBERALISM AND ANTI-IMPERIALISM

J. A. Hobson is famous for his critique of imperialism and is also well known as a turn of the (nineteenth) century new liberal. Hobson explicitly followed J. S. Mill in his development of liberal political economy and his analysis of nationalism and of international relations. However, when Hobson was writing his classic, *Imperialism: A Study* (1902), a generation after Mill, he was able to incorporate a response to the failures of liberal theory in the face of social, political, and economic change in what has since been described as the Age of Imperialism (Hobsbawm 1987). The key historical developments nationally and internationally were the growth of the size of firms and the increased pace of imperialism. The last few decades of the nineteenth century saw the emergence of joint stock companies, and other innovations in industrial organization marked a period of monopolization and cartelization as big firms or groups of firms began to dominate their markets (Murphy 1994). At the same time, imperialism was gathering speed as the European states and the United States began competing for territorial acquisitions in the less developed regions of the world. Hobson's liberal internationalism reflected the troubles of the times, as the world plunged from competitive imperialism in the late nineteenth century into global war early in the twentieth. For these reasons Hobson is a good deal more critical in general regarding liberalism and also more gloomy about the prospects for its implementation than mid-nineteenth-century liberals.[5]

While Hobson learned his liberalism from his readings of John Stuart Mill, he was not content merely to apply laissez-faire and free trade principles to international relations (or to politics and economics in general). Though he was never an academic, Hobson was an important influence in twentieth-century liberal thought. He was one of a small group of "new liberals" who argued that liberalism à la Cobden and Mill had run its course. Instead, in the domestic context, these new liberals proposed that there was a role for government in countering poverty and unemployment, and for the liberal values of liberty and justice to be realized through state action.

Hobson described himself as an economic heretic. His work in international relations is best seen as part of a wider project to revise economic principles so that they conformed to social liberal ethics, whether on national or global questions. Hobson's new liberalism translated in international relations into an argument that it was time to move beyond Mill's and Cobden's nineteenth-century formulation of liberal internationalism:

> Modern internationalists are no longer mere noninterventionalists, for the same reason that modern Radicals are no longer philosophic individualists. Experience has forced upon them the truth that governments are not essentially and of necessity the enemies of personal or national liberty, but that upon certain conditions they may become its creators, either by removing fetters or by furnishing the instruments of active co-operation by which both individuals and nations better realise themselves. (Hobson 1918: 406)

For Hobson, imperialism is the imposition of foreign rule on subject peoples. He contrasts imperialism with colonialism where there is a significant influx of

colonists. Imperialism, according to Hobson, is not about populating a territory but rather the domination of less fortunate peoples. Hobson noted that
the special characteristic of modern, industrial imperialism was that it involved
the competition of rival empires, and the final closing off of all of the available
territory on the planet. This new global context was the cause of many of
the maladies of imperialism, especially war, that Hobson identified. Internationalism, by contrast, Hobson defined as the cooperation of nations, and
here he meant nations rather than states, but rarely moved beyond generalities
in his discussion. Because his analysis was general he was able to avoid the difficult issues that arise where nation and state are not coincident. Hobson distinguished internationalism from cosmopolitanism, which he associated with
a global mass society of unattached individuals related by little more than the
market. Hobson approved of internationalism and argued that it was built upon
the contributions of various nationalisms. But he strongly disapproved of cosmopolitanism because he saw it as disintegrative and lacking in a social basis.

Hobson was an interventionist liberal both domestically and internationally. Domestically, he argued for government involvement in the running of the
economy, primarily through redistributive fiscal policy rather than Keynesian-
style government spending. Internationally, he was an advocate of a form of
international governance. As a result, we might expect Hobson to be more interventionist internationally than his liberal forebears. Where Mill and Cobden
were both internationalists and yet strongly against intervention except in particular limited cases, Hobson was also an internationalist in his belief that nations
had no absolute right of self-assertion.[6]

However, the emergence of the new imperialism in late-nineteenth-century
international politics conditioned Hobson's views a great deal. In particular, it
made him very skeptical and critical of unilateral state action in international
affairs. Hobson's analysis of imperialism deserves the fame it has subsequently
garnered, though it is considerably more nuanced and wide-ranging than the
synopses of his argument in IR texts or his categorization as a theorist of economic imperialism would suggest.[7] Most important of all, Hobson's analysis
in a series of chapters in the second part of *Imperialism* is an uncovering of the
reality behind the rhetoric of empire, whether this rhetoric saw empire as the
inevitable result of power, the unselfish application of civilization, or a biolog-
ically determined outcome. He goes behind the principles that Mill and his
successors advocated to consider how they were used in practice by various economic and political interests.

Hobson effectively dissects the various misinformed and selfish motives
and justifications for the imperial enterprise and details the impacts on the subjugated as well as on the "civilized." He is at his most devastating in his critique
of "philanthropy and 5 per cent" (Hobson 1988: 201). Hobson was critical of
the full range of activities conducted by European peoples and their governments
in the extension and maintenance of their empires. Throughout his critique he

argued that profiteering and parasitism, as he called it, came at the expense of the subjugated peoples, up to and often including their extermination. A couple of examples will suffice here to give a flavor of the overall tone:

> War, murder, strong drink, syphilis and other civilized diseases are chief instruments of a destruction commonly couched under the euphemism "contact with a superior civilization." (Hobson 1988: 258)

> When the settlement approaches the condition of genuine colonization, it has commonly implied the extermination of the lower races, either by war or by private slaughter, as in the case of the Australian Bushmen, African Bushmen and Hottentots, Red Indians, and Maories, or by forcing upon them the habits of a civilization equally destructive to them. ... This is the root fact of Imperialism so far as it relates to the control of inferior races; when the latter are not killed out they are subjected by force to the ends of their white superiors. (Hobson 1988: 252–53)

In short, says Hobson, imperialism is devastating for the so-called lower races/ backward peoples as well as being bad politics and economics for the imperial nation.

HOBSON'S DEFENSE OF "SANE" IMPERIALISM

Despite his critique of imperialism, Hobson was not totally opposed to some form of imperial rule, as long as that rule was subject to conditions and international oversight. Indeed, Jules Townshend argues that in Hobson's outline of "sane" imperialism (as he called it), he "agreed with much of the imperialist case as advanced by the Fabians, [and the Social Darwinists] Kidd and Giddings." Hobson was arguing, that is, for imperialism with a human face (Townshend 1990: 108, 115). Like other liberal critics of his time, Hobson's apparently uncharacteristic defense of imperialism derives from his proposals for reform or remedy of imperialism. Indeed, he fits well with those anti-imperialists who have been criticized for being stronger in their critiques of the causes of imperialism than in their proposals for change in the context of the actually existing empires (Taylor 1958).

According to Hobson, "[A]ll interference on the part of civilized white nations with 'lower races' is not prima facie illegitimate." Indeed, "civilized Governments *may* undertake the political and economic control of lower races— in a word ... the characteristic form of modern Imperialism is not under all conditions illegitimate" (Hobson 1988: 232; emphasis in the original; see also Hobson 1932: 77). How did the strident opponent of imperialism come to such an apparently imperialistic conclusion? In place of the classical liberal touchstone laissez-faire, Hobson sought "a supreme standard of moral appeal, some conception of the welfare of humanity as an organic unity" that would give him a "general law for the treatment of lower races" (Hobson 1988: 233). Imperialism was not in principle illegitimate, according to Hobson, if it abided by three conditions. These reflected his new liberalism and also the rhetoric (if not the reality) of the new imperialism and its relationship to its purported civilizing mission. The conditions can be seen as Hobson's way of guaranteeing that imperial nations lived up to their promises with regard to their empires and colonial dependencies.

Hobson's three conditions were:

> Such interference with the government of a lower race must be directed primarily to secure the safety and progress of the civilization of the world, and not the special interest of the interfering nation. Such interference must be attended by an improvement and elevation of the character of the people who are brought under this control. Lastly, the determination of the two preceding conditions must not be left to the arbitrary will or judgment of the interfering nation, but must proceed from some organized representation of civilized humanity. (Hobson 1988: 232)

Thus, first of all, "every act of 'Imperialism' consisting of forcible interference with another people can only be justified by showing that it contributes to the 'civilization of the world'" (Hobson 1988: 234). This is Hobson's ultimate standard, a global utilitarianism. He went as far as to consider the propriety of extinction of certain subject peoples in the global good. He ends up rejecting this in significantly limited terms:

> On the highest ground of theory, the repression, even extinction, of some unprogressive or retrogressive nation, yielding place to another more socially efficient and more capable of utilizing for the general good the natural resources of the land, might seem permissible, if we accepted unimpaired and unimproved the biological struggle for existence as the sole or chief instrument of progress. (Hobson 1988: 234)

Hobson rejects this because "in the progress of humanity, the services of nationality, as a means of education and of self-development, will be recognized as of such supreme importance that nothing short of direct physical necessity in self-defence can justify the extinction of a nation" (Hobson 1988: 235).

The second condition was that the rights of and benefits to the native population should be of primary importance in the consideration of whether intervention to exploit natural resources might take place. As we see from the quote above, in Hobson's view these rights would be upheld not by the backward nations themselves but by international agreement of the "organized represen-tation of civilized humanity" (Hobson 1988: 232). Hobson stressed that "impe-rial interference with a 'lower race' must justify itself by showing that it is acting for the real good of the subject race." But he assumed rather than demonstrated that the subjected peoples will be beneficiaries in his internationalized imperial process: "because it seems obvious that the gain to the general cause of civiliza-tion will chiefly be contained in or compassed by an improvement in the char-acter or condition of the nation which is the subject of interference ... " (Hobson 1988: 235).

These two conditions for a "sane" imperialism rest on the inevitability of Western intervention. Hobson believed it was "beyond a shadow of a doubt" "that such development will take place, and such compulsion, legitimate or ille-gitimate, be exercised, more and more throughout this new century in many quarters of this globe.... It is the great practical business of the country to explore and develop, by every method which science can devise, the hidden natural and human resources of the globe" (Hobson 1988: 229). National iso-lation was now impossible because the science and technology of transporta-tion and communications had irreversibly transformed the world and made it intimately interconnected.

Hobson derived an "ought" from this "is." Interconnections of peoples made disinterest under the guise of laissez-faire "impracticable in view of the actual forces which move politics" and "ethically indefensible" because "[t]here can no more be absolute nationalism in the society of nations than absolute individu-alism in the single nation" (Hobson 1988: 225). And he suggested as a result that "[c]omplete isolation is no longer possible even for the remotest island; absolute self-sufficiency is no more possible for a nation than for an individual: in each case society has the right and the need to safeguard its interests against an injurious assertion of individuality" (Hobson 1988: 231).

Hobson believed that the new international context meant that the policy choice for Western nations was no longer between intervention and noninter-vention, if it ever was. Rather, Western nations faced the choice of rationally controlled intervention in the public good or chaotic self-interested exploita-tion of backward peoples and their territories. The question for Hobson was whether there was a role for government regulation of private activity that has taken place under the guise/rubric of imperialism. His position was clear: "The contact with white races cannot be avoided, and it is more perilous and more injurious in proportion as it lacks governmental sanction and control" (Hobson 1988: 231). As a new liberal and an internationalist, Hobson believed there was a role for government but not national governments deciding for themselves and taking action unilaterally. In the face of interconnectedness, it was the responsibility of Western governments to make sure that the process of open-ing up developing countries' resources was not overtly exploitative, as it would be if it were left to private business interests (Hobson 1919: 128). The direction

was clear: "To abandon the backward races to these perils of private exploitation … is a barbarous dereliction of a public duty on behalf of humanity and
the civilization of the world" (Hobson 1988: 231). A hands-off approach was
indefensible because it would

> let loose a horde of private adventurers, slavers, piratical traders, trea-
> sure hunters, concession mongers, who, animated by mere greed of
> gold or power, would set about the work of exploitation under no pub-
> lic control and with no regard to the future; playing havoc with the
> political, economic, and moral institutions of the peoples, instilling
> civilized vices and civilized diseases, importing spirits and firearms as
> the trade of readiest acceptance, fostering internecine strife for their
> own political and industrial purposes, and even setting up private
> despotisms sustained by organized armed forces. (Hobson 1988: 230)

Hobson briefly considered but dismissed the idea that backward peoples
could defend themselves, that is, a policy of actually leaving native populations
alone. Besides his concern that the military and technological superiority of
the imperial nations was overwhelming, Hobson was not in any case persuaded by nationalist arguments against such international interference. Anti-
interventionist arguments, he reasoned, rested on the absolute right of nations
to do what they wanted with "their" natural resources. Hobson rejected this
argument on the ground that there was no such absolute right to property.
The criterion for national as well as individual property was, for Hobson, a
social criterion rather than an individual entitlement (Long 1996; Freeden
1988).

Hobson's utilitarianism shaped his views here: specifically, he considered
that ownership depended on the ability to use the property. In cases where natural resources that could be exploited for the common good were in less developed countries populated by peoples unable or unwilling to exploit them, he
argued that advanced countries could benefit all of humanity, and not just
themselves, by developing these resources. Accordingly, advanced nations
should be allowed to exploit these resources, even if this was against the immediate wishes of the inhabitants of the area whose resources were to be developed. The indigenous population had no intrinsic right, according to Hobson,
to stand in the way of a development that would benefit humanity at large
(Hobson 1909: 256–57). This was not just a brute fact resulting from technological advances but rather was a moral position. According to Hobson, "It is
our duty to see that [natural resources] are developed for the good of the
world" (Hobson 1988: 227). It should go without saying that this is an imperialist argument that rests on an unproven and indeed unquestioned assumption
that the native occupants of the land are not making use of it.

But exploitation of natural resources was not the only context involving international interdependence that Hobson considered. He presented two persuasive hypothetical examples. One in which

> a people on the upper reaches of a river like the Nile or the Niger might so damage or direct the [226] flow as to cause plague or famine to the lower lands belonging to another nation. Few, if any, would question some right of interference from without in such a case. Or take another case which falls outside the range of directly other-regarding actions. Suppose a famine or other catastrophe deprives a population of the means of living on their land, while unutilized land lies in plenty beyond their borders in another country, are the rulers of the latter entitled to refuse an entrance or necessary settlement? (Hobson 1988: 225–26)

Hobson's answer was a categorical "no." The persuasiveness of the examples allows Hobson to slip over the fact that there is no justification for limiting such reasoning to the imperial context.

THE INTERNATIONAL FORM OF "SANE" IMPERIALISM

If Hobson's first two conditions focused on the benefit to humanity in general and the local population in particular, the third condition was in fact how Hobson saw the first two being guaranteed. According to Townshend, "One of Hobson's biggest departures from the Cobdenite tradition of non-intervention lay in his advocacy of trusteeship over the 'lower races' … by an 'organised representation of civilised humanity'" (Townshend 1988: 26–27). Hobson suggested the need of an international government to supervise the development of natural resources in the backward countries and to manage imperialism more generally. As such, he is rightly regarded as a forefather of League of Nations Mandates and the UN's Trust Territories (Brailsford 1948: 25).

Indeed, rhetorically at least, Hobson deployed the notion of trust a good deal more than mandates. Often, he was critical noting that "[t]he actual history of Western relations with lower races occupying lands on which we have settled throws, then, a curious light upon the theory of a 'trust for civilization.'" (Hobson 1988: 252). Against imperialists, he argued that the

> claim to justify aggression, annexation, and focible government by talk of duty, trust, or mission can only be made good by proving that the claimant is accredited by a body genuinely representative of civilization, to which it acknowledges a real responsibility, and that it is in fact capable of executing such a trust. (Hobson 1988: 238)

Following this logic of the trust, the third of Hobson's criteria for sane imperialism was its formal internationalization, which was necessary because "[i]t is surely unreasonable to take as proof of the fulfilment of the conditions of sane Imperialism the untested and unverified *ipse dixit* of an interested party" (Hobson 1988: 237). In other words, imperial countries should not intervene on the basis merely of their own claim that their self-interest accorded with the global good or that their self-interest had priority over the common good of humanity. Such self-assertion was indeed, for Hobson, the "radical moral defect" of imperialism (Hobson 1909: 259). The only way of being sure that the interests of humanity and of the local population were being advanced, according to Hobson, was international oversight.

In *Imperialism*, Hobson proposed international government as one of the necessary elements of a just solution to the problem of imperialism and the development of less developed countries, as well as an institution to oversee the control of world population growth and a guardian of free trade (Hobson 1988: 191–93, 232–39). According to Hobson, what came to be called Mandates in the League of Nations system would be territories where the international government would be the arbiter of the rival claims of the great powers. The international authority would have the power and duty to monitor the respective mandated power to ensure that development policies were not prejudicial to the welfare of the native population or the interests of other nations or humanity as a whole (Hobson 1988: 232; cf. H. N. Brailsford: 25).

International government overseeing imperialism would have a number of roles, the first of which was preserving insofar as possible nonintervention. Hobson argued that states should agree not to come to the aid of their nationals in the latters' dealing with foreign countries, particularly in the case of less developed societies (Hobson 1988: 360). While this looks like a return to classical liberal internationalism, it is not for two reasons. First, Hobson believed that nonintervention would not just happen but had to be guaranteed by an international organization. Second, Hobson in actual fact here refuted the classical liberal notion that intervention was indeed justified in the case of less civilized peoples (Long 1996b). Such arguments Hobson understood as the pretext for imperialism that they were.

Beyond nonintervention, international government fulfilled three functions for Hobson. First, it would arbitrate the claims of the great powers in order to avoid as far as possible global conflict. Second, it would institutionalize the norms of an international economic order of free trade. And third, it would supervise the development of natural resources in the backward countries, and more generally oversee the development of the "lower races." As Jules Townshend has contended, Hobson envisaged in outline, a "kind of international welfare state" (Townshend 1990: 108; for a more extensive discussion, see Long 1996: ch. 8).

However, *Imperialism* is also notable for Hobson's worries that any international governmental structure would be dominated by the advanced nations and used to their benefit. He suggested that while "treaties and alliances hav-ing regard to the political government and industrial exploitation of countries occupied by lower races may constitute a rude sort of effective internationalism in the early future," nevertheless, common international policy on "lower races" more closely approximated a business deal than a moral trust (1988: 241). After writing *Imperialism*, Hobson became increasingly concerned by the possibility of what he called inter-imperialism, "an economic international co-operation of advanced industrial peoples for the exploitation of the labour and the unde-veloped natural resources of backward countries, chiefly in Africa and Asia" (Hobson 1930: 115). This would be a "world-order" where "the ruling classes of the most powerful Western allies undertake in the name of pacific inter-nationalism the political government and the economic exploitation of the weaker peoples and the less developed countries of the world" (Hobson 1915: 20; see also Hobson 1917: 191). With the fervor for a new world order during and immediately after World War I, Hobson predicted that the new League of Nations might become a vehicle for inter-imperialism. It would be

> a League from which all non-European States, except perhaps the United States and Japan, were excluded, [and] would be exceedingly likely to develop a wide conscious "imperialism" which would in the long run prove not less dangerous to the peace of the world than the national antagonism of the past, in that it was the expression of the joint ambitions and pretensions of a group of powerful white nations masquerading as world government. (Hobson 1915: 15)

Even if an international council was "representative of all the Powers," "collu-sion of the dominant nations [is] the largest and gravest peril of the early future," because "[t]here would still be grave danger lest the 'powers,' arroga-ting to themselves an exclusive possession of 'civilization,' might condemn to unwholesome and unjust subjection some people causing temporary trouble to the world by slow growth, turbulence or obnoxious institutions, for which lib-erty might be the most essential condition of progress" (Hobson 1988: 239). In addition to the overtly exploitative dimension to this world order, Hobson also predicted rather apocalyptically that any such parasitical pax Europoea, as he called it, would fail in the same manner as the pax Romana of the Roman Empire (1988: 194–95).

But these worries about the future of international governance did not prevent Hobson pondering other roles of an international body in *Imperialism*. Among his more now seemingly outlandish ideas, Hobson (1988: 193) pro-posed a hypothetical international organization for population control because "[e]ffective internationalism is the only sound basis of competition and rational selection among nations." He argued that the rational rejection of "unsound racial stock implies the existence of an international political organization which has put down war and has substituted this rational for the cruder national selection and rejection of races". The international organization would also protect "weak but valuable nationalities, and can check the insolent brutality of powerful aggressors" (Hobson 1988: 191, 193).

Morality aside, in *Imperialism*, Hobson's focus is more on the "scientific" arguments and the practicalities than about the humanity of the international control of population. He was most concerned to refute Pearson's idea that conflict must continue in the society of nations. At the same time, he accepted key elements of the racial selection theory, arguing that "[b]iology demands as a condition of world-progress that the struggle of nations or races continue; but as the world grows more rational it will in a similar fashion rationalize the rules of that ring, imposing a fairer test of forms of national fitness" (Hobson 1988: 188).

But Hobson applied a domestic analogy claiming that "[a]s in the case of individuals, so now of nations, the competition will be keener upon the higher levels; nations having ceased to compete with guns and tariffs will compete with feelings and ideas" (Hobson 1988: 185). And the conclusions of this analogy and the logic of population control were brutal but clear to Hobson, though he noted that the argument derived strictly from the biological, scientific view of the likes of Pearson rather than being a moral perspective.

> If the ordinary processes of physical degeneracy within the nation do not suffice for the elimination of bad stock, but must be supplemented by some direct prohibition of bad parentage, it must be necessary in the interests of humanity that similar measures should be enforced upon the larger scale by the mandates of organized humanity. As lower individuals within a society perish by contact with a civilization to which they cannot properly assimilate themselves, so "lower races" in some instances disappear by similar contact with higher races whose diseases and physical vices prove too strong for them. A rational stirpiculture in the wider social interest might, however, require a repression of the spread of degenerate or unprogressive races, corresponding to the check which a nation might place upon the propagation from bad individual stock. (Hobson 1988: 190–91)

International organization of population would, then, eliminate the pain and misery of the millions born in poverty. "It is not necessary for the safety and progress of society that 'unfit' children should die," he thought, "it is necessary that they should not be born ... " (Hobson 1988: 1964).

In short, "Rational humanity would economize and humanize the struggle by substituting a rational, social test of parenthood for the destruction of children by starvation, disease, or weakness" (Hobson 1988: 163). Such a drastic view of the role and function of international government was not one that Hobson maintained throughout his career. Indeed, the authoritarian tone of parts of *Imperialism* contrasts with other more considered sections, the latter of which are more readily reflected in his later work. Certainly the work written in 1902 reflected the spirit of the age, which was permeated by a considerable strain of Social Darwinism, though it must be noted that Hobson left the third edition of *Imperialism*, published more than thirty years later in 1938, substantially unchanged.[8]

HOBSON'S PATERNALISM: "LOWER RACES" AS CHILDREN REQUIRING EDUCATION

In his prescriptions for an international organization to oversee imperialism, Hobson looked for "general principles of guidance in dealing with countries occupied by 'lower' or unprogressive peoples" (Hobson 1988: 225). However, his general principles contain a number of unjustified and undefended assumptions about the peoples who were subject to imperialism, the most important of which rely on a paternalist view of the relationship of the imperial countries and the subject populations. In fact, there are two analogies at work here. First of all, Hobson assumes that one can understand the relations of nations in much the same way as one might understand the relations of individuals in society. This is the well-known and widely criticized domestic analogy (Suganami 1989). In combination with the idea that nations can be metaphorical persons, the paternalist assumption reads the Western nations as adults and the many peoples of the developing world as children. So Hobson argues for example that, "[t]he economy of internationalism is the same as that of nationalism. As individuality does not disappear, but is quickened and raised by good national government, so nationality does not disappear but is raised and quickened by internationalism .... As in the case of individuals, so now of nations..." (Hobson 1988: 185). However, the paternalist assumption can work alone, as it does above in Hobson's notion of fitness to be born or in the notions of education that Hobson deploys.

Hobson's paternalism is most obvious in his use of terminology. In *Imperialism*, he is occasionally critical of the misuse of the metaphor of less developed peoples as children (Hobson 1988: 222).[9] More often, though, he embraces the metaphor and uses it to advance his arguments about the need for imperial control despite his critique of the reality of Western imperialism. "The analogy furnished by the education of a child is prima facie a sound one," he argued, "and is not invalidated by the dangerous abuses to which it is exposed" (229). In particular, Hobson suggested that "[t]he races of Africa it has been possible to regard as savages or children, 'backward' in their progress along the same general road of civilization in which Anglo-Saxondom represents the vanguard, and requiring the help of more forward races" (285).[10]

Hobson's construction of imperialized peoples as children clearly underlies his notion of a trust. In his view of "sane" imperialism, the imperial power has a trust for civilization in looking after and assisting the dependent people in their development. "[I]t is generally agreed that the progress of world-civilization is the only valid moral ground for political interference with 'lower races,' and ... the only valid evidence of such progress is found in the political, industrial, and moral education of the race that is subjected to this interference". In the trust, the metaphor of the parent-child relationship is significantly double-edged, involving both control and responsibility, education and coercion. A good deal of Hobson's criticisms of imperialism focus on the lack of responsibility exhibited by imperial nations because "the true conditions for the exercise of such a 'trust' are entirely lacking." In fact, imperialism "lacks the first essential of a trust, viz. security that the 'trustee' represents fairly all the interested parties, and is responsible to some judicial body for the faithful fulfilment of the terms of the trust" (Hobson 1988: 237). However, this critique centering on irresponsibility suggests what is wrong with the relationship between the imperial powers and the subject peoples is the quality of the relationship—that the imperial nations are bad fathers, so to speak—rather than the unequal relationship itself as such.

The child metaphor drives the idea of a trust. This meant responsibilities for the trust holder, according to Hobson:

> If we or any other nation really undertook the case and education of a "lower race" as a trust, how should we set about the execution of the trust? By studying the religions, political and other social institutions and habits of the people, and by endeavouring to penetrate into their present mind and capacities of adaptation, by learning their language and their history, we should seek to place them in the natural history of man; by similar close attention to the country in which they live, and not to its agricultural and mining resources alone, we should get a real grip upon their environment. Then, carefully approaching them so as to gain what confidence we could for friendly motives, and openly discouraging any premature private attempts of exploiting companies to work mines, or secure concessions, or otherwise impair our disinterested conduct, we should endeavour to assume the position of advisers. [sic] Even if it were necessary to enforce some degree of authority, we should keep such force in the background as a last resort, and make it our first aim to understand and to promote the healthy operations of all internal forces for progress which we might discover. (Hobson 1988: 243)

This lengthy quotation demonstrates the hierarchical view of the relationship that Hobson held. Furthermore, the construction of whole populations of the world as lower, backward, as children, generates a question that needs an answer in Hobson's mind: "The real issue is whether, and under what circumstances, it is justifiable for Western nations to use compulsory government for the control and education in the arts of industrial and political civilization of the inhabitants of tropical countries and so-called lower races" (Hobson 1988: 228). "This real issue" is how one trains the child, which is ultimately an issue "of safeguards, of motives, and of methods. What are the conditions under which a nation may help to develop the resources of another, and even apply some element of compulsion in doing so?" (Hobson 1988: 229). In short, because subject peoples are children who require education and thus have to be taught, not only should there be control and a system of education but in addition certain amounts of legitimate force may be applied.

As a consequence of the metaphor, while education and development are the main aims for Hobson, coercion and violence (compulsion in Hobson's terms) are not wholly illegitimate. Again using the analogy to the control of a child, he claimed that "[f]orce is itself no remedy, coercion is not education, but it may be a prior condition to the operation of educative forces. Those, at any rate, who assign any place to force in the education or the political government of individuals in a nation can hardly deny that the same instrument may find a place in the civilization of backward by progressive nations" (Hobson 1988: 228–29). And this then leads inevitably, it seems, to a coercive conclusion with regard to the subject peoples, as "there can be no inherent natural right in a people to refuse that measure of compulsory education which shall raise it from childhood to manhood in the order of nationalities" (Hobson 1988: 229).

This legitimation of force was not the only way that Hobson envisaged the 'education' of subject peoples. He argued that

> if under the gradual teaching of industrial arts and the general educational influences of a white protectorate many of the old political, social, and religious institutions decay, that decay will be a natural wholesome process, and will be attended by the growth of new forms, not forced upon them, but growing out of the old forms and conforming to laws of natural growth in order to adapt native life to a changed environment. (Hobson 1988: 279–80)

Hobson does not tell us how we would discern such a natural development from the encounter with "civilized" diseases, habits, and institutions.

Given this construction, it may seem somewhat ironic that Hobson's ideal for the future of the subject peoples was self-government, as he claimed that "[n]atural growth in self-government and industry along tropical lines would be the end to which the enlightened policy of civilized assistance would address itself" (279). So much was he captured by his paternalist assumptions that it hardly seems to have occurred to Hobson that these peoples would be self-governing if they had been left alone! And yet elsewhere Hobson is utterly clear-sighted about the negative implications of the international government of dependencies. He doubts feasibility of a "genuine international council which shall accredit a civilized nation with the duty of educating a lower race" (239). But Hobson's problems here are not with the notion of control over subject peoples but rather the competition among the Western nations for control, that is, as bad fathers or bad teachers.

Paternalism is also evident in what Hobson does not say as much as what he does. In *Imperialism* and elsewhere, Hobson routinely discussed the peoples of Europe using the idiom of nationhood, an idiom that clearly makes them members of the wider international society. By contrast, the so-called backward peoples or lower races are rarely described as nations by Hobson. This is a significant omission since it is clear that for Hobson as for Mill before him the rules of civilized societies only apply to nations.

The paternalism of Hobson's schema for international government is confirmed by his treatment of the political representation of the mandated territories. Even in his later work, such as *Towards International Government* (1915), Hobson is vague on this issue, but he does not seem to consider the possibility of representation. If mandated territories were not to be represented, it would appear that international government is merely an institutionalization of the inter-imperialism of advanced nations Hobson hoped to avoid. If mandated territories were to be represented, interference by other states and by the international government, justified by whatever means, would give them a lower status than that of the rest of the world. Hobson was apparently untroubled by such contradictions and blatant paternalism in his ideas. This is a strange conclusion for someone who was supposedly so concerned about questions of welfare and just peace in the relations of developed and less-developed peoples (Hobson 1929: 391).

It is difficult to see how Hobson's internationalized "sane" imperialism could avoid producing exactly his dreaded inter-imperialism, the collusion of the Western nations in the exploitation of the rest of the world. Hobson foresaw such a development and viciously criticized the League of Nations for actually instituting it: "[T]he ruling classes of the most powerful Western allies undertake in the name of pacific internationalism the political government and the economic exploitation of the weaker peoples and the less developed countries of the world" (Hobson 1915: 20; 1919). More generally, Hobson did not confront the question of what justifies the use of force. He assumes that particular interests render the use of force illegitimate. But he seems to embrace the opposite, that force in the general interest is legitimate. This is not obvious, especially if the international body is not truly representative. Hobson elides the question of how international organization legitimizes imperial aggression in the past or present.

CONCLUSION

Despite their commitment to equality and liberty, liberals have had little trouble justifying imperialism. For nineteenth-century liberals such as John Stuart Mill, the liberal verity of nonintervention did not apply to backward peoples (Long 1986b; Mehta 1999). By contrast, at several points in his arguments, Hobson implicitly acknowledged the prima facie case that liberal principles should apply to the so-called lower races too. However, both his interventionist new liberalism and his paternalist assumptions compromised his egalitarianism. Thus, he called for the creation of an international body to control and oversee rather than remove Western imperialism.

Because of his new liberalism Hobson was much more predisposed to international organization and cooperation as a solution to the problems of imperialism. But his paternalism has deep roots in liberal international thought. Hobson's liberal internationalism is based on premises concerning the primacy of individual liberty, an emphasis on the greatest happiness of the greatest number of people, the importance of democracy, the growth of civilization, and the development of peaceful international relations based on these. Yet Hobson's liberal humanism, wherein international relations between liberal, civilized peoples were governed by a set of mutually agreed and mutually beneficial rules, stopped short of the international relationship of so-called civilized peoples with those peoples considered less civilized and thus either unable or unwilling to be governed by liberal principles. Where humanism ends, paternalism begins. Paternalism is manifested in Hobson's writings in the characterization of the Western nations as knowledgeable adults, wordly-wise and trustworthy, and of the "backward peoples" or "lower races" as children who required the tutelage of a benevolent father.

I have briefly argued the parent-child metaphor is not an irredeemably oppressive one: the education and other care of a child is a serious responsibility, and Hobson is quite clear that he is issuing a moral injunction of care. Yet, the construction of the father and child relationship is at best based on a partial understanding of the imperial relationship. Paternalism justifies the suspension of those liberal rules of equality, representativeness, and fairness that are based on the presumption of the autonomy and agency of peoples, rules that were also intended to buttress rights of people and peoples. Because these liberal rules are taken not to apply, serious breaches of liberal ethics follow, including the justification of imperial control and aggression. At the same time, paternalist assumptions legitimize coercive control, and even violence and destruction.

Hobson differed from earlier liberals in that he was prepared to acknowledge the variability and multidimensionality of civilization, while earlier liberals saw civilization as a single absolute standard by which peoples can be measured (see Mehta 1999; Gong 1984). He argued that "the notion that civilization is a beaten track, upon which every nation must march, and that social efficiency, or extent of civilization, can be measured by the respective distances the nations have gone, is a mischievous illusion" (Hobson 1988: 188). And he suggests that it is naïve to believe "religion and other arts of civilization are portable commodities which it is our duty to convey to the backward nations, and that a certain amount of compulsion is justified in pressing their benefits upon people too ignorant at once to recognize them" (Hobson 1988: 237).

I have examined Hobson's arguments regarding the international government of "lower races." Admittedly, it is easy to catch Hobson's inconsistencies, unsubstantiated rhetorical flourishes, and the like. And given that he wrote so much, it is not difficult to find that he changed his mind, very sensibly and reasonably in most cases, in fact. Hobson was not a rigid thinker. For instance, Hobson's *Economic Interpretation of Investment* contradicts many of the arguments about the value and import of foreign investment and international finance that appeared less than ten years before in *Imperialism*. As a result, a critical reading must be a balance of an evaluation of consistency and analysis of particular arguments with an overall appreciation of the admittedly flawed yet frequently insightful work of an important liberal humanist.

Indeed, it is not enough that we criticize the paternalist assumptions in Hobson's work. The mere unfamiliarity of some of his more extreme statements makes this an easy task. However, the contemporary terms we are left with, most obviously "development" itself, derive from the very same paternalist metaphor: developing nations were (are) expected to develop as the child's psychology and physical capabilities develop. At some point, we need to ask if it is possible to escape such metaphors, or as Manning (1975) suggests, whether the best way forward is not to try to avoid them but rather to see them for what they are and to create others that may be more appropriate. The passage of time not only shifts the meanings of words but can also shift attitudes to the notions those words describe. In this case, not only do the metaphors "lower," "backward," and "children" strike us as jarring today, but Hobson's ideas with regard to the role of force in education and the development of children reveals a more authoritarian attitude, which was prevalent in Hobson's day.

Finally, the lessons of the analysis of Hobson's rationalizations and the paternalist assumptions behind them can be applied to more recent incarnations of liberal internationalism. For instance, the recently published report of the International Commission on Intervention and State Sovereignty, *The Responsibility to Protect* (2001), replicates many of the liberal and paternalist themes that we have seen in Hobson. Where liberal ideals are absent, it is the responsibility of state leaders to ensure their guarantee, and if this cannot be fulfilled by local leaders, the burden falls to developed Western states to guarantee human rights, development, and progress to these people. At the same time, relations of the so-called advanced West and the less-developed worlds are, as Hobson argued, unavoidable and a hands-off attitude is not clearly the most ethically defensible response. Paternalism is replicated in, for instance, the (less than liberal) discourses of Russia's "Near Abroad" and the U.S. attitudes toward intervention globally as well as in the discussion of what the UN should do about "failed states." These issues suggest two things. First, liberal internationalism evokes paternalism whenever it encounters difference or perceived weakness. Second, the paternalistic construction of the inequality, and the relationship of the West and the rest, generates particular types of questions leading to a limited set of answers, answers that are usually interventionist, calling on the West to intervene. The consideration of Hobson's paternalism in this chapter suggests we should be very careful with such constructions.

NOTES

1.   That his rationalizations should be so fundamentally similar suggests that it is not a happenstance but rather may be intrinsic to (their) liberalism. Elsewhere (see Long 1996b), I have shown the relationship between Hobson's ideas and those of J. S. Mill. Specifically, the changes in liberalism and liberal internationalism in their approach to international institutions are superimposed on this paternalist attitude, creating different modes of expression of liberal paternalism at the historical junctures at which Mill and Hobson were writing.

2.   Hobson used quotation marks around the terms backward peoples and lower races very deliberately in most of his work, being concerned to note that this was a case of labeling which should not simply be taken for granted. However, while this was a deliberate technique, it was one that Hobson was not entirely consistent in using, creating some confusion in his actual meaning.

3.   Lakoff argues that such metaphorical reasoning usually is at some point "embodied," that is, it relates to some direct physical experience.

4.   See George Lakoff (1987) for the significance and functioning of metaphor in categorization. Indeed, the negative and authoritarian assumption relating to this metaphor may well reflect as much on contemporary attitudes to children in Western societies as it does to the past of international relations.

5.   For an excellent discussion of the outlines and development of new liberalism in the UK, see Michael Freeden 1978.

6.   One of the particular special cases was with respect to the so-called lower races where Mill defended intervention in very strong terms. For a discussion, see David Long 1996b.

7.   I cannot consider the various aspects of Hobson's analysis of imperialism. For a deeper analysis, see Long 1996a: chs. 4–5.

8.   One might account for this in a number of ways. Certainly, by this time Hobson was into his eighties, though he was nevertheless healthy enough to write and publish an autobiography and a new introduction to *Imperialism*.

9.   And at another point (217) he is very critical of the role of the school system in imperial countries in fanning imperialist sentiment.

10.   Hobson follows this with the comment that "[i]t is not so easy to make a specious case for Western control over India, China, and other Asiatic peoples upon the same ground" (285). Hobson rated Indian and Chinese civilization highly. For instance, on China, see Hobson 1988: 322–23. Elsewhere (225), Hobson distinguishes between "low-typed unprogressive races, countries whose people manifest a capacity of rapid progress from a present low condition, and countries like India and China, where an old civilization of a high type, widely different from that of European nations, exists."

Chapter 4

"A Liberal in a Muddle"

Alfred Zimmern on Nationality, Internationality, and Commonwealth

Jeanne Morefield

From the moment Alfred Zimmern's book *Nationality and Government* (1918) was first published, fellow liberals found it troubling. How, wondered *The Nation* in its November 23, 1918, review article entitled "A Liberal in a Muddle," could a man with such liberal credentials place such faith in the ineffable qualities of nationalism? Had this influential Foreign Office employee and soon-to-be professor of international relations abandoned liberal individualism altogether for a hazy internationalism based on the correctly channeled flow of nationalist sentiment? Ironically, in *The Twenty Years' Crisis* ([1939] 1964), E. H. Carr would make precisely the opposite critique. The problem with all of Zimmern's work, according to Carr, was not that Zimmern had rejected liberalism for nationalism but rather that he was too liberal, that he relied too completely on the thoroughly liberal "harmony of interests" doctrine—the notion that when all nations worked to improve their individual circumstances, internationalism would inevitably follow. It was this belief in an expanded liberal vision of the world, argued Carr, that made Zimmern's diagnoses of world problems seem "almost ludicrously disproportionate to the intensity and complexity of the international crisis" (Carr 1961: 39).

The inability of his contemporaries (much less those of us who study him in retrospect) to summarize Alfred Zimmern's politics neatly has, over the years, led many scholars to throw up their hands, reject him as simply "utopian," and dismiss his impact on the discipline of international relations (IR) and the theory and practice of internationalism altogether. The paucity of scholarship on Zimmern and his legacy, however, is troubling for two reasons. On a purely historical level, Alfred Zimmern wielded a considerable amount of power within international relations circles in Britain both before and after

World War I. As a young Fellow at Oxford before 1910, he influenced a number of students who would go on to play key roles in the formation of IR as a discipline in Britain, including Arnold Toynbee, Reginald Coupland, and several future members of the Round Table Society.[1] As the first professor of international politics in the world (at the University of Wales, Aberystwyth), the first Montague Burton professor of international relations at Oxford, and one of the founding members of both the Institute of International Affairs in London and the Geneva Institute for International Relations, Zimmern himself was intimately involved with the creation of the discipline of IR (Markwell 1986: 280). Likewise, as this chapter will discuss further, Zimmern's impact on the League of Nations' Covenant (and thus on internationalism between the wars) was also considerable.

On a more theoretical level, the intellectual foundations of Zimmern's liberalism were never simply muddled. Rather than merely reflecting a naïve faith in the unifying possibilities of nineteenth-century liberalism, as Carr contends, or an outright rejection of liberal individualism, as the editors of *The Nation* claimed, they demonstrated a deep attachment to the far more complicated and internally contradictory qualities of the late-nineteenth-century liberal idealism associated with Oxford. This was a liberalism that, in the tradition of T. H. Green, struggled to reconcile individualism and collectivism, spirituality and rationality, capitalism and morality, and a deep fear of the state with a belief in limited state intervention. Green himself addressed these tensions by coupling his liberalism with a Hegelian inspired notion of "Spiritual Principle." Later, Zimmern's work labored to hold together national and universalist strains in international politics by rooting the impetus to global morality in the "spiritual heritage" of all nations.

It was Zimmern's repeated insistence that nationalism provided the key to world peace that made his work seem so patently inscrutable and naïve to future generations of IR critics. And, in the case of both nationalist imperialism during World War I and the rise of fascism in the 1920s and '30s, these observations seem perfectly correct. It thus appears almost stunningly counterintuitive that Zimmern would develop a theory based on a commitment to the morality of nationalism precisely at a time when nationalists in Europe were behaving in a clearly power-driven, expansionist fashion. At the same time, it seems equally counterintuitive that he would continue to champion the moralizing potential of nationalist passions throughout the 1920s and into the 1930s, well after Mussolini's 1922 march on Rome and the Nazis' rise to power.[2] Perhaps, then, the only way to understand Zimmern's commitment to nationalism is to try to make sense of just how pointedly and powerfully the nation spoke to his internationalist imaginary.

The bulk of this chapter attempts to do this by exploring Zimmern's faith in the world-unifying possibilities of nationhood, paying particular attention to the way he organized his nationalist internationalism through the idea of commonwealth. In order to do this, it first looks at the intellectual origins of Zimmern's politics, origins rooted in the idealist-inflected liberalism that so permeated Oxford during his undergraduate days. The second section looks more closely at Zimmern's attempt to reconcile liberalism with the transcendent qualities of spirit and the "intimacies" of national life. It was his desire for intimate and authentic communities, this section concludes, that drove him toward a philosophical reliance on the metaphor of the family and, ultimately, toward a paternalistic politics grounded in a conservative approach to empire. The third section focuses on the effects of Zimmern's imperial vision on his developing theory of "commonwealth." In particular, this section examines the way Zimmern's notion of the commonwealth as "voluntary" served to obscure underlying relationships of imperial power.

The overall conclusions of the chapter are twofold. First, at its worst, Zimmern's political vision was deeply hierarchical, grounded in an almost preliberal understanding of the relationship between the familial and the political, between imperial children and the motherland. Second, despite this, there is still something redeemable in Zimmern's work that points beyond the limitations of the texts themselves toward an interesting and timely reconception of sovereignty and an understanding of international ethics that refuses to abandon national culture. In other words, Zimmern's theory of commonwealth gives us a glimpse of a politics that respects the importance of national culture to individual identity formation while challenging national sovereignty itself, and a global ethics rooted in both the particularities of nationhood and a broader concern for world affairs.

In its historical capacity, the goal of this inquiry is not simply to follow the developing strands of Zimmern's thought in order to demonstrate their internal coherence. Instead, with Foucault, this chapter rejects the possibility of discovering either the presence of a seamless internationalist discourse in Zimmern's works or the reputed "origins" of such a notion. As Foucault notes, "What is found at the historical beginning of things is not the inviolable identity of their origin; it is the dissension of other things. It is disparity" (Foucault 1984: 70). And disparities run deep throughout the palimpsest of Zimmern's life work. What ultimately emerges from his writings is a constellation of conflicting political visions, some gesturing toward a kind of enriched liberalism, others toward spiritual idealism, some toward an equality of nations, others toward the lingering existence of imperial union. These disparities should not, however, prompt us to reject Alfred Zimmern's work as purely contradictory. Rather, as Uday Sing Mehta cautions with regard to John Stuart Mill, the complexities that emerge from the "extended link between liberalism and empire" should be taken "as an invitation" (Mehta 1992: 8). In Zimmern's case, his vacillation between a call to internationalism and a vision of commonwealth that often appeared as a renewed imperialism should also be taken as an invitation, an enticement to examine the space that lies between these competing world visions. In the final analysis, the overlapping political images that inhabit this space have much to tell us about the fractious relationship between liberal internationalism and the politics of national difference more generally.

ZIMMERN, OXFORD, AND LIBERAL IDEALISM

All of us were then deeply under the German spell.

—Gilbert Murray

Born in Surbiton in 1879, Alfred Zimmern began his intellectual career at New College, Oxford, in the late 1890s. He continued on at Oxford as a Classics Fellow until 1909. Although he did not return to teach there until 1933 (as the Montague Burton Chair of International Relations), he maintained a close affiliation with the institution and his papers were eventually donated to the Bodleian library after his death in 1957. As the place that first inspired Zimmern to think critically about liberal politics, Oxford (and New College in particular) remained an important ideological focal point for Zimmern throughout his career. Understanding Zimmern's approach to both domestic and international politics thus requires a closer examination of the philosophical and political environment that produced him, an environment he associated with a "discipline and quality of mind" that was "precisely what is needed most for the study and interpretation of international relations in the present age" (Zimmern 1931: 20).

From the moment he first entered New College in 1897, Alfred Zimmern was what his student Arnold J. Toynbee would later describe as a "whole hearted liberal" (Toynbee 1967: 49). Liberalism at Oxford in the 1890s, however, carried particular valences. In the decades immediately prior to Zimmern's debut as an undergraduate, liberal students and professors were inspired largely by the ethical theory and political reformism of Balliol professor T. H. Green and his followers. What one sees in Zimmern's own political writings is, in many ways, a continuation or a working through of the philosophical and political antinomies produced by these earlier social theorists, antinomies that tended to cluster around their approaches to individualism, spirituality, and organicism.

Thinkers such as Green, Edward Caird, Bernard Bosanquet, Henry Muirhead, and David Ritchie were, before all else, critics of orthodox liberalism (as associated with Locke and Ricardo). They maintained that this approach to political and ethical life placed too great an emphasis on the individual, resulting in a kind of social atomism, a general disregard for morality among both politicians and philosophers, and massive economic disparities between rich and poor. And yet, as committed political liberals and firm believers in laissez-faire economics, these thinkers intended neither to call the entire legacy of liberalism into question nor to develop a theory that might provide ammunition for Tory politicians and their Burkean longing for tradition (Green 1906: 365–86). At the same time, Green and his colleagues viewed socialism with dread as, in Caird's words, "the reduction of the individual under the control of society" (Boucher 1997: 179). In the end, what they hoped to achieve was the creation of a philosophical "middle way" between these alternatives by theorizing a more collectivist liberal society.[3]

For a variety of historical reasons, new liberal thinkers turned to German idealism and, most importantly, to the work of G. W. F. Hegel to help them imagine what this theory might look like.[4] Indeed, as former New College student H. A. L Fisher remembered the 1880s, "Hegel, as interpreted by T. H. Green ... was the reigning philosopher of my undergraduate days" (Fisher 1940: 50). "All of us were then," concurred Gilbert Murray, "deeply under the German spell" (Murray 1940: 4). The Hegelian concept of *Geist* allowed these scholars to theorize the existence of an objective good found in both individuals and in the universal realm beyond. Green, for instance, argued for the existence of a "Spiritual Principle," an explicitly Hegelian concept that he defined as an "eternal intelligence realized in the related facts of the world, or as a system of related facts rendered possible by such an intelligence [that] partially and gradually reproduced itself in us" (Green 1884: 146). In addition, because they agreed with Hegel that rights originate within society rather than in an imaginary state of nature, these liberal idealists shared, to some extent, Hegel's commitment to an ethical state theory. In this context, the state was seen as a moral extension of society and an expression of the "public good" or the "Spiritual Principle."[5]

Nevertheless, as self-identified liberals whose own philosophical heritage and political experience required a certain level of wariness toward absolute government, these social theorists were uncomfortable with the Hegelian idea that the state alone provided the critical nexus between individuals, society, and *Geist*. In response to this parting of ways, many of the Oxford liberals sought to resolve the contradiction between their liberal discomfort with state power and their belief that the end of community was the establishment of the "good life" by turning to an organically conceived notion of society that was distinct from the state, a "social whole" whose origins predated the state and whose members constituted the "parts or organs of a living body" (Bosanquet 1958: 20). The result was a school of thought saturated with what Charles Taylor has referred to as an "oddly transposed variety" of Hegelianism (Taylor 1975: 537).

Ultimately, for Bosanquet and other more organically inclined Oxford liberals, the language of nature allowed them to theorize a moral community and yet avoid the totalizing implications of a Hegelian state that was the "ultimate expression of Spirit in the world." In the process of focusing on the organic to provide explanations of social understanding, however, these thinkers also came to place a considerable amount of emphasis on natural institutions (especially the nuclear family). Hence, for example, Muirhead argued that "society depends for the strength of its tissue on the health and strength of the cells that compose it, and especially of the primeval cell we call the family" (Muirhead 1900: 126). In turn, this emphasis on the family as the primary moral "cell" in the social organism led many new liberals to espouse some quite conservative political stands, on both domestic and international issues. On a domestic level, these thinkers were largely absent from liberal discussions concerning women's suffrage and many of them saw the movement of middle- and working-class women into the public realm as a sign of social collapse.[6] On an international level, many of them expressed extremely conservative views regarding empire, views that amounted to a literal replacement of the liberal state with a more broadly understood notion of family (Ritchie 1916: 262; Ritchie 1891: 73).

Political liberalism at Oxford at the turn of the century was dominated by this form of paternalist social theory initially inspired by Hegel. By the time Zimmern was an undergraduate and active in the liberal community, however, Hegelian liberalism was beginning to experience its initial decline within the British academy as the result of increased tensions between Britain and Germany.[7] Zimmern's political thought is illustrative of this transition. From the early twentieth century onward Zimmern's writings were explicitly anti-German in character, consistently equating Hegelian state theory with "Prussianism."[8] Indeed, his particularly virulent anti-German attitudes during the war largely influenced his attitude toward the benefits of a world organization based on the commonwealth. "The fact is," he wrote to F. S. Marvin in 1915, "that in my political philosophy the bond between London and Nigeria is closer than the bond between London and Düsseldorf" (Stapleton 1994: 104). And yet, at the same time, many of the same "oddly transposed" Hegelian ideas that wove their way so conflictingly through the work of thinkers such as Green reemerged with Zimmern's liberalism. Tutored by liberal idealists while at Oxford, Zimmern's philosophical and political thought reverberates with the sentiments of an earlier generation of scholars particularly in its emphasis on the relationship between "spirit" and liberalism and its tendency toward a paternalistic politics of community.

The belief that liberalism was more than a political theory, embodying a kind of spiritual and moral force at work in the world, was a central feature of Zimmern's political philosophy throughout the course of his career. As he noted in 1918, "[F]or Liberalism, spiritual forces are the centre of life; and the supreme aim is the application of moral and spiritual principles both to politics and to industry" (Zimmern 1918: xix). For Zimmern, these "moral and spiritual principles" were deeply entwined with the "spiritual welfare of the community," or what he had referred to in an earlier essay as "home spirit" (Zimmern 1918: 65; Bodl. Ms. Zimmern [136], fol. 127). Members of such a community, Zimmern maintained, necessarily understood themselves first in terms of "corporate life, corporate growth, and corporate self respect" (Zimmern 1918: 65). At the same time, spiritual liberalism demanded that the individual citizen be ready "to apply his reason to public affairs without fear and prejudice" (Zimmern 1921: 338).

On a policy level, Zimmern's vision combined a liberal appreciation for the individual and the market with a spiritualized notion of "corporate life," resulting in a politics that ultimately contained within it vestiges of a hesitant support for the emerging welfare state, a more orthodox liberal discomfort with state intervention, and an odd Burkean desire for social order. Thus, Zimmern described economic activity as fundamentally geared toward the good of the community. In domestic terms he argued that "[p]olitical economy is not, what Mill and other writers define it to be, the 'Science of Wealth.' It is the art of community housekeeping ... consciously ministering to the real needs of the community" (Zimmern 1916: 192). At the same time, Zimmern's economic policy was hardly socialist in its focus. As with an earlier generation of new liberals, Zimmern was ultimately uncomfortable with the idea of a state redistribution of wealth, arguing that "elaborate control and direction from above, dislikes the free play of human groupings, and discourages all spontaneous or unauthorized associations" (Zimmern 1918: 13).

Simultaneously, Zimmern's focus on communal needs and social traditions appeared strikingly pre-liberal in its reverence for tradition and hierarchy. Too much state intervention in the lives of the poor might disrupt both the natural flow of economic progress and the "parallel progress of social imitation" by which "class merges into class"(Bodl. Ms. Zimmern [135], fol. 26). For Zimmern, class conflict was a foreign importation, born out of a continental tradition of establishing "social gulfs" between workers, landowners, and the bourgeoisie. In England, by contrast, a shared sense of values had led to the establishment of a kind of spontaneous social order based on universal conceptions of right conduct. Rigid notions of human equality were not necessary in a society where classes understood their relationship to one another through tradition.

In sum, the quintessence of Zimmern's liberalism lay in its conservative appreciation for social order and tradition coupled with an understanding of the relationship between spirit and community that was inflected by idealism, an approach he would cling to throughout the Edwardian period and into the 1920s and '30s. As a whole, Zimmern's liberalism was redolent with Greenian idealism, despite the absence of any explicit debt to its "oddly transposed" Hegelianism. Unlike J. A. Hobson, L. T. Hobhouse, Bertrand Russell, G. Lowes Dickinson, and other Edwardian "new liberals," Zimmern never fully rejected the metaphysical, never fully rejected the existence of a spirit moved to reconcile individual autonomy with life in community. This was a liberalism that also tended to stress the capacity of communal life both to shape the individual's moral conscience and to structure an ethical order. Ultimately, Zimmern's belief in the reconciliatory power of spirit, the moral necessity of social traditions, and the ethical imperative of life in community would seriously impact his approach to international politics as well.

Zimmern's Internationalism and the Emergence of Commonwealth

.... the road to Internationalism lies through Nationalism
—Alfred Zimmern, *Nationality and Government*

After he left Oxford in 1910, Zimmern traveled to Greece and then taught sociology at the London School of Economics (Markwell 1986: 280). During the war he became involved full time with the intelligence division of the Foreign Office and participated in drafting the then secret British plans for a postwar League of Nations. In 1919 he was appointed to the first independent professorship of international relations in the world at the University College of Wales, Aberystwyth. Scandal propelled him from Wales to Cornell University where he spent two years in 1922–1923. From there, Zimmern worked professionally with the League of Nations and eventually ended up back at Oxford in 1931 as the university's first Montague Burton Professor of International Relations. He was knighted in 1936 and served in the Foreign Office again during World War II (Quigley 1981: 90).

As with his domestic political theory and, in the tradition of his intellectual predecessors, Zimmern crafted his wartime and postwar internationalism largely in response to the individualism of orthodox liberal theory. In his words, "Treitschke and Nietzsche may have furnished Prussian ambitions with congenial ammunition," but it was social theorists such as Bentham, "the high priest of individualism," who also contributed to the general atmosphere of excessive self-indulgence, greed, and a lack of global, civic consciousness on the part of states and individuals alike (Zimmern 1928a: 11). This move toward universal selfishness, argued Zimmern, had led to the devastation of the Great War and would, if given a chance, bring about another general unraveling of world order. In response Zimmern argued for a new world politics based on universal, moral principles, a world as truly "interdependent in its spiritual relations just in the same way it is in its material and economic relations" (Zimmern 1926a: 22). During the war and in the years that followed, Zimmern maintained that such an ethical system would require both states and individuals to take the good of the international whole rather than the competitive principles of orthodox liberalism as their moral compass in world affairs. In this new world order, argued Zimmern, "government and business must judge both economic and national issues from an ethical standpoint" (Zimmern 1917: 72). After 1919, Zimmern imagined the League of Nations itself as just one important component of this larger, ethical cosmos, "only enlightening in so far as it points beyond itself to the forces in the mind of man upon which its own future and that of our present-day civilization depend" (Zimmern 1917: 72). Above all, Zimmern believed in the animating power of what he and his internationalist colleagues termed the "international mind," a spiritual awareness at work in the world that offered to resolve intractably polarized economic and political forces.[9]

As Green and Bosanquet's "Spiritual Principle" had embraced both individuals and the greater social and spiritual good, so too did Zimmern's conception of "international mind" encompass both the particularities of citizens and states and a divine engine of progress—what Toynbee referred to as a "higher end"—capable of uniting the world's peoples on a more ethical plane (Toynbee 1915: 499). A world shaped by "international mind" implied the cultivation of a more forthright and reasonable understanding of international affairs in the minds of the individual citizens.[10] Simultaneously, Zimmern used the term to describe a kind of universal, higher power weaving through history, bringing humanity "into harmony with the great moral forces which rule the destinies of mankind" (Zimmern 1928a: 20).

The concept of "international mind," however, in no way implied "international government" for Zimmern. Indeed, throughout his internationalist writings, Zimmern's aversion to socialism and to all forms of "statism" shone through in his constantly reiterated discomfort with any kind of centralized power on a domestic or an international level. The "great moral forces" at work in the world, according to Zimmern, had to be allowed to arise spontaneously without the unifying mechanism of a "super-state." Internationalism, in other words, must base itself on the moral energy of the "international mind" while rejecting the potentially coercive powers of world government. In a political and philosophical move that was striking in its similarity to an earlier generation of Oxford liberal idealists, Zimmern attempted this balancing act not only by rejecting the possibility of a world state but also by rooting his understanding of moral internationalism in the organic qualities of the modern world. For instance, in 1916 Zimmern stressed that internationalism was possible because "the world has already, in many respects, become a single organism" (Zimmern 1916: 164). Ten years later, he compared the League itself not to "a super-state" but rather, to "a living, organic mechanism" (Zimmern 1926a: 26). For Zimmern, the chrysalis of organic internationalism lay just beneath the surface of the contemporary world. Hence, theorizing international politics was, he believed, a method of discovery, of unearthing natural processes at work. Zimmern imagined these processes in distinctly corporeal terms, particularly through his repeated references to an international "nervous system." In many ways, his use of the term is a testament to the consistency of his organicism throughout the war and well into the interwar era. Thus, in 1918, Zimmern described the movement of communications and capital as flowing through a "single world nervous system" (Zimmern 1918: 23). In 1926, he located the dynamics of a "moving, changing world" within "the adequate functioning of this international nervous system" (Zimmern 1926a: 22). By 1928, this world body had taken on even more biological qualities as "trade and industry" were expected to "respond," like efficient limbs and organs, to the "reactions of a single, world wide nervous system" (Zimmern 1928b: 327). In sum, for Zimmern, the peaceful functioning of the world depended upon the existence of a natural, organic movement that, like the processes of the human body in the hands of the skilled anatomist, awaited discovery and explanation.

In the final analysis, it was this faith in the workings of a living world body that made it possible for Zimmern to insist, even in the absence of an international organization with coercive authority, that the harmonious and peaceful development of "organic citizenship" amongst the world's peoples was not only probable but natural (Zimmern 1928b: 379). And, just as nineteenth-century Oxford liberals had once looked at a similar domestic "social organism" and identified the family as the most fundamental and moral "cell" in the social body, so too did Zimmern's naturalist approach to internationalism lead him to identify metaphorically similar families—national families—as the key constituents of the international body politic.

Zimmern most fully elaborated his theoretical understanding of the relationship between nationhood and internationalism in *Nationality and Government,* although one can see rudiments of this idea in lectures going back as far as 1905.[11] The theory itself entailed four key assumptions. First, Zimmern maintained that "natural" differences between people could only be understood in national terms. Second, he argued that these national differences were necessary for both the creation of global society and the true progress of humanity. Third, Zimmern identified nations as distinctly *familial* units; and fourth, Zimmern assumed that, like families, nations produced the spiritual and moral energy necessary both to animate the social organism and to ensure international cooperation.

In notably Hegelian terms, Zimmern argued that nations performed the same functions in the ethical development of the individual-engaged-with-the-world as the family did in the ethical maturity of the individual-engaged-with-the-state. In other words, nations, like families, facilitated that process whereby world citizens recognized other nationalities as both distinct from and inherently similar to themselves by giving them a moral focus, a resting place, a space from which to interact with the "life of the world" from a position of safety.[12] Although not necessarily ethnically coherent, once a people had reached a certain level of "corporate self consciousness," once they had begun to feel particularly intensely and intimately about their "home country," they took on those natural "sentiments" and "qualities" that distinguished them from all groups and provided for them all the unquestioning love and security of home (Zimmern 1918: 52).

Ultimately, the particular "qualities" produced by the intensity and intimacy of the nation distinguished it from all other social institutions. In addition, these "qualities"—what Zimmern's friend and colleague Cecil Burns described as "local and spiritual differences"—made each nation uniquely suited to meet the moral and spiritual needs of its citizens (Burns 1917). Thus, Zimmern maintained that "true internationalism is the contact between nations in their highest and best and *most distinctive* representatives and manifestations" (Zimmern 1929: 93). For Zimmern, nations at their "most distinctive" were also the most spiritual, and "true internationalism" implied that individuals both engage that spirit in themselves and appreciate it in others. In Zimmern's words:

> Any fool can book a ticket for a foreign country, just as any fool can learn Esperanto. But contacts so established effect nothing.... It is through a deeper exploration and enjoyment of the infinite treasures of the word's nationalities, by men and women whose vision has been trained and sensibilities refined because they themselves are intimately bound up with a nation of their own, that an enduring network of internationalism will some day be knit and a harmony of understanding established in a world of unassailable diversity. (Zimmern 1929: 93)

Zimmern also argued that nations were *natural* entities, the most organic, germinal elements of the international organism. Thus, the sensibilities of nations and states come across as quite different in his work, mirroring almost exactly the enlightenment dichotomy between passion and reason, subjectivity and objectivity, nature and civilization.[13] Feelings within nations, Zimmern argued, were based on "instinctive tendencies and primary emotions" rooted in "the half-conscious assumptions and dim feelings of life in a community" (Zimmern 1918: 348). In Zimmern's words, "[N]ationalism is not a mere fashion and foible ... but springs from deep roots buried in man's inherited nature" (1918: 99).

This metaphorical equation between the nation-as-natural-and-subjective and the nation-as-intimate-and-familial was hardly incidental for Zimmern. Rather, it was precisely their familial qualities that made nations so uniquely moral. Within the nation, within this home saturated with genuine, natural intimacy, internationally minded individuals first learned to respect themselves and others. For Zimmern, the nation functioned as "a school of character and self respect." World citizens, he maintained, learned respect for others in the *international* community only through their prima facie awareness of and respect for themselves as part of a *national* community (1918: 54). Zimmern's internationalism thus necessitated that *every* person in the world have a place to call home. Likewise, Zimmern's internationalism also required that individual nations have distinct spatial identities, that they occupy "a definite home country" (1918: 84). While this identity did not necessarily entail sovereignty, it did necessitate "an actual strip of land associated with the nationality, a territorial centre where the flame of nationality is kept alight" (1918: 52).

Just as an earlier generation of liberal idealists had argued that any shift in the fundamental makeup of the nuclear family would have dire consequences for the morality of the nation, so too did Zimmern argue that the loss or rejection of one's national homeland would lead inexorably to moral decay. For Zimmern, nothing was quite as disturbing as the "moral degradation the loss of nationality involves" (1918: 52). To illustrate this point, he wrote extensively in *Nationality and Government* of the "drab cosmopolitanism" of the Levantine merchant whose lack of a home country rendered him such a potent example "of the spiritual degradation which befalls men who have pursued ... cosmopolitanism and lost contact with their own national spiritual heritage."[14] For Zimmern, nationality was the ultimate antidote to the "insidious onslaughts" of a materialist transnationalism (1918: 53).

In the end, for Zimmern, internationalism meant not a forgoing of national identity but an "inter-communication between the families of mankind" (1918: 38). Not only was cosmopolitanism undesirable, but ultimately, untenable; national sentiment, like all natural forces, could not be suppressed. Indeed, according to Zimmern, "[n]ationalism thwarted, perverted, and unsatisfied ... is one of the festering sores of our time" (1918: 100). Instead, he maintained, nationalism must be channeled and guided to take on a more internationalist form. Thus, as Zimmern saw it, one of the most important missions of the League of Nations was the creation of an institutional framework wherein the "true" aspirations of nationalism could flourish. At the same time, the League of Nations must somehow help discourage individual nations from falling prey to the Mussolinis of the world, dictators bent on warping the nobility of national sentiment to their own ends. In other words, the League, in its educative capacity, was to encourage nationalisms that were consistent with the goal of internationalism. Thus, Zimmern argued that the League's educational mission could be "best defined as a process of harmonization between the inner and the outer," between the national home and the international world (Zimmern 1927: 30). "Nationality," he insisted, "rightly regarded, is not a political but an educational conception"(Zimmern 1918: 53).

In the internationalist imaginary of Alfred Zimmern, nations were moral, life-giving, spiritual entities. "Nationalism rightly understood and cherished," he argued, "is a great uplifting and life giving force, a bulwark alike against chauvinism and against materialism—against all the decivilising impersonal forces which harass and degrade the minds and souls of modern men" (1918: 100). The most natural, animating, and spiritual component of the great global organism thus resided in "living spirit of patriotism" (Zimmern 1913: 497). Within nations individuals first learned to love, just as wise men throughout the ages have "loved their home land as they loved their parents" (Zimmern 1918: 100).

Unfortunately, this equation between parental love and politics also allowed Zimmern more easily to rationalize a paternalistic world politics based on imperialist understandings of colonized peoples as children. Thus, the majority of his prewar writings on commonwealth and empire reveal an almost insouciant assumption that full citizenship rights be denied to nonwhite "dependencies" based on their well-understood immaturity. Democracy, he contended, in *Nationality and Government*, was not a "magic formula. It is open to limitation obvious enough to the student of non-adult races" (1918: 15). Likewise, Zimmern frequently described the relationship between the "motherland" and her imperial subjects in terms of parental responsibility for the "millions of less civilized human beings" whose "moral destiny" was entrusted to British hands (Zimmern 1913: 494). After the war, Zimmern tempered his language with regard to race, going so far as to argue at a public lecture in 1926 that the "League of Nations is still too white." And yet, during the same speech Zimmern also restated his position that colonized powers currently unrepresented in the League were by and large weaker economically than Western nations and thus required more "constructive" action before they could be allowed admittance (Zimmern 1926: 16).

In many ways Zimmern's approach to the empire appears to almost exactly mirror a long-standing tradition within British liberalism, a tradition that resurfaces within the works of thinkers as diverse as John Stuart Mill and J. A. Hobson.[15] As with these thinkers, Zimmern's understanding of nonwhite peoples as morally and politically immature allowed him to elide some glaring political inconsistencies. In particular, it allowed him to champion a liberal doctrine based on universal equality while denying political autonomy to millions by relocating political power from the realm of liberal civil equality and positing it in the loving, but deeply hierarchical, shelter of the family.

However, Zimmern's own political theory did not have to stretch nearly as far as more radical liberals such as Hobson to justify such an exclusionary vision. That is, Zimmern's liberalism—in contrast to more mainstream liberal understandings of the relationship between the public and the private—was already premised on a kind of melding of the political and the familial in all contexts (not just in relation to the empire). Thus, for Zimmern, the role of the family in ancient Athenian life made full citizenship possible. Likewise, the nation supplied individuals with the "intimate" atmosphere necessary to be true world citizens. The constant reiteration of political morality as family morality spilled over into Zimmern's understanding of empire, creating a fairly seamless connection between parental love and extant relations of imperial power.

This emphasis on the connection between the family and politics ultimately had much more in common with Green's Hegelian understanding of liberalism than with the social theory of "new liberals" such as Hobson, Hobhouse, and Lowes Dickinson. It is hardly surprising, therefore, that Zimmern would be drawn to join the Round Table Society, a powerful, pro-imperialist organization that was explicit in its debt to Green and the other Oxford idealists. Established at New College in the mid 1880s by Alfred Milner, the Round Table Society supplied much of the intellectual justification for Victorian and Edwardian imperialist expansion. Milner and his young colleagues (often referred to as "the kindergarten") were all self-proclaimed disciples of T. H. Green. In particular, they were drawn both to Green's simultaneous support for free trade and to his belief that the state could create a moral environment for its citizens by expanding educational and economic opportunities. In this sense, they argued that while the market itself was moral the mercantilist impulses of British imperialism were not always so. Instead, they suggested that Britain should approach its imperial mission in a manner that set a moral example for colonials. Indeed, Zimmern himself perhaps best expressed the core tenet of the Society in his 1913 article for the *Round Table* in which he argued that if "the British Empire is destined to endure, it will be only as the guardian of the moral welfare of its peoples. Faith in this mission alone can justify the effort to further its consolidation" (Zimmern 1918: 484).

Zimmern was a member of the Round Table Society from 1913 and, along with Lionel Curtis, was one of the leading forces behind a major rethinking of the Society's mission in the years just prior to World War I. During this time, Society members such as Curtis, along with other participants in the Society's "London Group" (including Zimmern, Phillip Kerr, and Ramsey Muir) began working on a number of papers for circulation focused on something Curtis called the "principle of commonwealth." The ideas behind this principle were developed largely in reaction to the statism of "Prussianism" and Bolshevism. In a classic liberal idealist move, Zimmern, Curtis, and their colleagues, attempted to come up with an alternative vision of empire that decentered the role of the state. Thus, in a manner highly reminiscent of Bosanquet and Ritchie and their relocation of moral authority from the state to the social organism, key thinkers of the Round Table argued that what bound the empire together was not a powerful state, but rather, a sense of community, a shared existence, in essence, a united "commonwealth" based on higher moral ends (Kendle 1975: 172). Zimmern's own work on *The Greek Commonwealth* was of central importance in the creation of this idea, particularly his notion of Greek citizenship and its relationship to what he claimed were the largely communal, not state-centered, ethics of Athenian life.[16]

For the Round Table Society as a whole, the most significant result of this new emphasis was a change in terminology and, from around 1911 on, the use of the word *empire* in the Society's publications was largely replaced by *commonwealth*. By contrast, for Zimmern, the importance of "commonwealth," as a political ideal, went beyond semantics. Rather, as his works during this period demonstrate, it quickly became the central axis around which the rest of his developing sense of internationalism would revolve. The idea of a "supernational commonwealth" was, in many ways, the practical manifestation of Zimmern's spiritually rooted internationalism.

Inherent in Zimmern's approach to the commonwealth were two basic principles: voluntarism and diversity. The former, I argue, worked to obscure the underlying power relations of the empire. The latter opened the door to a reconsideration of national sovereignty that balanced the particularities of nationhood with universal ethics. The next section and the conclusion follow the threads of these often conflicting ideas through Zimmern's work.

THE VOLUNTARY COMMONWEALTH

If the State ... is a body whose perfection consists in the variety of the functions of its several members—there has never been on the earth a political organism like the British Empire....
                                        —Alfred Zimmern, *The War and Democracy*

As the most fundamental assumption of contract theory, "voluntarism" has long stood at the heart of liberal approaches to both social institutions and the state. Liberals as diverse as Mill, Locke, and Green all understood the relationship between the citizen and the state as essentially "voluntary." Likewise, "voluntary principles" have historically guided liberal understandings of the family (Green 1884: 232). Rather than arising from a preordained patriarchal order, liberal thinkers have tended to regard the nuclear family as a voluntary commitment between a man and a woman. In response, feminist theorists argue that it is precisely this notion of free, voluntary union that has obscured actual relations of patriarchal power within the liberal family (Butler 1991: 90–91; Eisenstein 1981: 47–49).

Implicit in Zimmern's blending of familial, national, and imperial politics is a similar slippage that allowed him to continue regarding himself as liberal, while at the same time relying so heavily on a conservative, quasi-Hegelian conception of the social order. As Zimmern understood it, there was nothing inherently exclusionary about the spiritual bonds that developed within nations. Rather, he argued that nationality could be voluntarily adopted, not in the liberal sense in which a citizen explicitly or tacitly agrees to live under the influence of a state, but in the familial sense in which parents adopt children or individuals join a family through marriage. It was thus possible, in Zimmern's words, to literally marry the nation and still feel about it as one might feel toward one's biological family:

National sentiment is intimate: whether it be mainly compounded of influences of heredity (as in Europe), or of environment, as in the older Americans, or whether it be something newly acquired and deliberately cherished as among the new arrivals, it is something that goes deep down into the very recesses of the being.... The nationality

of a European and the nationality of a recent American may perhaps
be compared to a man's relation to his parents and his relation to his
wife. Both sentiments are intimate; both can legitimately be compared, in the sphere of personal relations, to the sense of nationality in
the wider sphere of corporate relations. But the one is hereditary and
the other is elective. (Zimmern 1929: 85)

Zimmern thus actively combined two apparently antithetical notions of family: the liberal ideal of the family as a voluntary commitment between a man
and a women, and idealist understandings of the family as a "natural" institution. At the same time, Zimmern also brought together two seemingly contradictory notions of nationhood: the liberal understanding of nationhood as
something one enters into by choice, and the more German idea of *Volk* or a
blood nationalism based on a shared ethnic parentage. In this manner,
Zimmern transformed nationhood into both a voluntary and natural—liberal
and organic—phenomenon.

What gets lost in Zimmern's understanding of nations as voluntary families is an analysis of internal power relationships. For Zimmern, nationalism
was familial and the family was loving. The more national sentiment grew
within a community, the more loving and inclusive its politics. Thus, Zimmern
argued quite forcefully in *Nationalism and Government* that social injustice,
racial inequality, and civic strife all found their antidotes in a growing sense of
nationalism. Zimmern thus lauded the education of immigrants in America as
a testament to the salving powers of nationality. Likewise, he argued that
encouraging a sense of nationality among African Americans would eventually
speak to "the thorniest of all the many thorny problems of American
life" (Zimmern 1918: 81). Never did it occur to Zimmern to ask whether
membership in a nation, as in a family, might be circumscribed by a politics
based not on loving *inclusion* but on an internal form of *exclusion*—and might
be far from voluntary.

The language of voluntary consent reemerges within Zimmern's approach
to the Empire and, later, within the idea of commonwealth. Early in his career,
Zimmern described the "Imperial Union" as a type of polity "less rigid than a
federation but more intimate than an alliance" (Bodl. Ms. Zimmern [135], fol.
124). Implicit in this idea was a notion of free "union" between "self governing
political units." By 1928, the language of imperial union had changed and now
it was the "commonwealth" that was both intimate and free, that combined
both the characteristics of an organism and the liberal rule of law (Zimmern
1928b: 369). Almost ten years later, the organic qualities of the commonwealth
were still held together, for Zimmern, by consent, by the actions of national
actors who chose to throw in their lot together (Zimmern 1936: 282). Such an
organization needed no state coercion, according to Zimmern, because at its
heart it was freely cooperative.

At the same time, as with his conception of nationhood, Zimmern's notion of the commonwealth as a "free union" of consenting states obscured many underlying power relations between England, the "white dominions," and non-white imperial holdings. While Zimmern maintained that the British Commonwealth was, essentially, a voluntary association of free and equal nations, the reality of the commonwealth was something quite different. In actuality, it was only during a brief three-month period in 1917–1918 that heads of state from the "white dominions" were invited to participate in the creation of imperial policy (Low 1991: 37). Likewise, nonwhite dominions were easily dismissed from even the pretense of cooperative politics. Zimmern himself blithely assumed that, because they had not yet reached a stage of development where they were capable of voluntary consent, certain national members of the Empire would not be allowed admittance. "I am not speaking at all of India or of our Tropical dependencies," he argued in 1905, "but of the self governing portions of the Empire" (Bodl. Ms. Zimmern [135], fol. 153).

Yet, at other times, Zimmern seemed happy to include such imperial "dependencies" in his notion of commonwealth and argued that one of its strengths was its flexibility, its capacity to encompass "races and peoples at varying levels of social progress which is its peculiar task" (Zimmern 1918: 17). In his desire to balance liberal philosophical commitments with a hierarchical, idealist politics, Zimmern maintained that the commonwealth was sometimes voluntary, sometimes familial, and sometimes both, comprised solely of "white dominions" able to achieve self-government, and, at other times, leading "non adult races" toward civilization. In essence, the language of voluntarism (and, indeed, the very language of "common"-wealth) allowed Zimmern to have it all: to don the mantle of liberalism while infantilizing millions; to theorize organic cooperation while centralizing politics in the motherland; to believe in the impartial rule of law while cherishing all that was intimate in family life.

Zimmern's vision had substantial policy implications for the League of Nations Covenant. After his appointment to the Political Intelligence Department of the Foreign Office, Zimmern authored what came to be known, in late 1918, as the "Foreign Office Memorandum," a document that laid the foundations for the famous "Cecil Draft" which the British delegation took to Paris in 1919 (Markwell 1986: 280). Taking the idea of commonwealth as its intellectual center, Zimmern's "Foreign Office Memorandum" spelled out the official British objection to Woodrow Wilson's "more ambitious ideas" for a League of Nations with potentially coercive powers, specifically Wilson's desire to include "guarantees" in the Covenant that would require states to respond in a forceful way to the unlawful actions of both member and nonmember states (Long and Wilson 1995: 82). Instead, Zimmern's report maintained that this international organization should ultimately resemble less a centrally organized bureaucracy and more a loosely associated version of the existing British Commonwealth. Hence, the "Foreign Office Memorandum" argued that any postwar arrangement of international relations ought to be purely voluntary, a cooperative society "maintained by the contributions of its members, who expect in return to draw from it regular benefits" (Zimmern 1936: 282).

In model Zimmern style, the memorandum ultimately reads as a juggling of compromises, a kind of complex meliorism that depended more on the assertion of international commonwealth than on the specific (often conflicting) details of how to bring about this commonwealth. And yet despite its lack of clarity—or maybe precisely because of it—when Robert Cecil became the head of the Foreign Office League of Nations Section in October 1918, he chose Zimmern's memorandum as the foundation from which to work and had its various organizational suggestions summarized in a "Brief Conspectus of League of Nations Organizations" (Egerton 1978: 99). This draft, later named the "Cecil Draft" but largely the work of Zimmern, went with the British delegation to Paris in early 1919, where it was presented to the Americans (Quigley 1981: 26).

The meeting between Cecil's committee and the American delegation produced the Hurst Miller Draft, a combination of American suggestions and British concerns which substantially reduced the powers of the League from those originally articulated by Wilson's Fourteen Points (Zimmern 1936: 195).[17] In particular, the British delegation insisted that the League's commitment to "preserve as against external aggression the territorial integrity and existing political independence of all State members of the League" be seen as a "principle" rather than an "obligation" (Zimmern 1936: 242). In this way, Zimmern's draft significantly altered the original American plan in a direction favored by the Lloyd George government and the members of the Round Table Group, a direction favoring what the League's own Information Section would term in 1925 "a sort of loose, continuous, organic relationship" rather than world government (Information Section 1925: 8). Carr would later refer to this assertion of political cohesion in the absence of power as a "body politic without a policy" (Carr 1961: 8).

Conclusion

An ordinary old fashioned State may be no more than a Sovereign Authority, but a free State or Commonwealth is and must be invested with what may best be described as a moral personality.
—Alfred Zimmern, *The War and Democracy*

Despite its limitations and its dampening political effect on the League however, there are aspects of Zimmern's international commonwealth that gesture toward the possibility of a world politics grounded in an appreciation for the diversity of national and minority cultures and the creation of an international politics based on shared political goals. In other words, the notion of commonwealth suggests the possibility of cooperation without coercion and thus, while it might also have obscured the obvious inequalities inherent in the empire, it simultaneously serves as an interesting model for consideration. This is particularly true for contemporary liberal theorists and IR scholars who seek a solution to nationalist violence by challenging the utility of the sovereign nation-state while, at the same time, honoring national cultures. In sum, at its core, Zimmern's internationalism contained within it the seeds of a politics capable of speaking to nationalist conflicts that emerge out of a desire for sovereignty while still recognizing the importance of national cultures to human (and liberal) identity formation.

Recall that for Zimmern, nations were valuable insofar as they molded the individual's moral vision. In this regard, the politics of internationalism could not develop in the absence of those initial moral lessons individuals learned first within their nations of origin. At the same time, Zimmern was also clearly aware that the expansionist policies of nationalists in Europe had played a key role in instigating the violence of the Great War. In fact, he not only wanted to free national sentiment from cosmopolitanism—he also wanted to free it from statehood, from the "vague nineteenth century shibboleth" that "every nation has a right to be a sovereign state" (Zimmern 1929: 89). Zimmern argued that only "those who are blind to the true course of human progress can fail to see that the day of the Nation-State is even now drawing to a close in the West." In an expansion of Lord Acton's argument, Zimmern maintained that uncoupling nationality from statehood would direct nationalism, as a political and deeply emotional force, outward toward "a better patriotism than that of a single nation and culture" (Zimmern 1927b: 8). This could be done, Zimmern insisted, by creating global institutions capable of providing nationhood with "a community more responsive to its true demands" (Zimmern 1928b: 370).

From early on in his career Zimmern argued that his idealized understanding of the British Commonwealth—as a kind of quasi-international government based on a loose, organic confederation of semi-sovereign nations—provided the world with a clear model of what such a community might look like. "It is perfectly possible" Zimmern argued in the 1920s, "for several nations to form a single sovereign state; but as a general rule all such nations will be allowed to manage their own internal affairs." This composite state would take the form of a "commonwealth of nations freely associating together within the confines of a single sovereign state" (Zimmern 1928a: 21). Zimmern claimed that the commonwealth would simultaneously avoid the specter of a "world-state," protect local and national cultures, and challenge the potentially endless proliferation of "self-determined" nation states. "It takes all sorts of men, says the old proverb," Zimmern noted rather whimsically in 1928, "to make a world. It takes all sorts of nations to make a modern state" (Zimmern 1928b: 370).

Beyond this, the commonwealth was Zimmern's answer to what he saw as the ethical limitations of "sovereign authority" and liberalism itself. Sovereign states, argued Zimmern, had no ethical obligations to one another. Likewise, citizens of a Lockean state could remain blithely unconcerned with the needs of the social whole. In contrast, membership in a commonwealth that embraced a diversity of national cultures meant "more than mere obedience to its laws or a mere emotion of pride and patriotism, more even than an intelligent exercise of political duties." Rather, in their capacity both to revel in and to move beyond their own national experiences, citizens of the commonwealth could potentially think in terms that were inherently international, centered on a "personal dedication to great tasks and great ideals" (Zimmern 1929: 59). When this happened, the commonwealth itself would be transformed into a "moral personality" and true internationalism, the kind that looked inward to what was unique about national culture and outward to the "life of the world," became possible.

At its worst, then, Zimmern's approach to commonwealth internationalism took on many of the same deeply paternalist qualities of his domestic politics and the domestic politics of idealist-oriented liberals before him. In particular, his reification of "the family" as the model upon which both domestic and national communities ought to be based spilled over into his understanding of "non-adult races." Likewise, his acceptance of the "voluntary" status of the commonwealth served to obscure what were in effect its nonvoluntary origins. At its best, however, Zimmern's theory was radically unwilling to uncouple the national and the local from the international, to separate domestic from world ethics. Internationalism imagined through the commonwealth would, Zimmern assumed, speak to both national characteristics that differentiated human beings from one another and to those "eternal things which unite, to the rock bottom level of our common humanity" (Zimmern 1918: 52). Like his nineteenth-century intellectual forebears, Zimmern refused to acknowledge the "old opposition" between individual and society, or nationalism and internationalism. Instead, he demanded the creation of a "better patriotism" able to negotiate both of these human concerns.

In this regard, Zimmern's approach to commonwealth bears a remarkable resemblance to the work of some contemporary liberal theorists of nationalism. Both Yael Tamir and Will Kymlicka, for instance, argue like Zimmern that national cultures play an important role in both individual personality formation and in the production of liberal values. For Kymlicka, the choices that an individual makes as she pursues her vision of the good life are not produced from within a cultural vacuum but are informed, constrained, and enhanced by her linguistic and social environment, an environment that Kymlicka refers to as "societal cultures" that "tend to be national cultures" (Kymlicka 1995: 92).[18] Tamir likewise argues that one's nationality plays an important role in the liberal citizen's process of identity formation. National societies, she argues, provide the individual with the freedom to "develop without repression those aspects of his personality which are bound up with his sense of identity as a member of his community" (Tamir 1993: 9). In other words, like Zimmern, Tamir and

Kymlicka argue for the centrality of the nation in nurturing liberal identity. Kymlicka even goes so far as to cite Zimmern as a progenitor of a now forgotten style of liberalism that took the issue of national minorities seriously. Further, because these theorists, like Zimmern, recognize that nationalisms focusing exclusively on the attainment of state sovereignty can, and do, lead to ethnic conflict, they each articulate a system of political organization based on graduated levels of sovereignty. For Tamir this system would resemble a kind of expanded idea of European Union, while Kymlicka's solution suggests that already multi-ethnic states relinquish certain sovereign rights to national minorities.

Beyond the fact that the approaches of both of these authors echo Zimmern's systematic vision, however, Zimmern's own theory continues to suggest ways in which such creative approaches to sovereignty might be expanded in a more explicitly internationalist direction. For instance, while both Tamir and Kymlicka are guided primarily by a concern to save nationality for liberalism, Zimmern's theory consistently brings the international back into the equation. For Zimmern, internationalism was an inevitable byproduct of rightly structured nationalism and this assumption compelled him to theorize a liberal subject who was both cosmopolitan and culturally situated. Such an approach might help to expand both Tamir's and Kymlicka's theories beyond what is now a more limited concern with reconciling liberalism and nationalism toward an understanding of the relationship between nationalism, liberalism, and international ethics.

In essence, Zimmern's work on internationalism and commonwealth may speak the language of empire, but it also speaks to a normative question that continues to fire the imagination of contemporary international ethicists: Is it possible to construct a world politics and a world ethics that take both the particularities of nationality and the universalist claims of an ethical human order into consideration? While his approach to nationalism was based, in part, on an outdated, nineteenth-century organicism that relied heavily on the conservative politics of the family, it also made a valiant effort to theorize the importance of nations to the formation of the liberal subject. Simultaneously, it was also concerned with developing a kind of international culture that would encourage these same individuals to consider their actions in light of the "spiritual bearings which affect each individual living soul born or to be born in the world" (Zimmern 1969: 187). Finally, it maintained that we could challenge sovereignty and respect national diversity by creating an international community through commonwealth. While it was precisely Zimmern's insistence that the world could have its cake and eat it too that placed him so firmly within the category of the "utopian" for Carr, this chapter suggests that in an era plagued by nationalist conflict, an ever-expanding corporate culture, and an emerging form of global governance based on the dictates of nondemocratic institutions such as the WTO, a utopianism that refuses to engage the easy dualism between nationality and internationality—or individual and community—offers a refreshing counterbalance to the contemporary debate.

Notes

Author's Note: The author gratefully acknowledges the Bodleian Library for making the Zimmern papers available. Attempts to obtain permission from the copyright holder were unsuccessful.

1.   See Toynbee's account of Zimmern in *Acquaintances* (1967: 48–61). Also, Carroll Quigley, *The Anglo-American Establishment: From Rhodes to Clivenden* (1981: 89).

2.   For critics such as Konni Zilliacus, it was precisely this refusal to challenge the morality of nationalist sentiment that ultimately gave the Nazis the green light "for their career of world aggression" (Zilliacus 1946: vii).

3.   And in this quest, British liberal idealists were not alone. Many of their contemporary liberal brethren (including John Stuart Mill and the American Progressives) also sought to explain why individuals in a liberal society should care about one another and about their community.

4.   The decision of some English liberals to turn to Germany for idealist solutions to their liberal questions reflects a more general, early- to mid-nineteenth-century, British fascination with German culture and thought. See, for example, Kennedy 1987.

5.   In Bosanquet's words, "[T]he end of the State ... is the end of Society and of the Individual—the best life, as determined by the fundamental logic of the will" (Bosanquet 1958).

6.   Bosanquet went so far as to oppose a free, national school lunch program because it would interfere with family responsibilities (Vincent and Plant 1984: 111).

7.   This decline would eventually expand, during and immediately after World War I, to a mass rejection of all German-inspired theory by most British new liberals. For more on this see Band 1980.

8.   This move on Zimmern's part, to distance himself from German theory precisely at the moment it became least fashionable was most likely due, in no small part, to his own German heritage (Bodl. Ms. Zimmern [135], fol. 18). For more on antiforeignism at Oxford in the late nineteenth century see Deslandes 1998.

9.   For the origins of the term *international mind* see Murray Butler, *The International Mind: An Argument for the Juridical Settlements of International Disputes* (1913).

10.   Zimmern sometimes defined the "international mind" as the "intellectual integrity, of applying one's reason to all and not only to selected problems" (Zimmern 1926b: 3).

11.   See Bodl. Ms. Zimmern (135). This box contains a number of relevant early lectures given between 1900 and 1905.

12.   See Hegel's theory of "the corporation" in *The Philosophy of Right* (Knox 1967). The "life of the world" was a favorite phrase of Zimmern's.

13.   "Nationality," Zimmern argued, "like religion, is subjective; Statehood is objective. Nationality is psychological; statehood is political. Nationality is a condition of mind; Statehood is a condition in law. Nationality is a spiritual possession...." (Zimmern 1918: 51).

14.   The term *Levant* has historically referred to a nexus of cultural and economic contact between Europe and the Middle East (Ziring 1992: 19). Zimmern's use of the term "Levantine merchant" also had clear associations with anti-Semitic evocations of the "wandering Jew." While Zimmern's intentions with regard to this similarity are unclear, both Jews and "Levantines" would have served the same, derisive metaphorical purpose; both were defined by a diasporic, transnational ethnic identity and both were assumed to be driven by material greed. Zimmern's clearly conflicted relationship to his father's Judaism further complicates his characterization of the "Levantine."

15.   See, of course, J. A. Hobson, *Imperialism*, Part 11, chapter 4, "Imperialism and the Lower Races." For an excellent analysis of John Stuart Mill's approach to imperialism, civilization, and "savages" see Mehta, *Liberalism and Empire* (1992).

16.   As Kendle notes, Curtis referred to Zimmern's work frequently in his 1915 "The Project of Commonwealth" (Kendle: 171).

17.   A letter to Zimmern from Eustace Perry with the British Delegation in Paris in 1919 makes it clear that most of the American representatives at the conference were equally worried about what was seen as a kind of abstract utopianism on Wilson's part (Bodl. Ms. Zimmern [16], fol. 2).

18.   Unlike communitarian critics of liberalism, Kymlicka maintains that these cultures do not need to hold any particular, universal vision of the good.

Chapter 5

Fabian Paternalism and Radical Dissent

Leonard Woolf's Theory of Economic Imperialism

Peter Wilson

Leonard Woolf was a remarkable man who achieved many remarkable things. His report for the Fabian Society on international government (Woolf 1916) was influential on the creation of the League of Nations, particularly its economic and social functions. For more than a decade it was essential reading for all serious students of the international scene. His writings on imperialism, and work for such bodies as the Labour Party Advisory Committee on Imperial Questions and the Fabian Colonial Bureau, contributed to the erosion of the moral and intellectual foundations of empire, and had a significant impact on the shape of British colonial policy in the 1940s. He was a central figure of the Bloomsbury Group, one of the most influential artistic and intellectual coteries of the twentieth century (Edel 1981; Bell 1995). He nurtured the genius of his wife, Virginia, whom he adored, and jealously guarded her literary reputation after her premature death in 1941. With Virginia he founded, in the basement of their house in Richmond-upon-Thames in 1917, the innovative and highly successful Hogarth Press, a landmark of twentieth-century publishing. He managed the editorial side of the press for more than fifty years, finally bowing out shortly after the consummation of its largest project, *The Standard Edition of the Complete Psychological Works of Sigmund Freud*, in 1966 (Spotts 1990: 265–76). In the intervening period he somehow found the time to write more than a dozen books, mainly on international issues, co-found and edit the center-left journal *Political Quarterly*, write literally thousands of book reviews, work energetically for the Union of Democratic Control (UDC) and the League of Nations Society, and occupy what today would be called "high-profile" (though Woolf always sought to keep his profile quite low) posts with the *Contemporary Review*, the *Nation*, and the *New Statesman*. But his crowning achievement was his five volume autobiography written in the last decade of his life (Woolf 1960, 1961, 1964, 1967, 1969), which former UK Chancellor of the Exchequer

Denis Healey described as the "best general introduction to the history of the early twentieth century yet written" (Healey 2002).

The argument of this chapter is simple. Like so many of his fellow supporters of the League, Woolf has gone down in International Relations (IR) historiography as an idealist. But this label distorts more than it reveals. Woolf's writings on imperialism, while they may be open to criticism on various counts, are not especially marked by their idealism. Fabian paternalism and radical dissent, rather than idealism or "utopianism," characterize Woolf's thought in this sphere. Certainly Woolf had ideals, but he recognized the need to be realistic in pursuit of them. Thus, a careful study of Woolf's thought on imperialism adds another nail in the coffin of the idealist-realist dichotomy, a dichotomy that has had a baleful influence on IR as a serious social science. (Booth 1991; Smith 1992; Wilson 1998; Ashworth 1999: ch. 5). This chapter shows that this putative idealist certainly did not ignore facts and "reality" when it came to that most important of twentieth-century questions: imperialism.

In what follows I begin by saying a few words on the nature of the exercise conducted in this chapter, broadly one of disciplinary history. I then specify the nature of Woolf's relationship with IR, before moving on to the main body of the chapter, an account of his theory of economic imperialism. Following this, an account is given of how this work was received at the time. Finally, I assess Woolf's theory of economic imperialism as it looks today, concluding with some illustrations of the components of radical dissent and Fabian paternalism in Woolf's thought.

DISCIPLINARY HISTORY

This chapter is an exercise in disciplinary history in the broad sense of being concerned with past thinkers, the way they conceived their subject, the way they went about studying it, the concepts they used, the ideas they considered important, and the impact they had on future thought. It is not concerned with telling a chronological story so much as correcting certain distortions in current understandings of this past. In the spirit of E. H. Carr, it sees history as a living subject; one in which the narration of a sequence of past events is of only secondary importance (being contingent on the historian's purpose and criteria for determining historical significance); one in which the processes of reappraisal and reinterpretation, however at times unsettling, are central to its character. This is because history is about how we understand the past from the viewpoint of present preoccupations, and how we understand the present from our analysis and understanding of the past. According to this view, the notion of history as the study of an objectively knowable past is rejected as methodologically and epistemologically untenable. History is inescapably a product of perspective. Historical knowledge is always provisional and a product of dialogue: "an unending dialogue," as Carr put it, "between the present and the past" (Carr 1961: 30).

It is very much in these terms that I see the disciplinary history of IR. It is a product of debate and dialogue between present scholars of the subject, and between present scholars and the past. No transhistorical, objective account can be given, but a certain class of scholar, the "intellectual historian," sees it as her job to refine past and present judgments, challenge those interpretations she considers unhelpful and/or erroneous, and offer new interpretations based on the discovery of new facts, or the utilization of a more rigorous and/or appropriate theoretical framework.

To this end, the warnings of Quentin Skinner in his much-discussed essay on the subject are apposite (Skinner 1969). Any satisfactory exercise in disciplinary history must contain close attention to both text and context. Until recently both have been largely neglected by scholars in the field (Schmidt 1998; Osiander 1998; Holden 2002). This is mainly because they have not seen themselves as specialists in the history of IR thought. Rather, their interest in the past has been driven by certain theoretical interests. Thus, Waltz delves into the history of political theory in order to discover patterns of thought on the causes of war, and Bull delves into the history of international political theory in order to retrieve a classical tradition (Waltz 1959; Bull 1977). A standard criticism of Waltz is that his analysis contains a large Procrustean element: the topping and tailing of a wide range of thinkers in order to squeeze them into his preferred theoretical framework. Historical accuracy is sacrificed to theoretical neatness. A standard criticism of Bull is that he not so much retrieves a classical tradition as invents one in order to legitimize a particular worldview. A pantheon of great names is constructed in order to demonstrate the excellent pedigree of his preferred concept of international society.

Careful textual analysis of the depth and rigor recently applied to the thought of E. H. Carr (Jones 1998; Cox 2000) has been a rare occurrence in IR. But this scarcity cannot be accounted for by a preoccupation with context. Greater attention to context there has been, but this attention has by and large focused on the general economic and political context of the times (the Great War, the Depression and the "crisis of capitalism," the cold war, detente). The intellectual context in which an author wrote, considered so important in political theory, has been largely overlooked in international political theory. Yet this intellectual context—why an author was writing, for what purpose, for whom, under what influences—can throw a tremendous amount of light on the author, her times, and her work.

It is for this reason that in my own work I have given a lot of attention to contemporary reviews. Discovering how any given work was received at the time and what debates it engendered is a vital first step in reconstructing the intellectual milieu in which it was written. Strangely, though a number of key texts have been much debated in IR, commentators have rarely taken the trouble to ascertain how these works were first received. Again the work of E. H. Carr provides a good example. Only recently has the critical reception of *The Twenty Years' Crisis* been analyzed in detail (Wilson 2000).

WOOLF AND IR

The problem with writing about the history of IR prior to the end of World War II is that the discipline, in the sense that that term is understood today, existed only in embryonic form. By 1930 there were three chairs of IR in the UK, two university departments, a handful of lectureships, a dozen or so courses, but no degrees devoted exclusively to the study of international relations, and only a few score students taking courses in it. It was in all essential respects a minority field, though one that was becoming less so.

Woolf never held an academic post. Nor, after doing badly in the second part of the Cambridge Classical Tripos, did he ever aspire to one (Spater and Parsons 1977: 44; Spotts 1990: 8–9). It is difficult to determine the nature of Woolf's affiliation with the discipline of IR since there is no evidence to suggest that he conceived international relations as a distinct field of academic enquiry. Whether he was aware of the fact or not, however, there can be little doubt that Woolf was a significant figure in the formative years of the discipline. He was a life-long friend and Labour party colleague of Philip Noel-Baker, the first professor of International Relations (1924–1929) at the University of London (Lloyd 1995). In his obituary of Woolf, Noel-Baker emphasized the importance of *International Government* in shaping British thinking about international relations in the early postwar years (Noel-Baker 1969). Alfred Zimmern described the book as "masterly" and borrowed from it extensively in his important, and still valuable, study of the League of Nations (Zimmern 1936: 171–72, 40–60). Martin Wight cautioned readers of the *Observer* not to read *The Twenty Years' Crisis* without Woolf's "deadly reply" in *The War for Peace* (Wight 1946). He included the latter along with *International Government* as "essential reading" in his International Theory syllabus (Wight 1991). These examples of the regard in which Woolf was held by three important figures in the professionalization of IR, give some indication of the nature of Woolf's contribution to and relationship with this emerging field. While never formally a part of the field, his work was widely read, respected, and influential within it.

WOOLF ON IMPERIALISM: AN OUTLINE

In the 1920s Woolf became one of the foremost British critics of imperialism. Like J. A. Hobson, he wrote about the subject in broad theoretical terms combining the detailed empirical analysis of the Fabian social investigator with the moral passion of the radical pamphleteer. Woolf's importance lies in his continuation of the Hobsonian tradition (see Long 1996). In many ways he assumed Hobson's mantle as Britain's foremost anti-imperialist theorist (Feuer 1989: 154).

Many of his ideas developed *pari passu* with his work as secretary of the Labour Party's Advisory Committee on Imperial Questions and his work, in various capacities, for the New Fabian Research Bureau, and the influential Fabian Colonial Bureau. In the 1920s Woolf was the Labour Movement's leading anti-imperialist thinker, and his opinions carried weight well into the 1930s (Feuer 1989: 157; Etherington 1984: 177). In 1920 he drafted, with Charles Buxton, the first policy document committing the British Labour Party to the "ultimate aim" of a "political system of self-government" in Africa. (Labour Party 1920; Hetherington 1978: 16; Luedeking and Edmonds 1992: 73–76).

Woolf was one of several prominent men—Olivier and George Orwell among them—whose anti-imperial ideas were shaped by personal experience of empire. Having fallen out of love with academia, and not yet in love with Virginia, he began his career as a colonial administrator in Ceylon. He later claimed that it was Ceylon, where he rose rapidly up the ranks from 1904 to 1907, that had turned him into a "political animal." His first published work was a novel based on these experiences, *The Village in the Jungle* (Woolf 1981 [1913]). In this work Woolf explores the complex relationship between traditional village society (charming but brutal), its natural jungle environment (beautiful but cruel), and British colonial rule (necessary but perverse).

Though its praises go largely unsung, *The Village in the Jungle* ranks alongside *Heart of Darkness* and *Burmese Days* as one of the great fictional explorations of the impact of the West upon the non-Western world (Barron 1977: 57–58). Unlike these works, however, *The Village of the Jungle* looks at its subject from the inside out rather than the outside in. Loathing the expatriate life, Woolf "went native," immersing himself in traditional life and culture, and acquiring fluency in Sinhalese in the process. As vividly recounted in the second volume of his autobiography, Woolf gained an understanding of traditional Sinhalese life and village society that was unique (Woolf 1961).

The publication of *The Village in the Jungle* was followed a decade later by the publication of a collection of shorter fictional works in which the same themes are further explored (Woolf 1924). During the intervening period Woolf wrote his major work on imperialism, *Empire and Commerce in Africa*, the more popular orientated *Economic Imperialism*, and a number of articles along similar lines (Woolf 1920a; Woolf 1920b).

Above all it was Woolf's voluminous *Empire and Commerce in Africa*, written for the newly formed Labour Research Department, that established his reputation as a leading anti-imperialist thinker. The incorporation of a vast amount of statistical data—gathered largely from the LSE library—made the book an invaluable work of reference for anticolonial publicists and campaigners. It soon joined Hobson's groundbreaking but empirically thinner study as a standard work on the subject (Etherington 1984: 182; Luedeking and Edwards 1992: 22–23).

Shortly after the publication of *Empire and Commerce in Africa*, Woolf turned his attention away from economic imperialism toward the question of mandates under the League of Nations. This change in focus was accompanied by certain modifications in outlook. The predominantly monocausal thesis of *Empire and Commerce in Africa* gave way to the more pluralistic perspective of *Economic Imperialism* and *Imperialism and Civilization*. The latter book is Woolf's most mature work on the subject. Its central theme, in contrast to earlier works, is that imperialism is best viewed as a "clash of civilizations": as a tremendous conflict between disparate and contending values, ideas, and beliefs. In the kind of questions it asks it can be seen as a forerunner, albeit in a more populist and radical vein, of Bull and Watson's *Expansion of International Society* (Woolf 1928; Bull and Watson 1984).

The darkening international scene in Europe dominated Woolf's thoughts in the 1930s. But he returned to the imperial question in the 1940s, writing several articles on colonial responsibilities and the preparation of African peoples for self-government. Woolf's interest in these more practical aspects of imperialism is a reflection of the fact that by the mid-1940s the anti-imperialists had largely won the day. The key political agendum now was no longer the aim or purpose of colonial rule, but the most appropriate means of bringing about its dissolution.

For the student of imperialism, therefore, Woolf is an important figure. His involvement with the subject spanned more than half a century; he wrote extensively; he was concerned with both theory and practice; he had a considerable impact on progressive opinion; and he was one of the few critics of empire who was at one stage involved in running one. He was, moreover, the only major critic of Western imperialism of the early twentieth century—among whom I include Hobson, Brailsford, Luxemburg, Morel, Olivier, and Lenin—who lived to taste the fruits of victory with the dissolution of the British and French colonial empires in the 1950s and 1960s.

WOOLF'S THEORY OF ECONOMIC IMPERIALISM

Woolf's analysis of economic imperialism is divided into two parts: the first concerning the causes of late-nineteenth-century imperialism; the second, its consequences.

Causes

Woolf's thesis was that the imperialism of the late nineteenth century, unlike previous imperialisms, was motivated purely by economic factors. The cause of this was the profound change that had occurred in the "structure and sphere of the State," the most immediate symptom of which was the "immense and almost overwhelming importance" that the state had assumed in economic affairs. This development was of relatively recent origin. "In its present form and with its present attributes it [the state] did not exist even in 1820" (Woolf 1920a: 4–5). But the pace of change had been rapid. By the first decade of the twentieth century there was hardly a department of individual life that had not been "subjected to State control or interference" (Woolf 1920a: 8–9).

Woolf attributed this change in the structure and sphere of the state to three phenomena that had begun to emerge in the late eighteenth century: democracy, nationalism, and industrialism. Democracy and nationalism ensured that the autocratic state conceived as the personal property and preserve of kings, was replaced by the democratic nation-state organized for the pursuit of national interests conceived as "the greatest good of the greatest number," "the realization of the best life," or "the materialization of the mysterious and sacred general will." Interacting with democracy and nationalism, the growth of industrialism ensured that the state became increasingly preoccupied with economic efficiency and commercial well-being. "Nobody in the eighteenth century thought of asking whether the state was efficient, for the main functions of the state were not economic: to-day, despite the enormous increase of patriotic nationalism, we instinctively regard the state as a kind of super-joint-stock-company" (Woolf 1920a: 6).

The changing role of the state was part and parcel of a general shift in ideas and beliefs. Industrialism and commercialism had begun to permeate every walk of life. In this respect the capitalists of Manchester were no different to the Mercantilists of an earlier or the imperialists of a later era: all assumed that material profit was the main standard of value and that the chief duty of the state was to promote, or at least not impede, its maximization. During the mid-Victorian era the policies of free trade, noninterference, and anti-imperialism were held to be the best means of attaining this end. But with the "intensive growth of industrial and commercial organization" in the late nineteenth century things began to change. "Vast and complicated organizations"—the big factory, the trust, the cartel, the syndicate, and the multiple shop—came into being and were increasingly seen as essential for industrial and commercial efficiency. The possibility of using the power and organization of the state for economic ends was not for long overlooked. This chain of cause and effect—from the emergence of nationalism, democracy, and industrialism, through the change in the state, to the "active and aggressive" use of the "power and organization of the state" for the economic purposes of its citizens—culminated, around the year 1880, in economic imperialism (Woolf 1920a: 15).

So what did Woolf mean by imperialism? Unlike other theorists of the time, he provided a clear definition:

> Under this term I include the international economic policy of the European States, of the U.S.A., and latterly of Japan, in the unexploited

and non-Europeanized territories of the world. The policy of
Economic Imperialism includes colonial policy and the acquisition by
the Europeanized State of exploitable territory, the policy of spheres
of influence, and the policy of obtaining economic control through
other political means. These various kinds of policy are all distinguished by one important characteristic; they all aim at using the
power and organisation of the European form of State in the economic interests of its inhabitants in lands where the European form
of state has not developed. I call it imperialism because the policy
always implies either the extension of the state's territory by conquest
or occupation, or the application of its dominion or some form of
political control to people who are not its citizens. I qualify it with the
word economic because the motives of this imperialism are not
defence or prestige nor conquest nor the "spread of civilization," but
the profit of the citizens, or of some citizens, of the European state.
(Woolf 1920a: 19)

The method adopted by Woolf was essentially *verstehen*, that is, interpretive
understanding of actor behavior. His evidence was drawn from the writings
and speeches of those statesmen, soldiers, and businessmen to whom the
formulation of state policy and the control of state action was entrusted.

Woolf cites many passages from the speeches and statements of such prominent continental statesmen as Bismarck, Clemenceau, and Etienne in order to
prove his contention that the motivating force of the new imperialism of the
late nineteenth century was economic gain. But he highlights the statements of
two British spokesmen: Joseph Chamberlain and Captain, later Sir Frederick,
later Lord, Lugard. Chamberlain claimed in 1894 that it was the government's
job to ensure that "new markets shall be created and old markets ... effectively
developed." There consequently existed "a necessity as well as a duty for us to
uphold the dominion and empire which we now possess" and "a necessity for
using every legitimate opportunity to extend our influence and control in that
African continent which is now being opened up to civilization and commerce"
(Woolf 1920a: 18).

Chamberlain explicated this view in more detail in a speech to the
Birmingham Chamber of Commerce in 1896:

All the great offices of state are occupied with commercial affairs. The
Foreign Office and the Colonial Office are chiefly engaged in finding
new markets and defending old ones. The War Office and the
Admiralty are mostly occupied in preparation for the defence of those
markets and for the protection of our commerce. ... Commerce is the
greatest of all political interests. (Woolf 1920a: 7)

Speaking about his recent expedition to Uganda for the British East Africa Company, Woolf's second star witness, Sir Frederick Lugard, claimed:

> The scramble for Africa … was due to the growing commercial rivalry, which brought home to civilized nations the vital necessity of securing the only remaining fields for industrial enterprise and expansion. It is well to realise that it is for our advantage—and not alone at the dictates of duty—that we have undertaken responsibilities in East Africa. It is in order to foster the growth of the trade of this country, and to find an outlet for our manufactures and our surplus energy, that our far-seeing statesmen and our commercial men advocate colonial expansion. … I do not believe that in these days our national policy is based on motives of philanthropy only. (Woolf 1920a: 26)

Through such statements Woolf was able to show that economic considerations were of immense importance in motivating nineteenth-century imperialism. He was also able to show that these considerations assumed progressively greater importance as the century unfolded. The era of Ferry, Rhodes, and Chamberlain differed markedly from the era of Metternich, Wellington, and Talleyrand. For this latter group, imperialism was about alliances, the balance of power, national and international prestige. But by the ninth decade of the nineteenth-century economic imperialism had "fully and finally established itself." "In the great States of Europe, now completely industrialized, political power passed from the hands of birth into the hands of wealth, and the political ideals of rule and power and prestige gave way to those of commerce, industry, and finance." European policy became "dominated by rival imperialisms, colonial policies, spheres of influence, commercial treaties, markets, and tariffs" (Woolf 1920a: 24, 57–58).

Woolf's evidence, however, is not entirely consistent. He is unable to sustain his initial contention that imperialism was motivated *purely* by economic factors. Bismarck may have become more interested in economics in the 1880s, but as Woolf's own account shows, questions of strategy and great power competition were never far from the forefront of his mind. Although Bismarck eventually complied with the wishes of German trading and financial interests, thereby initiating Germany's imperial policy, Woolf does not prove that he did so for *their* reasons. The German chancellor was clearly perturbed by the expansion of British power in Africa and was eager to check it—as revealed by his involvement in the Congo controversy of the early 1880s, culminating in his convening of the 1884 Congo Conference at Berlin (Woolf 1920a: 38–45). But why exactly did he abandon his earlier indifference to colonialism? The arguments of those representing economic interests may have been an important factor, but they were not the only, nor necessarily the most important one. The quotations Woolf selects from Bismarck's speeches do not clinch the matter in quite the decisive way he assumed. The following statement taken from Bismarck's public announcement of his new policy could be interpreted as evincing an abiding concern with "Power and Prestige" as much as a new desire for "money-making and markets":

> It is not possible to conquer oversea territories by men of war or to take possession of them without further ceremony. Nevertheless the German trader wherever he has settled will be protected, and wherever he has assumed possession of territory there the Administration will follow him, as England has continually done. (Woolf 1920a: 36)

This statement contains a tacit acknowledgment of both Britain's naval mastery and the importance Bismarck attached to great power rivalry.

It is also significant that Woolf makes a distinction between North and Tropical Africa. After 1880 European statesmen began to "deal" with the latter in terms of the new policy of economic imperialism. But with respect to the former, the "older policy of Wellington and de Polignac" never entirely lost its hold (Woolf 1920a: 58). Furthermore, the spirit of the church missionary societies of Victorian Britain might be said to have also shaped the statesmanship of Chamberlain and Lugard. Lugard's references to the "dictates of duty" and to "motives of philanthropy" indicate that the idea of the "civilizing mission" was not entirely absent in his explanation of empire. The same could be said of Chamberlain's references to "duty" and "civilization." In addition, although it may have been correct to say that "all the great offices of state are occupied with commercial affairs," this does not mean that they were wholly so occupied.

Along with these specific problems with Woolf's analysis, there are problems of a more general nature. The determination of social causation through analysis of public declarations of social actors is not a hazard-free enterprise. Social purpose and setting invariably condition social pronouncements. The speeches and statements of politicians and major political actors are particularly conditioned by the political context in which they are made. The social investigator, therefore, must always be on her guard. She may be witnessing not social truth but the employment of an age-old political tool (Manning 1975: xviii–xx, 88–100).

Chamberlain in his speech to the Birmingham Chamber of Commerce was probably exaggerating for his own political purposes, rather than giving an "objective" account of what he felt to be the raison d'être of empire. Such statements often contain as much "ought" as "is." Similarly, the fact that Lugard was writing in defense of a much-criticized campaign cannot be ignored. He was at pains to point out to reluctant British ministers the considerable material rewards that could be reaped in East Africa. He wanted to convince them that official British involvement would not become the financial albatross that many feared. Lugard was not so much concerned with explaining and justifying past acts of imperialism, as making a case for its continuation and reinvigoration.

Another problem concerns selection of evidence. Woolf does supply a large number of quotations, but only ones that corroborate his thesis. This raises a general question with the interpretive method. How far should the analyst go in searching for counterinterpretations? As we shall see, a number of critics at the time felt that Woolf did not go far enough.

There is no evidence to suggest that Woolf was aware of these short-comings except for the fact that as *Empire and Commerce in Africa* unfolds, his determination to uphold his monocausal thesis becomes weaker. Claims to the effect that late-nineteenth-century imperialism was notable for "the singleness and purity of [economic] motive." become less frequent, and claims to the effect that economic factors were the "main" motive or the "ultimate" end of policy, more so (Woolf 1920a: 18, 22, 44, 58, 323–24).

A distinct trend away from monocausalism is clearly evident in later writings. In *Economic Imperialism* Woolf explicitly says that there was no single and simple cause of the "complex" phenomenon of imperialism, and he proceeds to examine some of the explanations commonly advanced. The "moral" explanation that colonial expansion was motivated by the "white man's burden"—the duty to spread Christianity, law and order, and other "blessings of Western civilization" (an ironic reference to the Final Act of the 1884–85 Congress of Berlin)—is dismissed by Woolf as a secondary cause (Woolf 1920a: 43–45; Woolf 1928: 78–79). This view was frequently used as an argument against withdrawing from a conquest once it had been made, or abandoning control once it had been acquired. Thus, in Woolf's view:

> [T]he connection between imperialism and moral ideas appears to be this: Europeans have acquired their Empires for selfish motives; they, or many of them, believe that they retain and maintain their Empires for altruistic motives. The white man's burden becomes a duty only after … he has placed it upon his own shoulders. (Woolf 1920b: 18)

The same could be said of "sentimental" reasons, such as the belief that "the acquisition and retention of imperial possessions and dependencies outside Europe reflects great glory on the European State". This explanation, according to Woolf, may have been valid as far as the retention of empire went, but belief in the glory of empire had done little to set the policy in motion (Woolf 1920b: 20–23).

Military and strategic reasons had more weight, especially with regard to French and Italian imperialism in North Africa. There was also a sense in which imperialism had a strategic logic of its own. Britain sought to control Egypt not because such control afforded any strategic value for Britain itself, but in order to protect India. Accordingly, "[m]ilitary reasons are … not to any great extent a cause of imperialism, but they are a reason for making an empire large, and a large empire larger" (Woolf 1920b: 24).

At a glance *Imperialism and Civilization* seems to mark a return of Woolf's initial monocausalism. He began the book by pointing out that the relations between civilizations prior to the nineteenth century were largely tolerant and indifferent. "But the new European civilization of the nineteenth century changed all that. It was a belligerent, crusading, conquering, exploiting, prose-lytizing civilization." Vastly superior technology made this aggressive expansion of Western civilization possible. The need for new markets and new sources of raw materials made it necessary. The picture was as follows:

> Behind the capitalist, the trader, the manufacturer, and the financier, who had emerged from the industrial revolution and were now led by blind economic forces to stretch out their hands to the markets and produce of Asia and Africa, stood the highly organised, efficient, power-fully armed, acutely nationalist modern State which had emerged from the French Revolution and the Napoleonic Wars. Sometimes deliberately and sometimes haphazardly and unconsciously, the power of this terrific engine of force and government was invoked by the capitalist to aid him in developing or exploiting the other continents. The effect was stupendous. (Woolf 1928: 9–11)

But elsewhere in the book the picture is far from clear. Thus, the "inevitability" of the "stretching out" and "imposition" of European civilization on the rest of the world was "especially" due to economic impulses. Though these impulses were a primary cause of imperialism, strategic impulses were a "secondary" cause. The conquests of Greece, Rome, and the Renaissance were about glory and domination. In contrast, nineteenth-century imperialism was "primarily" about economic exploitation. The forceful control of the economic life of China by the imperial Powers of Europe, the United States, and later Japan was "exercised *primarily* in the interests of the commercial, industrial, and financial classes of the controlling Power." Similarly, the evils caused by imperialism were "*mainly* due to the habit of European civilization of subordinating everything to economic ends" (Woolf 1928: 32–47, 63–71; emphasis added).

The phrasing of these arguments amounts to a significant modification of Woolf's initial thesis. It is important to stress, however, that although he aban-doned the notion that late-nineteenth-century imperialism was motivated *purely* by economic factors, he continued to insist on their *primacy*. His label "economic imperialism" remains therefore a valid one.

Consequences

Woolf contended that the consequences of late-nineteenth-century imperialism were "almost wholly evil" (Woolf 1920a: 352). Economic imperialism was not only bad for the colonized, it was bad for the colonizers, too—except for a small band of traders, financiers, mine owners, and planters who in many cases accumulated great wealth.

The proponents of economic imperialism genuinely believed that great riches were to be won in the "opening up" of Asia and Africa. For Woolf this was pure delusion. The colonial parties in France and Germany, for example, held "vague and erroneous ideas" about the nature of the empire they wished to conquer:

> This was particularly true of Africa, the mystery of whose forests and lakes and rivers was only just being revealed to Europeans. Undoubtedly a vision of "many goodly states and kingdoms" swam before the eyes of patriots, who dreamed dreams of German or French Australias and Canadas rising by the side of great rivers, or in the tropical forests of Asia and Africa. (Woolf 1920a: 30)

The Congo, to give one example, was seen as an "Eldorado" of rubber, precious metals, and—oddly, given Woolf's original thesis—"savage souls" (Woolf 1920a: 38).

Such views were delusory because the historical record showed that the benefits of economic imperialism had been small. Woolf provided a wealth of data to substantiate this claim. In 1913, for instance, all of Britain's tropical possessions in Africa accounted for only 1.04 per cent of UK imports and 1.4 per cent of UK exports. This meant that tropical Africa was of no more importance economically to the UK than Chile. In terms of UK exports, Argentina was three times more important, and six times more important in terms of imports. The average value of food and raw materials imported from British East Africa between 1909 and 1913 amounted to 0.15 per cent of the UK's total imports of these commodities, and British East Africa imported only 0.19 per cent of total UK exports. It had been claimed in the early 1890s, by Chamberlain, Lugard, the London *Times*, and others that Britain should colonize Uganda because it would provide a vital market for British exports and vital jobs for British workers. In classic dissenting fashion Woolf responded as follows:

> Uganda, that country which was to secure the British workman from unemployment, actually takes no more than .006 per cent of the total exports of British industries. It is clear that the incorporation of Uganda in the British Empire has had no more and no less effect upon British trade, industry, and employment, than if it had been sunk in the Indian Ocean and blotted off the map of the world. (Woolf 1920a: 334)

Woolf also pointed out that imperialists assumed that colonial markets would be closed to foreign competition. But this was not the case. For the period 1898–1913, for example, the increase in value of raw materials imported by British industries from German East Africa was far greater than the increase in value of those imported from British East Africa. Similarly, the rate of increase of British exports to German East Africa was far greater than the rate of increase of British exports to British East Africa. Woolf continued:

> The significance of this fact is obvious when it is remembered that Mr. Chamberlain and the economic imperialists of the British East Africa Company argued that the main reason why Britain should seize and retain Uganda and British East Africa was in order to keep the Germans out and prevent them from closing these territories to the products of British industry. (Woolf 1920a: 333)

Even at the height of the empire, Woolf concluded, the importance of Britain's tropical possessions in Africa to the metropolitan economy was at best marginal. The belief that they provided an important market for British manufactures was a delusion. "The few score inhabitants of Park Lane," he exclaimed, "have a far higher purchasing power and are a far better market for British industries than the millions of Africans in these British possessions" (Woolf 1920b: 59).

The importance of British Africa as a source of raw materials was similarly delusory. British imports from East Africa were negligible. Her imports from West Africa were greater but still relatively modest: palm oil, the major export of the region, was a commodity of minor importance when set against cotton, wool, copper, and iron ore; so too was Nigerian tin when set against the much greater amounts of tin imported from Bolivia.

Although not identical, what was true of British possessions was also generally true of French and German. For example, the trade between France and her Algerian and Tunisian colonies was not insignificant, these colonies accounting for 5.5 per cent of French exports in 1912. But this figure was only marginally greater after France established a system of colonial preference, in 1885, than before. Colonization had resulted in only a marginal increase in trade. Moreover, the value of French exports to Algeria and Tunisia was two and one-half times greater than the value of the exports to all other French colonial possessions. In 1910 the French Empire accounted for 8 per cent of French exports and 7 per cent of imports. This meant that, as trading partners, Germany and especially Britain were far more important to France than her colonies: British imports of French goods were twice the value of French goods bought by the entire French colonial empire, and Germany imported 15 per cent more. Together Britain and Germany exported to France three times the total exports of the whole French Empire. "Nothing could show more clearly,"

Woolf concluded, "that the economic beliefs behind economic imperialism are dreams and delusions" (Woolf 1920a: 330).

If the European side of the colonial balance sheet made a bleak picture the African side was even more so. The so-called blessings of European colonialism amounted to little. "Law and order" had to some extent been established, but only in the wake of "persistent and ruthless slaughter of the inhabitants in wars and through 'punitive expeditions'" (Woolf 1920b: 65). Brutal systems of administration existed in many colonies and especially in the Belgian Congo, the French Congo, and German South West Africa. Christianity had been spread to some extent but its adoption was more apparent than real. Many of the nine million Africans (out of a total population of 170 million) who had been converted by 1920 were Christian only nominally. The spread of education had fared little better. Even in British colonies, which tended to have a better record on education than the others, the provision of education in any of its forms was dismal. Local taxation far outstripped local public expenditure. In 1917, for example, the expenditure on schools in Nigeria amounted to only 1.7 per cent of taxation raised. In British East Africa the total expenditure on education for the year 1909–1910 was a meager 1,835 pounds while the expenditure on the post office, which served only the interests of white settlers, was 26,700 pounds, that is, 1,400 per cent more. The colonial authorities, indeed, spent little of the revenue they raised on schemes designed to benefit "the native":

> Though the native is heavily taxed, the revenue derived from such taxation is devoted by Government not to native requirements, but mainly to European interests, e.g., the Chief Native Commissioner of Kenya stated that the Kitui Akamba tribe paid 207,749 pounds in taxes in ten years, and that the only Government expenditure in the Kitui Reserve during this time had been on collecting the taxes. (Labour Party 1920: 15)

Similarly, the attempt to establish the "Europeans' economic system" and the "principle of economic efficiency" had produced few benefits for Africans. The colonial record in East Africa was particularly appalling. Local economic systems had been ruthlessly destroyed rather than adapted. No attempt had been made to improve traditional agricultural techniques. The best land had been expropriated to white settlers and local populations forced into inadequate "native reserves." By various means, some direct, others indirect, the native had been compelled to work for poor wages. In many cases the exploitation of African labor by white capitalists amounted to slavery (Woolf 1919: 28–32; Labour Party 1920: 12–16).

In Asia, although the pattern of economic imperialism had been different the results were equally grave. Economic imperialism brought corruption, civil war, indebtedness, and foreign intervention. China, for example, had been reduced to "anarchy and economic chaos."

Thus, the phenomenon of economic imperialism stood indicted on all sides: neither Africans, Asians, nor Europeans benefited from it except for a tiny commercial elite.

THE ASSESSMENT OF WOOLF'S THEORY IN CONTEMPORARY OPINION

Woolf's books on imperialism were published to widespread critical acclaim. A reviewer of *Empire and Commerce in Africa* opined that "the labours Mr Woolf has undertaken ... put all students of politics and economics under a great debt. His analysis is thorough, impartial and convincing" (UDC 1920a). A further review in a later issue of the same journal came to an even more favorable conclusion: "A clearer exposition of the relations between imperialism and finance has never been penned, and the whole book rests on a masterly marshalling of indisputable fact" (UDC 1920b). In the same vein, a reviewer in the *Commonwealth* remarked: "Great credit is due to the Labour Research Department and Mr Woolf for the issue of such a well-balanced and exhaustive work" (*Commonwealth* 1921). The founder of the UDC and fellow anti-imperialist, E. D. Morel, described the book as "a piece of historical research of great value ... [which should] be widely read and deeply pondered" (Morel 1920).

One might expect such enthusiasm from such eminently Left-leaning publications. But *Empire and Commerce in Africa* was also enthusiastically greeted by publications without any obvious Left or radical bent. A Canadian academic journal described it as "a contribution to the literature of international relations of cardinal importance ... [one] which all students should familiarize themselves and which statesmen must reckon" (Barnes 1921). The *Nation* considered it "masterly," "thorough," "powerful," "courageous," and "conspicuously honest in the handling of facts" (*Nation* 1920). The *Glasgow Herald* declared:

> Whatever one may think of the political standpoint of Mr Woolf, there is no doubt that he has given us a most fascinating book, packed full of information, brilliantly written, and sound alike in statistics and judgment ... we question whether the whole field has ever been surveyed more boldly or with more advantage to the reader. (*Glasgow Herald* 1920)

Even the imperialist *Daily Mail* described it as "a penetrating study which no student of politics or history can afford to leave unread" (*Daily Mail* 1920).

Woolf's subsequent books on the subject enjoyed less attention, as befitting works more limited in ambition. They were nonetheless well received. The *New Statesman* described *Economic Imperialism* as an "extremely useful little book … admirably written … [and one which] ought to be in the hands of everyone who wants to understand the underlying causes of the foreign policy of the Great Powers" (*New Statesman* 1921). A reviewer in economically straitened postwar Germany similarly concluded: "Any person who wishes to have in a brief compass the facts about imperialism should consult this cheap and masterly summary" (*European Press* 1920). Of *Imperialism and Civilization* the weekly newspaper of the Independent Labour Party wrote: "Few wiser or more thoughtful books have been written on this problem" (*New Leader* 1928). A view echoed by an American reviewer who declared: "I know no clearer analysis of the nature of nineteenth century imperialism and its difference from previous movements of conquest than is contained in this little book" (Gannett 1928).

But the judgment of contemporary critics was not uniformly favorable. Morel, in the review cited above, criticized Woolf for accepting at face value the explanations given by capitalists and imperialists of their own actions. In Morel's view, "sheer individual will-to-power" as much as greed for gain accounted for a good deal of what went on in modern Africa. The *Economist* congratulated Woolf for "brilliantly exposing" the mistakes and iniquities of empire, but questioned his method of quotation without reference to context. In their view, Chamberlain, his clever rationalizations notwithstanding, was essentially no different to Disraeli: both regarded commerce not as an end in itself but as a means to national greatness, power, and prestige (*Economist* 1920). The *Manchester Guardian*, while considering the work "really valuable," nonetheless felt that its author had been arbitrary in his choice of cases. In addition, Woolf had been selective in his choice of quotations. Those emphasizing the motivating force of new investment opportunities were clearly significant, but passages of equal import could be found emphasizing native welfare (*Manchester Guardian* 1920). A reviewer for the *TLS* reached the same verdict. The book clearly contained evidence of much research, but it was

> always on one side and directed to proving what the author wants to prove. … The facts and figures may be accurate, as far as they go, but only one side is given or emphasized. … Authorities are regarded only so far as they square with preconceived opinions. (*Times Literary Supplement* 1920)

Even the *New Statesman* had some critical words to say about the volume. In a lengthy review it praised Woolf for having produced a "very remarkable," "detailed," "thoroughly documented," and "fascinatingly readable" book. It also praised him for his "intense intellectual honesty" which not only prevented him "from distorting the facts to suit his thesis," but saved him (*pace* the *TLS*) "even from any suspicion of having overlooked facts which might be inconvenient." It concluded that it was "far the ablest and most stimulating book that has been written about the subject from the democratic point of view."

Yet although Woolf could not be accused of unfairly presenting the facts, the standpoint from which he did so was "impossibly Utopian." It was impossible to question on general principles Woolf's moral indictment of European imperialism. But a "purely ethical judgment" of so great an episode seemed "curiously irrelevant." It was "as if one were to write a book showing that Julius Caesar had no moral right to invade Gaul or Britain." Superior civilizations, the *New Statesman* claimed, would always dominate inferior ones when they came into contact with them. It was wrong therefore to put the new imperialism down to economic motives. Such motives were for the most part merely camouflage. The key factor was "the development of transport which brought Europe in close contact with great areas over which an immensely lower civilisation prevailed" (*New Statesman* 1920).

Finally, along with criticism of his method and his moral standpoint, more than one skeptical eyebrow was raised at Woolf's prescriptions. The *Nation* questioned his call for a change in men's beliefs and desires, from economic imperialism to humanitarianism. Such a change—"so simple, so reasonable, so commonplace"—was difficult enough for an individual to accomplish let alone a nation. To ask for such a change was to ask for nothing short of a miracle. Indeed, Woolf was in effect requesting "the old change of heart of the evangelist" (*Nation* 1921).

From this overview of the critical reception of Woolf's works, three observations can be made. First, nearly all reviewers praised Woolf for his detailed enumeration of the facts. This alone should give us pause before dismissing Woolf's thought as "utopian." Second, several reviewers had reservations about Woolf's methodology, along much the same lines as those generic problems with interpretivism identified above. Third, criticism was leveled at the overtly moral tone of Woolf's approach, and his tendency to marshal facts for the purpose of drawing up a moral balance sheet. This betrayed an essentially evangelical attitude to political change, the central task being a mass conversion of hearts and minds. Hence, Woolf's stark and in some instances dramatic presentation of the errors of past ways. To change reality, perhaps a stubborn, deep-rooted reality, one first had to convince the public of its utter unacceptability.

ANALYSIS AND ASSESSMENT

The enduring value of a number of aspects of Woolf's theory—his clear definition, his combination of interpretive and empirical analysis, his balance sheet of the costs and benefits of empire—has been reaffirmed by a number of writers in the postwar historical literature (Hammond 1961; Fieldhouse 1984: 30–32; 63–76; Offer 1993). But the cumulative effect of this literature has been to cast doubt on the validity of Woolf's theory as a whole.

At the most general level, numerous detailed historical studies, based on documentary evidence not available until the 1950s, have demonstrated that what Woolf and others called the "new imperialism" was in fact an immensely complicated historical phenomenon that cannot be reduced to a single set of factors whether "economic," "political," "strategic," or "technological." The issue is still highly controversial. The weight of opinion suggests, however, that the causal matrix of late-nineteenth-century imperialism differed from one colonial power to another and from one part of the world to another (Fieldhouse 1984: Part III; Eldridge 1984).

The weight of historical opinion also suggests that both "peripheral" and "Eurocentric" explanations have their place in any general theory of why the pace and temper of colonial acquisition changed so suddenly in the final decades of the nineteenth century. The absolute superiority of one approach over the other, on which debate raged in the 1960s and 1970s, is now generally rejected in favor of a hybrid approach that postulates that crises erupting on the outer reaches of empire, requiring some kind of metropolitan response, interacted in various complex ways with internal socioeconomic and political changes that were simultaneously occurring in the metropolitan heartlands. Woolf's explanation—like Hobson's, Lenin's, and all the classical theorists'—was exclusively Eurocentric. To that extent, in the eyes of modern scholars, it is flawed (Robinson and Gallagher 1953; Robinson and Gallagher 1961; Fieldhouse 1961; Fieldhouse 1984: 3–84).

Along with these general points a number of more specific points can be made. Woolf contended that the growth of monopoly—the big factory, the trust, the cartel, the syndicate, the multiple shop—was an important factor in generating, "around the year 1880," the new, "economic" imperialism. It has been shown, however, that this could only have been an important factor in two countries—Germany and the United States—and even in these countries the industrial and financial combines that were undoubtedly rising at this time did not reach the level of dominance suggested by Woolf until the final decade of the century, that is, at least ten years *after* the events they allegedly caused had begun to occur. The countries with the largest empires—Britain and France— were the countries where the growth of monopoly was least advanced (Fieldhouse 1984: 3–38).

Secondly, it has been shown that references to the commercial benefits of the extension of empire—especially into the tropical zones—in the speeches of leading statesmen and politicians, only became pronounced in the final years of the century. Fieldhouse has shown that references to these benefits by Ferry and Chamberlain in particular were rationalizations of events that had already taken place, or justifications for keeping hold of territories that were already under imperial control, having been acquired for quite different reasons. The issue at stake was escalating administrative costs, and the feeling that newly acquired colonies were placing an intolerable strain on the public finances.

If they were to be retained they must, it was felt, be made to pay. Hence the appeal by imperialists to their untapped economic potential (Fieldhouse 1984: 3–87, 459–77). In this respect Woolf got his primary and secondary factors back to front. Economics, rather than being a primary factor, were a secondary factor in the sense that they were not so much a cause of empire as a justification for keeping and extending it.

Thirdly, as Etherington has shown, Woolf played fast and loose with chronology. What is flagged as a more or less discrete historical phenomenon—the *new* imperialism—becomes indistinguishable, as Woolf's analysis unfolds, from European colonizing activity in the nineteenth century as a whole. Woolf gives at least five dates for the beginning of the new imperialism ranging from 1839 to 1890 (Etherington 1984: 180). Ironically, this implicit recognition that the so-called new imperialism perhaps did not represent such a sharp break with the past as many at the time believed—Woolf included—is one that finds confirmation in one of the most important academic papers in the postwar literature (Robinson and Gallagher 1953).

Of all the sins of which Woolf can be accused, having an idealist or a utopian approach to imperialism is not one of them. He cannot be accused of ignoring facts and analysis of cause and effect. Woolf's contribution to theorizing about late-nineteenth-century imperialism largely consists of the vast amount of statistical data he brought to bear on the subject. Though Woolf's theory has clear normative underpinnings (the desire to discredit both commercialism and imperialism by linking them inextricably together), and though he drew strong moral conclusions from it (that imperialism was an unqualified evil for both the colonized and the colonizers), his theory is a causal theory par excellence. It stands or falls not on its normative underpinnings, its normative implications, or its practical usefulness, but on its empirical accuracy, its conceptual clarity, and its internal coherence. Nor can it be said that Woolf was guilty, in Carr's quasi-Marxist sense, of peddling some kind of bourgeois ideology, the hidden but real purpose of which was to promote and defend a particular status quo (see Carr 1939: 81–112). The whole thrust of Woolf's analysis was that the status quo was corrupt and dangerous and needed to be replaced as a matter of the first importance.

The only sense in which the charge of idealism/utopianism might be applied is that in exaggerating the importance of economic factors he underestimated the role of power: power, that is, in the "realist" sense of political and military power. The problem with this assertion, however, is that it comes close to suggesting that Woolf was utopian simply because he was not realist. It should also be pointed out that Woolf did not ignore realpolitik and the strategic factor. He emphasized, for example, that it continued to exercise a powerful influence in North Africa long after economic factors had become dominant elsewhere on the continent. In sum, therefore, although it is probably true—and key works by Langer and Fieldhouse suggest so—that the power-political/strategic factor was more important in determining the European division of the African continent than Woolf conceded, it would be unreasonable to cite this as evidence of utopianism. Woolf did not ignore the power factor in general. Nor did he ignore the influence of the power factor conceived in this particular way (Langer 1935; Fieldhouse 1984: 63–69, 459–77).

It is certainly true that this most slippery term *utopian/idealist* can be defined in a number of different ways. But in *The Twenty Years' Crisis* and other central IR texts, these three facets (concerning facts and analysis of cause and effect, ideological defense of the status quo, and power) are outstanding (Wilson 1995; Wilson 2003: ch. 2). However pronounced they may have been in other aspects of Woolf's political thought, this study reveals that these facets of idealism were not pronounced in his thought on imperialism.

CONCLUSION: RADICAL DISSENT AND FABIAN PATERNALISM

To label Woolf idealist, period, is to belittle his contribution, and that of his colleagues in Fabian, Labour, and liberal circles, to the erosion of the moral and intellectual foundations of empire. Woolf imbibed from the classics as an earnest pupil, and less earnest student, and from his mentor, the philosopher G. E. Moore, at Trinity, a great love of, and faith in, reason. But it was not blind faith. It was not based on shallow optimism in abstract human nature. Nor was it a product of the high-Victorian belief in inevitable progress. Rather, it was a product of an understanding and appreciation of what the carefully tutored human mind was capable of achieving.

It was this faith in the capacity of the tutored mind, along with a dedication to public service, that made Woolf a natural Fabian. It is the paternalism characteristic of early Fabianism, allied with evangelical zeal of English radicalism, which together most aptly characterize his thought on imperialism.

Radical Dissent

By "radical dissent" I have in mind that tradition of political thought described by A. J. P. Taylor in his masterly *The Troublemakers* (Taylor 1985). It is united by what it is against more than what it is for. Dissenters are vehemently critical of British foreign policy orthodoxy. They oppose the use of force, intervention, and power politics. They are deeply skeptical of the balance of power. They argue that war is little more than the sport of kings in which the vast majority of people have everything to lose but nothing to gain. They see diplomacy as an elitist and undemocratic activity, distant to the needs and interests of ordinary people. They deplore the unprincipled conduct of international affairs and demand greater attention to morality. They view the military as an oppressive, undemocratic force, and advocate either complete (or very substantial) disarmament or the concentration of armaments in the hands of a world authority.

The term *dissent* must be qualified by the term *radical* for three interrelated reasons. First, orthodox foreign policy is not only criticized but rejected root and branch. Second, the cause of international ills is located not at the international level but primarily at the domestic level. War and other forms of "dysfunctional" political behavior are seen, at root, as products of corrupt or unjust or obsolete or irrational domestic political structures. Third, the alternative policies prescribed by dissenters represent a fundamental challenge to the status quo. Cobden, for example, advocated a policy of pure nonintervention; Morel recommended open diplomacy and the democratization of the foreign policy; Wells proposed the abolition of the wasteful system of interstate competition and its replacement by a world society based on rational scientific organization.

Taylor rightly cites Woolf as a prominent dissenting voice in early-twentieth-century British history. The purpose of much of Woolf's work was to discredit orthodox or conservative policies and ideas. Throughout his career he arraigned them as variously irrational, myopic, immoral, stupid, deceitful, and impracticable. His tone was sometimes cool and skeptical but more often impassioned, indignant, sarcastic. The tone of these passages and their antiestablishment intent clearly mark out Woolf as a dissenter.

> The European went into Africa … desiring to exploit it and its inhabitants for his own economic advantage, and he rapidly acquired the belief that the power of his State should be used in Africa for his own economic interests. Once this belief was accepted, it destroyed the idea of individual moral responsibility. The State, enthroned in its impersonality and a glamour of patriotism, can always make a wilderness and call it peace, or make a conquest and call it civilization. The right of Europe to civilize became synonymous with the right of Europe to rob or exploit the uncivilized. (Woolf 1920: 352–53)

Woolf was at his most mischievous when commenting upon the astonishing arrogance of the Victorian imperialists:

> Until very nearly the end of the nineteenth century, Europeans … regarded … [their colonial conquests] with complacent pride as one of the chief blessings and glories of Western civilization. The white race of Europe, they held, was physically, mentally, and morally superior to all other races, and God, with infinite wisdom and goodness, had created it and developed it so it might be ready, during the reign of Queen Victoria of England, to take over and manage the affairs of all other peoples on the earth and teach them to be, in so far as that was

possible for natives and heathens, good Europeans and good Christians. (Woolf 1928: 12–13)

Fabian Paternalism

By "Fabian paternalism" I have in mind that approach to political change, central to early Fabianism, which assigned a special role to a highly educated, public spirited, scientifically minded, meritocratic elite. Progressive change would be brought about via a division of labor between several cadres of technical, scientific, and administrative "experts." In this respect social progress was analogous to technical progress. Through detached and systematic analysis of physical facts, the scientific expert was able to discover causes of physical phenomena and events, and use these discoveries in order to harness and control them. Through detached and systematic analysis of social facts, the social-scientific expert could do the same for the social world. It was to such experts that the communal good needed to be entrusted. Her special knowledge combined with her highly attuned social conscience made her the standard bearer of progress. In the modern world the expert knew best (Pugh 1984; Pimlott 1984: Part I).

A further hallmark of Fabian paternalism was belief in gradual change. This had both a positive and a normative dimension. On the one hand, gradual change would inevitably occur if society chose to be governed by reason and "the facts" rather than prejudice and opinion. Hence the Fabian motto, coined by Sidney Webb: "the inevitability of gradualness." On the other hand, change was best—more permanent, more just, more beneficial—when gradual. Only through gradual change could the evils of social turmoil, social injustice, and political reaction be avoided.

Fabian paternalism, in substance and in tone, is strongly evident in Woolf's thought on mandates (e.g., Woolf 1920c) Improving and extending the League's mandate system was Woolf's main recommendation for dealing with the vast problem of imperialism (Wilson 2003: ch. 5–6). For the most part, Woolf wrote about African peoples as if they occupied a much lower level of civilization and were helpless in the face of the superior civilization of the West. He accepted the late Victorian assumption that "the African" was "backward" and "savage." Such things as war, slavery, mysticism, and cannibalism proved this. He freely used such demeaning terms as "non-adult races" and "primitive peoples." But consistent with the self-consciously enlightened and progressive beliefs of his Fabian and Bloomsbury colleagues, he refused to put the parlous condition of "the African" down to race or color. Indeed, the main responsibility for his backwardness resided with the Europeans since they had failed to introduce a proper system of education.

He thus fully subscribed to the presumption of Article 22 of the League Covenant that, unassisted, they would not be able to "stand by themselves under the strenuous conditions of the modern world." The native was "no match" for the European and was unable to cope with the economic and political system that had been imposed upon him. It was consequently the job of the colonial authorities to "educate the people so that they may gradually take their place as free men both in the economic system and in the government of their country" (Woolf 1920c: 12). Accordingly:

> The end in view is an African population, with its own institutions and civilization, capable of making the most economic use of its land, able to understand Western civilization and control the forces it has let loose on the world, governing itself through organs of government appropriate to its traditions and environment. (Woolf 1928: 131)

The paternalism of all this is clear: it was the job and indeed the duty of Europeans—with the aid of expert bodies such as League Committee for Intellectual Co-operation—to work out the general lines of economic and political development in Africa.

The paternalism of the following passage, written as late as 1943, is particularly striking. Responding to the "extreme left" opinion that full independence should be granted immediately, Woolf stated:

> In my opinion to do that would be disastrous—disastrous for the Africans. Most of them are ignorant and uneducated, terribly poor, ravaged by tropical diseases. To think that they are capable of suddenly taking over the government of their countries under the political and economic conditions of the modern world is just nonsense. They would fall victims to the first private profiteers and exploiters and the first imperialist government who crossed their path.
>
> No, the right way to deal with our African colonies … is to begin at once to educate the Africans to govern themselves. (Woolf 1943: 180)

African peoples needed the paternal guidance of enlightened Europeans if they were to achieve real independence. They needed to be "gradually trained" in democracy and "the art of self-government." Only with such guidance would they ever be capable of "standing by themselves."

Chapter 6

Internationalism and the
Promise of Science

Jan-Stefan Fritz

This chapter analyzes the influence of science in shaping thinking about cooperative internationalism in International Relations (IR). At the turn of the twentieth century, there was a surge of interest in ways of making international relations more about cooperation than of competition, conflict or conquest. The question facing many early-twentieth-century writers was how best to make cooperation work, systematically and for the long term. Science was the answer they found. It was seen as providing an alternative basis for internationalism from the imperialist and state-interest-driven international relations of the nineteenth century. The application of scientific knowledge to the practice of international relations was seen by many writers as an invaluable means toward better understanding and tackling increasingly important economic and social concerns. That is, through scientific knowledge and technology, the lives of individuals could be improved worldwide. In turn, the focus on economic and social issues in the study of internationalism became equated with cooperation.

This chapter compares a cross-section of writers who contributed to the study of cooperative internationalism in IR during the early twentieth century. This serves to show that despite conflicting views over what cooperation and internationalism meant, many writers similarly looked to the sciences as a basis for their work. In particular, a number of Anglo-American writers, well known to students of IR, were among the most influential in the study.[1] These are, in approximate chronological order of their major works, Paul Reinsch, John Hobson, Leonard Woolf, and David Mitrany. These writers have been identified as having been particularly influential on the study and practice of cooperative internationalism. Paul Reinsch, for example, is often considered the founding father of the study of international organization (Potter 1945: 803–806) as well as being a leading international law scholar and senior

U.S. diplomat. John Hobson and Leonard Woolf were widely read publicists, who introduced the concept of international government; moreover, their ideas were influential in the creation of the League of Nations.[2] David Mitrany developed the concept of functional international government and influenced the creation of the UN specialized agencies.[3] In addition to referring to these writers, this chapter draws on a variety of sources to illustrate the context in which their ideas were shaped and how in turn these shaped the discipline of IR.

While each of the four writers focused on here has been studied countless times before, little time has been devoted to exploring the particular importance of the expectations that were held of the sciences (Cooper 1998 is a rare exception). It is argued here that these expectations were fundamentally important to those individuals listed above, who substantially shaped the discipline of IR early in the twentieth century. This chapter shows that, in particular, the study of cooperative internationalism as reflected in international institutions was shaped from its beginnings by the expectation that scientific knowledge and technological innovation held out the promise of both deeper and broader cooperation. In fact, it is probably not far-fetched to claim that the relationship between developments in the sciences and in international relations were not only first highlighted by these writers, but also that this aspect of their work seminally influenced later theories, including neo-functionalist regional integration theory, as well as various approaches to complex interdependence theory, regime theory, and the study of global governance. This chapter systematically assesses what promises were expected from the sciences and how these influenced the study of IR, and in particular the study of cooperative internationalism.

THE PROMISES OF SCIENCE

An important assumption in the study of international cooperation early in the twentieth-century was that, through the application of scientific knowledge to the practices of states and societies, these could learn to develop more pacific relations. According to the writers considered here, peace was all too rare. The general view held that international relations was dominated by a small elite, which, under the guise of national interests, primarily enriched itself through imperial plunder. This was seen to result in recurring conflict, which, in turn, was justified along Darwinian lines as the survival of the fittest. In the rare instances where peace was pursued, it was done haphazardly and, in any case, at best tended to find a cure to the problem at hand, rather than seeking a mechanism to prevent future conflict.

Among these writers, most critical of imperialism was Hobson (1902b), who strongly condemned imperialism as a perverted form of nationalism. Hobson argued that imperialism promoted national aggrandizement and militaristic competition. Economically, he believed imperialism reinforced an exploitative capitalism which, in turn, fostered an unequal distribution of wealth both within societies and between them. Reinsch (1922), too, criticized existing international relations, but focused on diplomatic practices and their, in his view, too secretive nature. He argued that these practices perpetuated existing inequalities within and between societies, and prevented the achievement of long-term peace.

These writers were not, however, pessimists in the Spenglerian sense, that is, that they saw the occidental civilization as being in decline. Instead, they observed developments that seemed to promise lasting cooperation in international relations. Perhaps the most important of these developments was the startling accumulation of scientific knowledge and its application to technological innovation. Before turning to the promises expected of the sciences, the concept of science, as it was used by the writers considered here, requires elaboration.

When Reinsch, Hobson, Woolf, and Mitrany used the term *science*, the aim was not to make the study but, rather, the practice of internationalism more systematic. Their concern was not to make the study of politics more inductive and thus scientific; this was, in fact, a criticism Pitman B. Potter (1923) levied at other writers of the time. Quite simply, there existed a general belief that cooperation on economic and social issues was intrinsically linked to the practices of scientific discovery and development of related technological products. In other words, the process of discovering empirical facts, when rationally applied, invariably supported technological developments, and thus contributed to what is commonly referred to as "progress." In practice, the aim was to have as much scientific content and process as possible reflected in political content and practice. Thus, for Hobson and Reinsch, scientific knowledge and its application provided a practical basis for exploring the problems of human relations, including economic and social ones such as poverty, for containing these problems by defining and managing them, and eventually for solving them systematically.

The height of expectations of what science could deliver was paralleled by a breadth in what was seen to qualify as "being scientific" or "the sciences." The writers considered here tended to refer simultaneously to both the natural or physical sciences and the social or human sciences, including sociology, psychology, and anthropology. Closer to home, there was also some discussion about exactly what political "science" should contribute to the study of international cooperation and organization (Potter 1923). Beyond this, there was also a tendency to equate the scientific and the practical. The writers believed that those disciplines often identified as using scientific knowledge for practical ends, such as engineering, medicine and even architecture, had shown that the application of knowledge to a practical pursuit could yield seemingly boundless results. Because such activities required expertise, the terms *scientist* and *expert* were taken to be synonymous. By extension, the writers also assumed an inextricable link between basic scientific knowledge and the technological products derived from it. For this reason, the terms *science* and *technical* were often used interchangeably.[4] Furthermore, the terms *technical* and *economic and social* were also used interchangeably; an equation that Mitrany in particular developed as the basis for his theory. In other words, "science" was conceived of in extremely loose terms. This probably stemmed at least in part from the fact that none of the writers considered here had studied in detail the sciences themselves, let alone the history or sociology of science, or science-technology-policy relations. Perhaps because of this, the expectations of what science could provide international relations were seen to be almost boundless. In sum, science was not only taken to be a set of academic disciplines involving systematic observation and experimentation, but a quasi-ideology that could serve as the basis for a new means of articulating and promoting inter- and intrasocietal cooperation.

As suggested above, this worldview gave an important place to economic and social issues. The term *economic and social issues* encompassed a variety of specific activities often cited as important issues at the heart of international cooperation, including such diverse matters as: commerce, policing, railways and transportation networks, sanitation infrastructures, the abolition of slavery, scientific research, telegraphic communications networks, as well as trade and industry. It is important to note that the term served not only to refer to specific issues, but also to exclude others, such as conflict and war, as well as related concerns with diplomacy and international law.

As stated earlier, when looking at the use of science as a leitmotif for shaping the practice of cooperative internationalism, a number of concrete promises that science was expected to deliver can be identified. First, the thinkers discussed here saw the promise of involving scientists in the possibility that such individuals could replace the dominant state-interest perspective of international relations with a knowledge-based one. Second, science promised a view of what could constitute a "natural" international community—centered around specific spheres of cooperation. The underlying assumption was that international discord was not the natural state of things, that under the right conditions, a feeling of international community could be realized through cooperation in specific economic and social areas. Third, science promised the possibility of cooperation without political prejudice. It was believed that science-based international cooperation could provide a universally acceptable method for organizing international negotiations and tackling the implementation of international agreements. Fourth, science promised more enlightened international governance. Scientific knowledge and interdependence were understood to be two sides of the same coin. Scientific cooperation was seen to underpin interdependence and interdependence reinforced scientific cooperation. Together they were seen to provide a means of institutionalizing cooperative internationalism for the long term without a formal, centralized governmental structure.

The Promise of Involving Scientists

The four authors each observed in the nineteenth century the emergence of
more pluralist international relations. Representative of this was that individuals and groups who had not traditionally been part of the policymaking elites
were beginning to participate in decision making at the international level.
Central to the interests of these new actors were not traditional concerns such
as diplomacy and war, but a concern for increasing wealth and improving social
conditions even for many of the most marginalized members of society. Based
upon empirical evidence cited in particular by Mitrany, Reinsch, and Woolf,
this observation certainly holds true as concerns the expanding role of technical experts, scientists, and nongovernmental interest groups in the industrialized, predominantly European world. In particular the following examples
were highlighted: the development of railways, telegraphic communications
networks, sanitation infrastructures, the abolition of slavery, and the internationalization of scientific research.

Reinsch was among the first analysts to note the increasing participation of
technical experts in negotiating public agreements. In the case of such issues
as railway expansion and sanitation, experts were often used simply because of
the technical character of international agreements being negotiated. At other
times, experts were involved as advisors to the diplomats. The usual process was for
agreements—whether originally negotiated by technical experts or diplomats—
to be in the end subject to the approval of diplomats or other government representatives. Reinsch (1909: 22; 1911: 2) saw the benefit of technical experts
in their tendency to view issues from a more "international" perspective.[5]
Diplomats, he believed, considered issues from the perspective of national freedom of action. The effect of involving experts both broadened international
relations in terms of participating actors and, more practically, encouraged
a "liberal"—meaning more democratic and more sensitive to the needs of
individuals—character to the legislation being passed. Reinsch also saw experts as
improving the technical awareness of international institutions, especially if they
were civil servants within those institutions, thereby improving resource allocation to an effective and efficient implementation of international agreements.

Briefly, the relevance of scientists to international institutions was important since these new bodies were observed to take on an ever more influential
role in international relations. The importance of international institutions was
strengthened by the fact that there now existed such a variety of bodies, including intergovernmental and nongovernmental ones. Even many of the intergovernmental bodies seemed intrinsically noncontroversial, covering such
scientific and technical issues as health, post, telegraph, as well as marine sciences and navigation. In an extensive review of institutions established during
the nineteenth and early twentieth centuries, Reinsch (1907: 579–623) highlighted communications and transportation; economic interests (including

trade and the protection of labor), sanitation, prison reform, police powers (including over fisheries and the slave trade), and science.[6] In short, to Reinsch, these examples of internationalism had successfully contributed to a broadening of international relations into something more than conventional diplomacy and the foreign policy of states.

To Mitrany, the importance of technical experts and scientists came in parallel with the decline of what he saw as the unitary, territorial state. Above all, Mitrany believed states to be overwhelmed by the expanding tasks associated with more complex international relations.[7] Mitrany believed the role of experts to be particularly important not only as advisors to diplomats and politicians, but also as public policymakers in their own right. The problem of traditional diplomacy and politics were evident not least in the outbreak of World War II. Mitrany saw the postwar period as an opportunity to change things and during this period the majority of his work focused on illustrating the potential of knowledge-based and technically driven international bodies. To justify the importance he attributed to scientists and technical experts, Mitrany envisaged that public decision-making entities needed to be judged by the direct impact their decisions had on improving standards of living, and not merely on whether agreements between states were signed or by the degree of interaction they promoted between individuals and social groups. As the bearers of "objective" data and information, Mitrany believed scientists to be ideally placed to identify what means were needed to achieve the improvements to the lives of individuals.

Though Mitrany did not elaborate upon the sociology or epistemology of expertise and the specific relations between the technical and the political, his functional theory of politics provided the first conceptual framework in IR for allowing experts in society a role in policy making. Mitrany claimed that his aspiration was not to stop "the public discussion of issues of public concern" as a classical definition of politics might suggest, but to take issues of public concern outside the exclusive jurisdiction of diplomats and governmental officials and put them in the hands of what he thought were more knowledgeable individuals. The attraction of Mitrany's work to audiences broader than those specifically interested in politics was one substantial reason why his work was so popular even outside IR and political science in the 1950s and '60s. An indication of Mitrany's popularity with scientists during this time can be seen in the articles, either written by him or about him, that appeared in the influential scientific journal *Nature*.[8]

For Reinsch and Mitrany, the promise of involving scientists in international relations was important in that it held many tangible benefits, and it was symbolic of what pluralist and enlightened international relations could look like. Though their works certainly contributed to shifting the focus in IR from its traditionally narrow concern with the state and intergovernmental relations, their potential contribution was not as unambiguous as they thought. At the very least, the sphere of what they considered to be "qualified" participants in international relations remained limited. The writers considered here failed to explain why, for example, scientists and other technical experts would contribute only objective knowledge and not personal or other interests. Underlying the works of each of the writers here is the assumption that state interests and the knowledge-led interests of scientists are somehow mutually exclusive. Similarly, none of these writers even touched on the question of why scientific knowledge should be treated as distinct from other types of knowledge and experience gathered via systematic observation and the carrying out of long-term practical tasks. For example, the particular knowledge of farmers certainly drives technological development and thus—by these writers' definitions—could influence international relations. Yet neither this, nor other trades, were considered.

The Promise of Natural Community

To Reinsch, Hobson, Woolf, and Mitrany, the knowledge provided by scientists was seen to play an important role in shifting emphasis in international relations from confrontation to community. There were two dimensions to this belief. First, scientific research in the nineteenth century had identified a certain unity in nature through the theory of evolution. This was taken by many observers at the time to be a plausible basis for believing that cooperative internationalism was in fact an expression of this unity among humans. This line of argument was used by most of the writers considered here as a basis for speculating that, under the right conditions, cooperation was as, or even more, natural than the competition and conflict analogies that had shaped so much of the imperial and balance-of-power policies of the nineteenth century. The second dimension of natural community was the fact the scientific community itself was seen to lead by example, with many international scientific organizations being established during the nineteenth century.

The belief in the link between biological and social unity was particularly prevalent in the works of Hobson (1902a: 460–89). The basis of this approach lies in his criticism of the use of Darwin's theory of evolution to justify imperialist politics.[9] He argued this was a perverted use of scientific knowledge. Instead, science had a more positive role as a "normative injunction to guide human conduct" (Long 1996: 13). Therefore, politics could learn from science about the "natural" conditions that encouraged cooperation. Hobson's belief in the possibility of a natural community among states and societies in international relations rested in part on what David Long (1996: 8–27) has called an "organic analogy." This analogy rejected state-centric interpretations of international relations in favor of socially based interpretations. From the natural sciences, Hobson extrapolated that, since humans were biological organisms and therefore part of nature, there was necessarily some harmony in the social relations between humans. Equally, he accepted that competitive behavior was also natural. However, through scientific and thereby rational analysis, Hobson believed cooperative behavior could be separated from the competitive and the former given emphasis in public policymaking. As Long (1996: 8) points out, Hobson saw science as providing the basis for linking the concepts of human development and evolutionary theory, which Hobson specifically applied to the cause of liberal social reform.

Hobson was not alone in understanding the concept of cooperation in such terms; Reinsch and Woolf, too, posited a metaphysical explanation for why individuals and groups would cooperate, given the right circumstances. Reinsch and Woolf believed that a metaphysical unity existed, or could be created, in international relations. For example, Reinsch (1900: 340–51) argued that, in spite of the pessimistic spirit of parochial nationalism that dominated the nineteenth century, a "new internationalism" had emerged. This new internationalism was supposedly reflected both in an increase in economic and financial cooperation, and in the growth of a psychological unity through communications and media. Such communications and media naturally included the exchange of scientific ideas and their relation to the general public. In short, Reinsch (1911: ch. 1) saw this as "world-wide unity" based on "positive and concrete concepts" and practical enterprise. What Reinsch expressed in terms of a pychological unity, Woolf (1917: 13) called "international communal psychology." According to this view, institutionalized cooperation was the expression of scientifically informed behavior that reflected a collective will, collective rewards, and, above all, commonly accepted principles of what the "right relations [between states] ought to be," as Woolf put it.

In contrast to the earlier writers, Mitrany sought to articulate a materially based theory of cooperation, wherein he downplayed the idea that a collective "we"-feeling could bring people actively together. However, like the writers before him, Mitrany presumed that international discord was not the natural state of things; it had to be due to some flaw in understanding and organizations. He believed that the international relations of economic and social issues, for example, were not about how to keep states and societies apart, but how to bring them actively together.[10] Mitrany argued that it was common sense that, given the appropriate knowledge, people would use it to improve their lives by bettering their economic and social conditions. Using science, one could thus pursue cooperation and community without interfering in the ways people lived their lives privately, culturally, or religiously. The supranational character and organization of the international scientific community provided a perfect illustration of this argument. Mitrany argued that as international society learned to cooperate in specifically defined areas, an ever more complex web of cooperation would emerge. This was the development of a "living material international community" or what he also described as a "way which would make it possible to build up a free world community, one which would have room for every country and people and which above all, would be liberal in spirit and performance."[11]

To claim that all four writers saw the emergence of international community as "natural" does not mean they did not see cooperation also being pursued out of self-interest. Reinsch, Hobson, Woolf, and Mitrany all pointed out that "enlightened" self-interest was evident throughout the history of international cooperation. They believed that, having experienced cooperation, individuals, social groups, and states would begin to develop shared expectations of collective rewards. A collective reward was generally understood to be one that was shared by all equally; exemplified by the belief that everyone benefits from clean drinking water in a similar manner and to a similar extent. In this sense, the writers all similarly attach their notions of unity to the growing importance of scientific and technological expertise. Expertise was to be the basis of "enlightened" self-interest in that it indicated the possible outcomes of cooperation. It enlightened decision makers as to the possible and, indeed, the best outcomes. Introducing scientific knowledge was important as a means of building international community without each actor having to compromise their particular interests. Science could show how different interests were reconcilable in practice, thus avoiding potential political disputes. In sum, science represented not only knowledge about the physical world and physical constructs, but science was also a leitmotif for how to organize international relations along more systematic and, as a consequence, more cooperative lines.

In the view of science as a leitmotif for political action, Reinsch, Hobson, Woolf, and Mitrany saw something that was almost akin to an antidote to the existing power political relations, dominated by states and diplomatic elites. The consequence of focusing their theories on this aspect of international relations was, however, that the issue of power was altogether omitted from their theories. In other words, by focusing all their attention on how to make cooperation work, they failed to provide their own theories of power in the relations of states and societies. To Mitrany, in particular, the separation between cooperation in economic and social areas and conflict in the realm of power politics was an integral tenet in his theory, yet he concerned himself only with the former. Ultimately, the writers considered here believed that scientists influenced international relations in only the most benevolent terms, by improving the capacity of decision makers to reach higher levels of consensus. More important for the purposes here, this bias meant that, in contrast to the detailed assessment of the relations between science and cooperation, these writers did not provide a similarly detailed analysis of the relations between science and imperialism. Beyond Hobson, who touched on this issue in his analysis of Darwinism, no writer considered here reflected on why scientific knowledge was necessarily tied to the practice of cooperation, or whether it could just as well be used in service of conflict and conquest. Though the writers considered here all published on the topic of imperialism, they failed to connect these two strands in their prescriptive work. That is, their theories of cooperation were developed in such a way as to assume that imperialism would be relegated to history. In short, science played an integral role in the shift from imperialism to cooperative internationalism. With regard to coercive international relations more broadly, a further consequence of this bias was the inability of these theories of international cooperation to respond to Hans Morgenthau's criticism that science can play no role in removing power from politics. Somewhat dramatically, he notes that the "Age of Science has completely lost [the] awareness [of the] tragic sense of life, the awareness of unresolvable discord, contradictions, and conflicts which are inherent in the nature of things and which human reason is powerless to solve" (Morgenthau 1946: 206).

The Promise of Cooperation without Political Prejudice

The potential of natural community required, in the minds of Reinsch, Hobson, Woolf, and Mitrany, some systematic process to structure and institutionalize these communities. In their empirical studies, all four identified the emergence of a new form of organizing and managing the process of international cooperation; a form they commonly referred to as "international administration." In international administration, they found a means with which international institutions could acquire and develop whole areas of competence and responsibility.

A problem with international relations observed by the writers considered here was that states spent too much time searching for consensus at the lowest common denominator. Even after this denominator had been agreed upon, traditionally there were no international means to implement, let alone enforce, agreements. By contrast, these writers believed that science could raise the denominator of consensus and provide a method for tackling the implementation of international agreements. The practical expression of this was found in "international administration." The first person to popularize the study of administration in a comparative political context was Woodrow Wilson (1887). Wilson defined administration as a "practical science," which had as its object "to discover, first, what government can properly and successfully do, and, secondly, how it can do these proper things with the utmost possible efficiency and the least possible cost either of money or of energy" (Wilson 1887: 197). As a practical science, administration could be considered in a comparative sense. Wilson argued that various states, whether democratic or not, shared the same understanding and practice of administration. Thus, it was not inappropriate for the United States to look toward Germany or France for insights into the better organization of government. In short, administration promised systematic cooperation without political prejudice.

Using this same logic, Reinsch and Woolf were among the very first writers to take administration to the international level and call it "international administration." The value of administration was that it could be similarly applied at any political level, and this made it seem as objective, and thus scientific, a process as could be defined. As discussed earlier, it was assumed that there were objective similarities worldwide in the material needs and conditions required for living a good life, regardless of how these needs were phrased in terms of interests. Although perhaps occurring in different places and at different times, it was believed that, through administration, a means had been found with which all economic and social issues could be tackled systematically.

Reinsch used the term *international administration* loosely to describe a systematic process of organizing cooperation necessarily involving "public international unions" (viz. international institutions) and excluding processes of settling disputes in a judicial manner. In practice, the administrative work of the union normally involved acting as a link between the members and organizing conferences or meetings. However, the importance of international administration was that it gave international institutions a seemingly independent means to become actors in their own right. Equally, by its very nature, the advent of administration served to promote an increased participation of technical experts in international relations. Reinsch observed that "in nearly every branch of [international] administrative activities it is necessary to conduct scientific investigations in order to provide a reliable basis for governmental action" (1911: 67). Woolf continued along the same lines, taking international administration to include all the "practical steps which from day to day the state takes to maintain law and order, and to regulate health or the despatch of telegrams or the coinage and issue of money" (1916: 116).

During the 1930s and through to the end of World War II, interest in international administration grew. Numerous prominent IR scholars, including Norman Hill (1931), Pitman Potter (1928), and Frances Sayre (1919), wrote on the subject. However, where Wilson had considered domestic accounts of administration, and Reinsch and Woolf had identified an emerging process in international relations, now the international version had been tried and tested, especially concerning the management of economic and social issues at the international level. Numerous references were made at the time to the fact that the only bodies of the League of Nations to survive World War I were its economic and social ones. In fact, some argued that the truly successful aspect of the League had been its economic and social work (Freeman 1948: 982; Greaves 1931). Concerned with similar issues, Harrop Freeman observed that in practice, over time, "the administrative agency has proved particularly adapted, offering the advantages of expertness, specialization, combination of private and public action and speedy, cheap and non-technical procedures" (1948: 976).

When Mitrany began writing on international administration, he likewise espoused its virtues. The difference between Mitrany and the earlier writers

was his criticism of the existing institutions as being subjected to power poli-
tics. In his estimation, the League had failed because of power politics.
Moreover, even before the United Nations Charter had been negotiated,
Mitrany (1946: 49) noted the disproportionate influence of the "Big Four
Powers" over what he viewed as an essentially technical agency, namely the UN
Relief and Rehabilitation Agency (UNRRA). This worried him, since finding
practical consensus in relief-related situations—a perfect example of what was
viewed as a scientific and technical "clean-water" issue—was being compro-
mised by power politics.

Nonetheless, Mitrany believed international administration to be an
expanding sphere of international relations. He saw the growth of administration most effectively represented in the numerous unions and bureaus that had
been founded, including the International Telegraph Union, the Universal
Postal Union, and the United Nations specialized agencies established after
1945. Mitrany considered these to be truly global services. These were entities
run by scientists and experts, as international civil servants, to serve impartial,
practical ends. Mitrany's own view is well reflected in a passage from George
Shipman (in Mitrany 1945: 458–59) he often quoted:

> The trend in international administration during the past twenty-five
> years has been away from political and diplomatic influence. More
> and more organizations are being set-up on the theory that purely
> technical problems can be separated from political problems, and that
> technical co-operation on the part of national administrative services
> can be brought about successfully in the international sphere without
> the interference of the political departments of the member states.

This statement reflects one of the most important biases found in the
works of the writers considered here: namely, that certain ends, such as the
implementation of collective decisions, should be achieved as quickly and cost-
effectively as possible. In itself this may seem desirable. However, a potential
problem in this position is that it assumes those ends identified by the scientific community, for example and above all, would be acceptable to all individuals and would thus require no further debate. In fact, the expressed desire of
these writers for more pluralistic, democratically accountable international
relations could undoubtedly have implications for institutional efficiency.
In short, an international institution whose existence and work is subject to
debate among its members is certainly more inefficient than one given clear
priorities unanimously agreed upon by its members. Ultimately, science was
viewed not as a means of expanding debate in international relations, but as a
means of spurring quicker, though more well-founded, collective action.
Neither Hobson nor Reinsch considered the possibility that settling with an
international bureaucracy could be counterproductive to their goals, though

both advocated the need for transparency and accountability in international relations. In the case of Mitrany, the consequence of this desire for technically expedient action, according to Cornelia Navari (1995: 223), was that he replaced earlier emphases on democratically representative methods of government with committees and quangos.

The Promise of "Enlightened" International Governance

Science was not merely seen as a systematic means of administering international agreements, but its underlying value was seen as a means for strengthening and reinforcing the interdependence of states and societies. Scientific knowledge and interdependence were both understood to be desirable and complementary; two sides of the same coin. In short, scientific cooperation was seen to underpin interdependence and interdependence reinforced scientific cooperation. The term often used to describe the institutionalized version of this process was international government—a term closely related to contemporary uses of the term global governance, as opposed to world government.[12]

Woolf has been identified as one of the pioneers of writing on complex interdependence (Wilson 1997: 160; also see Wilson 1995: 126–36). He observed that

> the chief characteristic of [international government] was that the existence of very large communities was recognized, that the existence of smaller communities of every variety and kind within the larger was recognized, that communities and parts of communities were to be left to manage for themselves matters which only affected themselves; but that where the relations of communities or parts of a community were many and intricate, organization and organs of government should be provided for joint regulation. ... And the great merit of such a system is that it consciously recognizes that where the units of a community are through their infinite relations dependent upon one another and not independent, an organized regulation of those relations reflecting that interdependence, must be provided. (Woolf 1916: 220)

When defining interdependence in these terms, Woolf was principally concerned with the increased economic and social exchanges between societies around the world. To the writers considered here, the interdependence of societies based on economic and social issues was fundamentally different and separable from cooperation concerning military or strategic matters or involving foreign office diplomats. Not only did this belief lead people such as Reinsch to write books condemning secretive diplomacy, but Mitrany, for example, developed his functional theory of politics around this argument.

Mitrany believed that removing economic and social issues from the domain of diplomacy was possible since these issues were inherently similar. For example, he assumed that everyone would agree that sanitation was a similar problem in all urban environments and its improvement would lead to an equivalent increase in living standards in all contexts. Moreover, Mitrany saw all issues of this type as technical ones. Contrary to political problems, he believed technical problems to be less likely to become sources of strife, since they could be solved by applying a particular technique. It was merely a question of deciding which one to use; the question of *who* decides, however, was never actually definitively answered by Mitrany. To Mitrany, the scientific-technological revolution provided the basis for the emergence of truly global issues that could not be governed through traditional international politics. Mitrany illustrates his view on the interrelationship between science and his proposals for functional means for governing international relations in the following statement:

> Functional arrangements are possible because they are necessary; and the necessity is caused by our restless scientific-technological cleverness. Every new invention, every discovery is apt to raise a new problem that needs to be jointly controlled. (1970: 834)

Mitrany (1946: 41) took the idea that individual activities in international relations could be "selected specifically and organized separately" and formulated it as an essential principle in his theory. Like the natural sciences, interdependence was viewed at once as being reducible to its individual constituent elements, while also being considered in its entirety as a collective set of processes—a system. By extension, the lessons learned in one area of cooperation were seen to be applicable in other areas of potential cooperation. This represented international government. In fact, this idea was first introduced by Reinsch, and later adopted by Mitrany. Reinsch predicted that cooperation would expand outward from particular areas "in constantly widening circles" toward what would become a universal web of cooperation in economic and social issues (1911: 2). Fostering this growth were specialized and expert international institutions:

> Universal cooperation is the watch-word which stands for positive action, for the development of concrete facts of human life corresponding to the actual needs of our economic and social order. For this purpose adequate institutions must be created to take international action out of the field of resolutions and to make it part of the realities of human life. (Reinsch 1911: 3)

Woolf also made some interesting observations on the complementary nature of scientific cooperation and international government. To Woolf, science served to expand international society and internationalize knowledge, thus broadening the concept and practice of international government. In discussing the relations between science and international government, Woolf stated that "what is not often realized is that though the interests of science are so obviously international, they cannot be adequately served without organized regulation; in other words without International Government" (1916: 197). Woolf argued that a certain minimum of uniformity in standards was needed to ensure that international transactions could be conducted effectively. To this end, the internationalization of scientific nomenclature was necessary, and was in fact already happening. Using the medical sciences as an example, Woolf argued that the first step of its internationalization began with the simple sharing of experiences and knowledge across state frontiers. The second step was to spread scientific knowledge through formal international congresses. Further steps followed, whereby scientific research was jointly pursued through international government; that is, the scientific agenda was developed and carried out in the international sphere. This last step ultimately leads to the building of international scientific knowledge. The standardization of nomenclature also had another feature of interest to Woolf. He viewed it as a process of unification at the international level, to the point that international government was even involved in the standardizing of chickens and apple breeds (Woolf 1916: 205). For Woolf, this was not an irrelevant or trivial fact since through such occurrences, international government would become a positive reality in the everyday lives of ordinary people around the world.

THE PROMISES OF SCIENCE IN THE STUDY OF COOPERATIVE INTERNATIONALISM

The aim of this chapter so far has been to demonstrate how the contributions of some of the dominant writers on cooperative internationalism in IR were substantially influenced by the expectation that the sciences would deliver on a number of promises. The assumption that these promises would be delivered meant that specific assumptions were made about the possibility of building more cooperative international relations by building international institutions around economic and social issues. By the same token, it was expected that theories of cooperation could thus avoid traditional concerns with confronting conflict and coercion directly through law and diplomacy. In short, the argument here is that this position is largely responsible for giving the study of international institutions its distinctive emphasis on cooperative internationalism.

The relevance of this development in the discipline of IR is twofold. Understanding the expectations and theories of early twentieth century writers is not only about understanding a historical set of debates or individuals; above all, it is about understanding both the origins of IR and its more recent developments. Throughout the twentieth century, various mainstream theories of IR continue to reflect an expectation that through scientific knowledge and technological development international relations will become more complex and, if governed appropriately, more cooperative. Although a comparative analysis between early-twentieth-century writers and more recent theorists is beyond the scope of this chapter, it can be claimed that similar views are also shared by neo-functionalist approaches to regional integration, as well as by many writers on complex interdependence, regime theory, and global governance. Many of the proponents of these theories have based their works on the argument that, due to developments in science and technology, IR as a discipline was in need of an "updated" theory of international cooperation.

By way of example, this claim is perhaps best illustrated in the origins of regime theory. By their own definition, Ernst Haas and John Ruggie developed regime theory as "a response to the international implications of the interdependencies forged by science and technology" (Haas 1975: 147). This was the view of Haas in an article that is credited with introducing the idea of regimes to IR. Haas continues with the observation that "once such interdependencies are experienced by men, they call for the creation of regimes—collective arrangements among nations designed to create or more effectively use scientific and technological capabilities." Later that same year, Ruggie edited a special issue of *International Organization* devoted to the study of regimes as responses to technological developments. This issue included articles on collective responses to such issues as nuclear nonproliferation, research and development problems, oceans and fisheries, as well as weather modification. This series of articles was compiled in the belief that "technological, ecological, political, economic and social environments are becoming so enmeshed that changes taking place in one segment of international society will have consequential repercussions in all others" (Ruggie 1975: 557). Ruggie continues that this process of change is "outpacing the capacities of our systems of international organization to manage them." This interpretation of the importance of science to cooperative internationalism has since become an integral part of regime theory, especially as a result of Peter Haas's work on epistemic communities as well as Oran Young's work on environmental regimes and global governance.

CONCLUSIONS

Historical analyses of the development of theories of cooperative internationalism are important for many reasons. In this chapter, the aim was to show that the conceptual links drawn between science as one field of human endeavor and cooperation between states and societies as another, fundamentally shaped the way in which certain issues have been and continue to be treated in IR. Most obviously, the emphasis has been on studying the linkages between scientific knowledge and cooperation, rather than scientific knowledge and imperialism, coercion, or power politics. Clearly, the study of IR then and now are not identical and any direct comparison would have to be worked out much more carefully than is possible here. Nonetheless, many mainstream studies of cooperative internationalism are grounded in thinking similar to that of Reinsch, Hobson, Woolf, and Mitrany about how international relations work. A substantial part of this rests on the belief that science can provide objective information to guide the vagaries of policymaking toward improved outcomes. This has been the case for students of IR focusing on economic and social issues, technology and interdependence, and, most recently, environmental concerns. This is not to say that to look toward the sciences is something negative. Yet if IR is to provide a better understanding of the world, the discipline itself must also understand the priorities, as well as biases, of the theorists and theories that have shaped it over the decades.

NOTES

1. Other writers, notably continental European ones, focused mainly on the need to harness power politics through international law. Many of the major works within this particular tradition tended to focus on the emergence of international legal frameworks and diplomatic conferences. This can be seen in such overviews as Jakob ter Meulen (1917, 1929, 1940) as well as Christian L. Lange (1919).

2. John H. Latané (1932) attributes important roles to Hobson, Reinsch, and Woolf in formulating ideas directly influential in the creation of the League of Nations in two edited volumes entitled *Development of the League of Nations Idea: Documents and Correspondence of Theodore Marburg*. This view is still reflected in the website of the League of Nations archives (http://www.unog.ch/library/archives/archives.htm), which includes extracts from Woolf (1916).

3. In the past twenty years continuing reference is made to the influence of functionalist thought on UN specialized agencies and its implications. Some more recent examples include: Evan Luard (1983: 677–92); Javed Siddiqi (1995); and Rosemary Righter (1995).

4. For an interesting discussion of the distinction and relations between science and technology in the context of a case study set in Victorian England, see Thomas F. Gieryn (1999: ch. 1).

5. A shorted version of this article reappears in Reinsch's most popular work, *Public International Unions, Their Work and Organization: A Study in International Administrative Law* (1911).

6.   This article reappears in revised form in *Public International Unions*.

7.   It was not only Mitrany who believed this to be the case, but many other political writers of the 1930s and '40s. See Peter Wilson (1996: 49).

8.   One example of such an article is Anonymous (1943: 134).

9.   For a more extensive discussion of this article, see also Brian Schmidt (1998: 145–46).

10.   See David Mitrany (1941: 39–43).

11.   Mitrany, no date. Political Science Slips and Historical Analysis of Political Thought. Mitrany archives.

12.   For a more detailed comparison of the terms *international government*, *international governance*, and *global governance*, see Jan-Stefan Fritz (2000: 187–205). The chapter argues that international government was actually understood in terms that are close to what is understood by "global governance" in the contemporary international relations literature.

Chapter 7

Birth of a Discipline

Robert Vitalis

[T]here can be no nonlegitimating or neutral stance from which a disciplinary history can be written. All such histories will be selective, and guided
by some commitment (or opposition) to a particular identity.
—John Dryzek and Stephen Leonard,
"History and Discipline in Political Science"

Born and raised in America, the discipline of international relations is, so
to speak, too close to the fire. It needs triple distance: it should move away
from the contemporary, toward the past; from the perspective of a superpower
(and a highly conservative one), toward that of the weak and the
revolutionary—away from the impossible quest for stability; from the glide
into policy science, back to the steep ascent toward the peaks which the
questions raised by traditional political philosophy represent.
—Stanley Hoffmann, "An American Social Science:
International Relations"

What parts do the invention and development of whiteness play in the
construction of what is loosely described as "American"?
—Toni Morrison, Playing in the Dark

A student taking classes in international relations in the United States may
sometime encounter the "man in the moon," one popular way to represent the
point of view of a profession that defines as its specialized object of knowledge
the state system. I did—at MIT in 1978. The trope in fact appears in print in
1925 in the first line of the best-selling American textbook devoted to a new
political science of *International Relations*, by Raymond Leslie Buell.[1] He had
the man in the moon looking down on the "world Island" and smaller "islands"
such as North America, intrigued by the social organization of the ant-like
men "scurrying hither and thither on land and sea."

If this other-world spectator is not color-blind, he would find that
these men are of different hues—in Europe and America, what are

159

called "white men," but in oriental Asia, 825,000,000 beings who mostly are yellow and brown. Beneath the dense foliage of the mysterious continent of Africa, he would see the home of the black man. ... If the Man in the Moon should gaze long enough, he would find that that these ant-like men differ not only in physical characteristics, but in material and mental accomplishments.

If the Man in the Moon had a political bent, he would soon learn that mankind had split itself into a large number of groups, some of which are called states, others, nations, and still others, races. (Buell 1929: 3–4)

These same groupings, the visitor learns, who act according to a mix of "economic considerations" and "racial factors" but above all "nationalism," have in turn shaped the new global order of national imperialism. "[M]odern imperialism does not object to the existence of separate nation-states of white men, but looks to the establishment of autocratic rule by such states over the colored people." Thus Buell assesses the prospects for an *emerging* source of conflict in the world—not in terms of nationalism but on a broader scale. "Important as national groups have been in modern history, their supremacy is being attacked by a new alignment based on 'race'" (Buell 1929: 5, 56–57, 306). What Buell calls the principle of White Supremacy was being both challenged and consequently reasserted in the post–World War I world. The challenge was the rise of anticolonial national (including the various *Pan*-African, Islamic, Slavic, etc.) movements. The reassertion was evident in a flood of new writings and theorizing in the 1920s on both race and on race war, in a decade said to mark the birth of the discipline of International Relations (IR) (Hannaford 1996: 348–68; Lauren 1996: 50–81).

While teachers of IR may still hang on to Buell's man in the moon or some related trope today, they have long since forgotten Buell. They have nothing to say about racism as a force or, in *au courant* language, an institution in world politics (Vitalis 2000). White supremacy is not generally discussed either as a historical identity of the American state or an ideological commitment on which the "interdiscipline" of international relations is founded. Nor is empire understood as the context that gives rise to this specialized field of knowledge. To be a professional IR scholar in the United States today means adopting a particular disciplinary identity constructed in the 1950s and '60s that rests on a certain willful forgetting. So, in the 1980s, Michael Doyle, the director of Princeton's Center for International Studies, could claim that the tradition of political science in the United States has never shown much interest in empire and imperialism (Doyle 1986: 11). Or, from the early 1990s critical margins of the field, Roxanne Doty could imagine that it was in the 1960s that IR theorists first began to consider the role of race in world politics (Doty 1993). Contemporary writing about IR turns out to share along with all other domains of American culture the powerful tendency toward "silence and evasion" about the four-hundred-year presence of Africans and African Americans in the United States (Morrison 1992).

This chapter begins to trace the contours of the twentieth-century color line in the American social science of IR, using critical methods pioneered in African-American studies. I show that these institutions need to be understood in a particular sociocultural context of racism in American life. In *Work of Democracy*, a study of popular representations of Lorraine Hansberry, Kenneth Clark, and ex-APSA president Ralph Bunche in post–World War II America, Ben Keppel calls the dialectic of avoiding and coming to grips with this racism the most important theme in the history of the United States (Keppel 1995: 1). American IR has so far made the choice to avoid it. Bunche, a political scientist who wrote what is still one of the most important theoretical statements on racism, empire, and international relations, *A World View of Race* (1936), goes unread and unrecognized along with *all* other African American and Caribbean intellectuals within the *tradition* of IR today.

One need not have turned to Toni Morrison or to any particular *theoretical* claim about American society and culture to see that white supremacy has a central place in the origins and development of IR. It is enough for any reasonably informed student of African-American studies and of the country's *herrenvolk* democracy simply to glance at the names of social science's founding founders in order to conclude the obvious—as Du Bois had done long ago. John Burgess who created the School of Political Science at Columbia (1880) and began publishing *Political Science Quarterly* (1885) and Herbert Baxter Adams who had hoped to follow Burgess and turn his famous seminary at Hopkins into another "great school of History and Politics," were the country's preeminent theorists of the race state. These institution builders were also the teachers respectively of, among dozens of other "historico-political scientists," William Dunning and Woodrow Wilson. Paul Reinsch (1869–1923), author of *World Politics* published in 1900, probably the most renowned political scientist after Wilson himself, who taught the first courses on international relations in the United States, was America's first expert in colonial administration. Reinsch participated alongside Du Bois in the Universal Races Congress in 1911. For these "founders" and countless other students of a new American science of IR, races *and* states were the discipline-in-formation's most important twin units of analysis, as our scientists might put it today.

In the years before the opening salvos of the Great War, G. Stanley Hall, the country's distinguished theorist of the race children, and his colleague at Clark, George Hubbard Blakeslee, who would head its new department of history and international relations, began publishing the *Journal of Race Development* (1910). This was the first IR journal in the country, renamed the *Journal of International Relations* in 1919. Three years later it became *Foreign Affairs*, the house publication of the New York Council on Foreign Relations. Following the war, Raymond Leslie Buell, whose man in the moon surveyed the course of race development in political science's first textbook with the name *International Relations*, also undertook the first field research by a political scientist in Africa, under the auspices of Harvard University and the Rockefeller Foundation. His two-volume work, *The Native Problem in Africa* (1928), would become a lightening rod for anticolonial critics in the post–World War II era, although Buell, who became research director and later head of the New York Foreign Policy Association, was an ally of and an influence on people such as Rayford Logan and a member of the board of Paul Robeson's Council on African Affairs.

The individualistic and ahistorical assumptions of liberal exceptionalism continue to shape the project of social science in America. There is no more relevant an example of these tendencies than the now canonical Myrdalian account of white supremacism as a vestigial prejudice of "the hinterland" and "backward areas of Anglo-Saxon North America." One can find an early version of this argument in the second edition of Frederick Schuman's *International Politics* (1937), where theories of Teutonism and Anglo-Saxonism are traced to "psuedoscientific apologists" rather than, more accurately, to the leading lights in his own profession. But Schuman had also been ousted in Chicago as a left-wing ideologue and spent the rest of his career in exile at Amherst College. In the *American Political Science Review*, Charles Merriam, the chief advocate of the break with historical and evolutionary theories of institutions and prophet for a new science of behaviorism at Chicago, where Schuman earned his PhD, claimed political science itself as "a precious asset of the race" (Merriam 1921: 176).

Today, the embrace of scientism that Merriam dreamed was the solution for the race's ills reinforces his descendants' myopia about their discipline's past. Practitioners are most likely to operate under the assumption that knowing the history of political science has no bearing on doing political science. Each new generation is socialized into the profession with the help of reliably Whiggish accounts of the epochs through which it has passed on its way to the present. Like all other organized fields of inquiry, and not just those that aspire to the status of natural science, political science has at particular moments revisited its history to legitimate a particular identity—"the present theoretical consensus"—or else perhaps to undermine the consensus. Because that aspiration to be just like physics remains unfulfilled, however, political scientists now typically tell stories of growing methodological sophistication and rigor rather than of cumulative lawful knowledge with predictive value as proof of true advance (Dryzek and Leonard 1988: 1255).

Finally, the discipline's characteristic sociology of knowledge works to constrain the historical imagination and fix the gaze of successive generations of expert observers in a way that makes not noticing natural. IR theorists are able to protect the stance of the detached, neutral observer, which is the essence of the social science profession's contemporary identity, with layers of distance-enhancing effects. The shared core is of course the fiction of occupying a position outside culture from which to observe the social world (Campbell 1998).

Critics of scientism within the profession have offered more complex accounts of the development of American political science than those of the self-identified scientists. Against such alternatives, the Whig histories learned by most practitioners appear especially clumsy and contrived. Recent efforts to reconstruct the foundations of IR make the contrivances that much more obvious (Schmidt 1998). Still, the discipline's new in-house historians have no answer to the challenge posed by Toni Morrison: "What intellectual feats had to be performed by the author or his critics to erase me from a society seething with my presence, and what effect has that performance had on the work? What are the strategies of escape from knowledge? Of willful oblivion?" (Morrison 1996: 24).

If we are to see these "feats," trace these "effects," and lay bare these "strategies" in the case of American international relations, we first need a reliable account of institutional origins. Stanley Hoffman is correct, IR "was born ... in America," but we have got the date—and thus much else—wrong. We need to move the date of the founding back to 1900–1910, midway in the era that was coming to be defined as a time of "increasing political and economic interdependence" or what now some say is the first round of globalization.

We also have to establish the context that actually matters to the ideas and institutions that comprise the field-in-formation. For lack of a better term I call it empire, the process whereby the northeast consolidated its control of the southern and western states and territories, and began to exert dominion over peoples and resources beyond the formal boundaries of the Republic. Gerstle (2001) calls this the founding of the Rooseveltian Republic, Lind (1995) the creation of the second Euro-American Nation. This period is also the moment of consolidation zones of domination and dependency worldwide.

Context clarifies for us why a community of scholars understood itself as focused primarily on accounting for the dynamics of imperialism and nationalism, and seeking practical strategies for better ways of administering territories and uplifting backward races, using what were seen as the progressive tools of racial science. The professors of the APSA depicted themselves as occupying a new intellectual space by right of the failure of the international legal scholars and *antiquo-historians* to deal adequately with the problems posed by empire. New race development and eugenics advocates vied and intersected with practitioners of *rassenpolitik* and with visionaries who predicted the inevitability of war between the Anglo-Saxons and one or more competing racial alignments.

This account complicates the standard view of the external events that typically matter to a field of knowledge that we imagine is exclusively concerned with spaces beyond the territorial boundaries of the United States. It forces us to think about boundaries we take for granted and to ask: events external to what? The lead article of the premier issue of the country's first IR journal, the *Journal of Race Development*, raises precisely this kind of question in making the case for a research agenda on the progress of backward races and states. The United States "has as fundamental an interest in races of a less developed civilization as have the powers of Europe. The key to the past seventy-five years of

American history is the continuing struggle to find some solution for the negro problem—a problem still unsolved" (Blakeslee 1910: 2). Fifteen years later, when Lord Zimmern, the first holder of the Woodrow Wilson Chair at Aberystwyth, the first ever created in the new field of international relations, lectured at Columbia in 1926 he would raise the stakes, insisting that the "race question" was "the most urgent problem of our time" and a "primary cause of war in the world" (Zimmern 1926: 81).

Fifty years later, in analyzing the "malaise" that was prompting government, foundations, and scholars to rethink international studies, James Rosenau ended up back where forgotten ancestors such as G. Stanley Hall, George Blakeslee, Raymond Leslie Buell, and W. E. B. Du Bois had started (and where we still seem to be today):

> with the surfacing of many new types of international issues—ranging from ecology to racial conflict to political kidnapping to traffic in drugs—which reflect the world's growing interdependence and which, consequently do not fall neatly or logically into any of the established disciplines. The new issues of the 1970s—the very issues that have brought on the economic, urban, and ecological crises—span the disciplines and work on them must perforce be interdisciplinary. And this means interdisciplinary not only among the social sciences, but among all the sciences, biological and physical as well as social.
>
> Finally, the mounting interdependence of the world and the emergence of new issues have been accompanied by a waning of the "Cold War" and a confounding of old issues. Where the main cleavages of the past stemmed from considerations of ideology and divided East from West, today they derive as much, if not more, from a stress on equality and divide rich from poor and black from white. Long-standing models of the world and its politics thus seem increasingly obsolete. (Rosenau 1973: 18–19)

Excavating this history is the necessary first step in answering Toni Morrison's challenge, since it allows us to see when the escape from knowledge of the supremacist origins of the field and the still-intact commitment to an apartheid of benign neglect takes shape. Whether one prefers to see America's postwar hegemony as vindication of the liberal creed or as a community in defense of a common heritage and civilization, the fact remains that it is a hierarchical, exclusionary caste order of superior and inferior states (Goldberg and Vitalis 2002). Before World War II it was conceived as a natural order among races. Now it is more common to find international inequality explained as a natural order among states, where "the strong do what they will, the weak do what they must." For others, it is common to write as if hierarchy did not exist.

Morrison's challenge ultimately leads here. Our time is one when it is hard for practitioners to imagine black people ever writing anything of relevance to the field, and when the "intercultural and transnational formation" that Paul Gilroy calls the *Black Atlantic*, where some of the most important critiques of empire and hegemony are found, is subject to strict quarantine by all but a handful. Were we to consider the institutional origins and norms of an equivalent intellectual project in any other settler colonial society at the exact moment when an apartheid system was being consolidated, we would be able to guess the history I am about to tell without much trouble. This story would not need to be told. As we know all too well, however, use the term *colonial settler state* to describe the United States today and objections will automatically be lodged. Such is the power of the exceptionalist myth that is so central to what Rogers Smith calls the American liberal tradition and Gary Gerstle calls civic nationalism.

A critical disciplinary history of IR is a part of the larger project, obviously, of exposing the competing and contradictory currents that they say animates culture, politics, state, and society. Empire exposes the cross-currents of liberal and exclusionary conceptions of the nation, as we now know, but it also points to problems in coming to grips with hierarchy and privilege in the world system. Both Smith and Gerstle have little difficulty in demonstrating that American progressivist thought was deeply entangled in the contradictory liberal/civic, republican, and racist visions of the American nation. One could reject imperialism on the grounds that it threatened what was most vital about the republican or liberal ideal *or* one could sound the alarm against miscegenation and race suicide. Defenders of empire made the opposite case. The health of the republic's institutions depended on expansion, and in that sense one might call them civic nationalists. Yet empire *requires* rather than simply allows the making of invidious distinctions.

One conventional understanding of the discipline of IR is that it is a system or tradition of justification for one set of practices "inside" and another "outside" the boundaries of the nation, and, famously, liberal theory is not easily adaptable to such a project. Many arguments mustered today for democracy promotion, institution building, and economic aid echo older ones about civilizing missions, tutelage, and uplift. If I read Smith and Gerstle correctly, these old arguments were no less rooted in beliefs about the naturalness of hierarchy than were arguments about the futility of trying to redeem the subject races. It may be that the approach taken in *American Crucible* and *Civic Ideals* gives way at "the water's edge" and in Gerstle's case, leads as well to misrepresenting Du Bois and others whose work was increasingly focused on global rather than national exclusions.

Empire, Race, and Academia

The fact of a continuing silence and evasion within the tradition of American IR might lead us to appreciate anew Dorothy Ross's *Origins of the American*

Social Sciences (1988). In contrast to the way practitioners reconstruct their own past, Ross's book is more reliable in its grasp of nineteenth- and twentieth-century American society and culture, and, not surprisingly, less compelled than are political scientists by the idea that their own discursive evolution is what matters to history above all else.[2] Ross instead sees in this discursive evolution the unmistakable stamp of the national ideology of American exceptionalism and the experience of civil war and rapid industrialization. The irony and flaw in a book dedicated to turning away from ideological national history and loosening the hold that exceptionalism has over the national imagination is its blind spot when it comes to empire, imperialism's relationship to the social questions of the Gilded Age and Progressive Era, and its consequences for the American social sciences (Kramer 1998: 380–83).

To observe that American imperialism shaped the course of institutional change in the professions should strike one as banal as my suggestion that white supremacism was at the core of what professors thought and wrote about empire, save that the history of the professors is much less studied than the history of racism. As Franklin Ng notes, few people today know that the University of Chicago once listed a "Colonial Commissioner for the University" (Ng 1994: 141) on its staff: Alleyne Ireland, journalist and author of the influential program for research in political science, "On the Need for a Scientific Study of Colonial Administration" (1906). Ireland failed in his bid to create the country's first department of colonial study at Chicago, but APSA's second vice president Paul Reinsch pressed for the profession's first organized subfield in colonial administration as American territorial expansion led after 1900 to a wave of new courses, publications, popular and scholarly journals, and the first opportunities for social scientists to assist in the development of the state's interventionist capacity. The real institutional origins of IR are to be found here, rather than the 1920s or 1940s, as generations of cold war Whigs would later claim.

Brian Schmidt makes the point in slightly different terms, borrowing from Olson and Groom to argue, after patient reconstruction of the discourse's first decades, that IR "had its real beginning in studies of imperialism, not world order, as has so often been suggested" (Schmidt 1998: 72). Empire is, as Michael Doyle shows, a particular type of world order, but the thrust of the point stands. To see the truth in it that later generations would work hard to forget, one can simply pull Buell's 1925 textbook *International Relations* off the shelf once more. This textbook, like any other one before and since, represents the accumulation of knowledge in circulation for one or two decades, presented, argued, refuted, and reformulated in books, journals, conferences, and seminaries, as they were then known. Its representation of the state of knowledge and debate is mirrored exactly in *Syllabus on International Relations* by Columbia University's Parker Moon, a book published the same year, organized conceptually around the three themes or units of nationalism and war, imperialism, and militarism and armaments.[3] Moon's own most famous work, *Imperialism and*

World Politics, appeared two years later, followed by Buell's *Native Problem* and a massive work on the future of colonialism by Chicago's Quincy Wright, *Mandates Under the League of Nations*, in 1930.

Two points in particular about this remarkable, thirty-year-long record of scholarship on race and empire deserve highlighting. One is the defensiveness in the perception of racial threats, which produces theories of race war and, more commonly after World War I, projects of *world racial uplift* on the part of states, foundations, and their university clients. The defensiveness suggests that resistance in both theory and practice needs to be brought back in to view. The second point is that not one but two unstable boundary lines—between states and between races—were at play as scholars attempted to define the domain of international/race studies.

American debate on empire turned on questions of race—race purity, miscegenation, white right and duty, and the threat posed to fundamental institutions. Race was itself the source or germ of these institutions, or so a founding generation of self-identified political scientists told us. This debate had generated fiercely productive ideas about the natural development of and struggle among races, about geopolitics, the need to end open immigration, about Anglo-Saxon and Teutonic genius, black disfranchisement, eugenics or race science, and about humanitarian norms of eliminating inferior races. The most important political scientist of the generation, William Burgess, founder of the School of Political Science at Columbia, taught these ideas (Gunnell 1993: 49–53).

Against the so-called Social Darwinist strands of imperialist thought, various counter-strands of strategic or defensive white supremacism may have been even more productive between 1865 and 1898. Arguments about the unrecuperable character of those who inhabited the peripheral zones and, thus, of the folly of humanitarian uplift were joined to warnings that overseas expansionism threatened the country, increasing the dangers of race war, the devolution of the Anglo-Saxon stock and the breakdown of republican institutions. Against these appeals to safeguard the *national racial security*, which mobilized many (not all) workers, Catholics, westerners, and southern anti-imperialists, expansionists found racial imperialist rationalizations a liability in the political arena (Trubowitz 1998: 68–75; Lasch 1958; Patterson, ed. 1973; Love 1997; Jacobson 1998: 205–13).

Strands of *racial realpolitik* and of a coming-clash-of-civilizations had emerged as well as the nineteenth century drew to a close. Akira Iriye singles out Alfred Thayer Mahan's 1897 essay in *Harper's Monthly*, "A Twentieth-Century Outlook," which predicted a twentieth-century race war with a rising East, in a pointed comparison with Samuel Huntington's late-twentieth-century variant on the same theme (Iriye 1997: 44–45, 70). The successful resistance to the Italian invasion of Ethiopia in 1896, followed by the fierce fighting in the American conquest of the Philippines in 1898 and the Boxer Rebellion in China in 1900, may have discomfited some intellectuals. The Japanese victory

in the Russo-Japanese War in 1905, however, presented white supremacy theory with a serious empirical problem. Sir Alfred Zimmern recalled having
walked into his classroom at Oxford the morning the news broke about the
sinking of the Russian fleet, and reluctantly putting aside his lecture on Greek
history. He told the class, "I feel I must speak to you about the most important
historical event which has happened, or is likely to happen, in our lifetime: the
victory of a non-white people over a white people" (Zimmern 1926: 82).

Intellectual work inside and outside the university elaborated on and popu-
larized this account of a critical juncture and apocalyptic reading of contemporary
history. Henry Adams, an ex-president of the American Historical Association,
was warning of the *last* struggle for power in Asia and the end of the white race by
1950 (LaFeber 1995). Madison Grant, the Manhattan patrician who was chair-
man of the New York Zoological Society and a trustee the National Geographic
Society, published *The Passing of the Great Race* in 1916, which argued against
education and environment as forces that shaped races and that might amelio-
rate differences among them. Grant wrote the introduction to *Revolt Against
Civilization* (1922) by T. Lothrop Stoddard, who received a PhD in history from
Harvard under Archibald Cary Coolidge, the first editor of *Foreign Affairs*.

The anxieties that were betrayed by Zimmern and Adams could be found
in other neighborhoods as well. For example, on July 4, 1910, white Americans
were stunned when Jim Jeffries, who was billed as the "Hope of the White
Race," betrayed the predictive power of Anglo-Saxonism by losing to the first
black world heavyweight boxing champion, Jack Johnson. Violence followed in a
dozen states, police thwarted an attempt at lynching a black man on the streets of
Manhattan, and the U.S. Congress passed a law that forbid movie theaters to
show films of the fight (Bederman 1995: 1–3). *Birth of a Nation* (D. W. Griffiths,
dir., 1915), the movie that Michael Rogin argues "founded modern American
mass culture," the first ever shown in the White House, drew millions into theaters for the first time where they were treated to an epic account of imminent
race suicide and salvation by the invisible empire of the Klan in a struggle with
"black political and sexual revolution" (Rogin 1987: 191–92).

The Klan's resurgence in 1915 is a reminder that conflict was not confined to
boxing rings and movie screens. Violence broke out repeatedly in the cities of the
North, where 250,000 African Americans had fled between 1915 and 1917, mirroring the pattern of riot and lynching in the South. The new NAACP, founded
in 1911, and its important journal, the *Crisis*, under Du Bois's editorship, drew
increasing attention to the struggle for self-determination at home and, by the
time of the war, abroad (Painter 1987). Nor would violence be confined to
American cities. In 1915, the Wilson regime launched its invasion and fifteen-
year occupation of Haiti. The NAACP sought to expose the record of atrocities
that was left in the wake (Weston 1972; Plummer 1982; Schmidt 1995).

The same NAACP and its indefatigable intellectual Du Bois fought
bravely over the architecture of the future in Paris in 1919 but the defenders of

a normative world ascriptive order and an expanded and reinforced color line would win the day. Du Bois had poured his energies into reviving the Pan-African Congress as a means to represent worldwide black peoples' interests in the peace process. The Woodrow Wilson administration had joined the other European great powers in hindering the organization of the congress and Wilson himself was the pivotal actor in defeating a proposed article on racial equality in the founding covenant of the League of Nations.

To black American observers it must have seemed very much as if this racist visionary, who in 1913 had extended the American apartheid regime known as Jim Crow to federal agencies and throughout the District of Columbia, was now enlarging the global reign of white supremacy. To the Japanese sent to negotiate in Paris, the course of diplomacy confirmed their worst fears of subordination to an Anglo-Saxon hegemony. Among the American white working class and more generally among the denizens of the West and South, the proposed racial equality clause had become the critical rallying point for opposition to the League (Shimazu 1998: 138–48). And the popular defense of privilege on the basis of race, which was fundamental to anti-imperialism in the United States, echoed similar currents elsewhere, for example, the "White Australia" plank which Labour and its breakaway faction the Nationalists had championed inside the dominions of the British Empire. When Japan's emissary reintroduced the equality amendment, with the word "races" removed and "nations" inserted in its place, a majority of the League's future members voted to include the principle in the preamble. Wilson, chairing the session, instead declared the proposal defeated because the vote had not been unanimous—a condition never applied before or again at the peace conference!

With equal rights once more denied to Africans at home and in the diaspora at war's end, a theorist such as Du Bois could perhaps console himself with seeing the prediction of a war of the Color Line, which climaxed his remarkable 1915 analysis "The African Roots of War," come true. In 1919 in Asia (the May Fourth Movement in China, and in Japanese occupied Korea), in the Western imperial domains (Afghanistan, Egypt, the Punjab, and Palestine), and across North America, rising protest and violent repression provided the sharp counterpoint to the peace negotiated at Versailles. It was "the greatest period of interracial strife the nation had ever witnessed," according to historian John Hope Franklin (Lauren 1996: 106). States and their reigning parties and organic intellectuals meanwhile all redoubled their efforts to buttress this white supremacist Anglo-Saxon order.

THE CONSOLIDATION OF IR

As American scholars began for the first time to identify themselves as experts in something called IR and began to introduce their students to the workings of contemporary history or world politics, as universities began to raise money to support these experts and institutionalize this expertise, as the philanthropies paid out, and as a canon was gradually accumulated and transmitted in professional association meetings, in classrooms, and in the first textbooks, this process was bound up with pressing issues of the day. A short list of such issues may be assembled, as viewed from the departments and chairs-in-formation in places such as Harvard, Columbia, Clark, Johns Hopkins, and Chicago. There were the "high" politics of conquest and transformation of the western, Mexican, and Indian territories; the reconstruction of the South; expansion into the Caribbean; the conquest of the Philippines; the prospects for the clash of national imperialisms; and the waves of migration that marked the industrial transformation of the country as indelibly as the factory, the mine, and the electric power station. In places such as Wisconsin, where Reinsch taught, or the new Leland Stanford College, where its president tried to woo Reinsch away in 1902 (Chicago had tried too), Asian races, markets, and migrants mattered a bit more than they did on the eastern seaboard. The end result was nonetheless the same on both coasts.

> An interesting innovation at the University of California is the establishment by vote of the academic senate of a university committee on international relations. This action has been taken in pursuance of a resolution adopted in 1915 to the effect that the university should "give increased emphasis to the work of instruction and research in problems of international and inter-racial relations; and that a committee of the senate be appointed to formulate a plan for the organization and expansion of instruction and research having the definite purpose of assisting in the promotion of amicable world relations." (Ogg 1917: 373)

To make a contextualist claim about knowledge is not in itself controversial, presumably, save now in the narrow sense of contesting one or another account of precisely how ideas and environment are related. Certainly, we find plenty of other practitioners-turned-disciplinary-historians making this move, as I have already noted. E. H. Carr's canonical 1939 critique of idealism is one example. Hoffman's 1971 essay is another. These more familiar contextualist arguments however all share a distinctive, truncated sense of the past that supposedly matters, corresponding roughly to the twenty years before the writers themselves appear on the scene. Put another way, presentism's account of disciplinary institutional origins invariably lacks depth.

In order to reduce the likelihood that readers in 2005 will misconstrue what follows by imposing their contemporary understanding of what it is that constitutes and distinguishes history from political science and international relations from comparative politics, area, and development studies, some basic points should be kept in mind. First, as Dorothy Ross makes clear, political scientists circa 1910–1920 wrote what she calls "historico-politics" that looks more like what is published today in *Studies in American Political Development* and *Diplomatic History* than in the *American Political Science Review*. Members of APSA, founded in 1903, who were university faculty were as apt to have PhDs in history (or in law) as in political science. The distinctiveness that its adherents claimed was the concern with *the contemporary*.

Second, as the publication of the premier volume of the *Journal of Race Development* makes clear, the boundaries we draw today between what is inside and outside the national territorial space and that are now distinct domains of expertise were not made in the same way in 1910. Perhaps more accurately, who is inside and who is outside the national space was not so much a territorial question as it was a biological one. So it was possible to imagine an interdisciplinary field of expertise and a journal to support it that would bring together men such as George Hubbard Blakeslee (1871–1954), the country's most famous scholar of U.S. relations with Latin American and Asia once Reinsch had left Madison for China; G. Stanley Hall, the country's most important psychologist after William James and the first president of the new graduate institution Clark University (the second one after Johns Hopkins); the great Franz Boas of Columbia; Ellsworth Huntington, the geographer at Yale who was a close colleague of Stoddard and Grant and a future president of the American Eugenics Society; and W. E. B. Du Bois (Kuehl, ed. 1983: 80–82; Ross 1972; Martin 1973).

Third, then, it must also be kept in mind that, as Victoria Hattam shows, the discursive terrain we now take for granted, in which one routinely distinguishes race from nation, nation from ethnicity, and ethnicity from race, was scarcely recognizable to most people in the first decade of the twentieth century (Hattam 2000). The differences that a reader today will insist are real and significant ones were only coming into play at the end of the period 1910–1920. Boas was of course a central figure in this process, as was Du Bois, and one is able to see the outline of these shifts as well as the first questioning of the scientific validity of race as a concept in their writings from this period, including papers presented at and discussions of the Universal Races Congress in London in 1911. The arguments were tentative and, needless to say, completely unacceptable within the neo-Lamarckian orthodoxy that Hall helped to create.

The arguments in support of a new interdisciplinary field called IR were, by contrast, bold, clear, and in retrospect obvious ones. A new world order of national imperialism had emerged, producing new pressing practical political administrative problems for the state and the sections, which begged for scientific study and solutions. Buell coined the term (in 1925!) *complex interdependence* to characterize this new order among the natural and historic races. Traditional approaches in political history, theory, and international law could not recognize let alone solve the problems introduced by this new form of imperialism. Chief among these problems was that of "race progress" and "how best to aid the progress of the undeveloped" (Blakeslee 1910). New, combined, and interdisciplinary forms of expertise were thus necessary, chief among them the social sciences of geography, eugenics, anthropology, contemporary history or political science, colonial administration, and so on.

One way to think of the *Journal of Race Development/Journal of International Relations* is that it was an early version of what *World Politics* is today, spanning the overlapping fields we now call comparative, development, and international studies. The first two 1910–1911 and 1911–1912 volumes included articles on the "French Scheme of Empire in Africa," the "Political Situation of Finland," the "Pacific Ocean in the Racial History of Mankind," "Islam as a Factor in West African Culture," the "Indian National Congress," "Turkey and the United States," "Physical Environment as a Factor in the Present Condition of Turkey," the "Contribution of the Negro to Human Civilization," "Constitution Making in China," "Japanese Administration in Formosa," "Bulgaria: The Dynamics in the Balkan Situation," "Relations of Japan and the United States," the "Japanese in America," "The Future of the Japanese in Hawaii," and the "Anglo-Saxon in India and the Philippines."

Two differences between *World Politics* and the *Journal of Race Development/ Journal of International Relations* are also important to keep in mind. *World Politics*, first published in 1948 under the auspices of Yale's Institute of International Studies, reflects a different moment in American expansionism, a moment when issues of European reconstruction and the cold war had moved to the top of the research agendas of a new generation of, most prominently, émigré theorists from Europe. The world looked different to an earlier generation, writing when American national imperialism was a project of limited rather than limitless geographic scope. A second, less-marked difference is that where in *World Politics* one typically does not find articles on the domestic politics of the United States as we now phrase it, in the *Journal of Race Development/Journal of International Relations* one did not find articles on the Anglo-Saxon race and its branches, but would find articles on the lower or undeveloped races, as was noted, on the "Japanese in America," and on interracial relations, such as the "Anglo-Saxon in India and the Philippines."

When World War I erupted in 1914, the new field-in-formation found its national imperialism perspective confirmed in the first structural accounts of the war's origins. One variant or another of the war as outcome of the "European system of nationalism, imperialism, secret diplomacy and militarism which sprang into full bloom from 1870–1914," reigned in American "new" progressive historians' circles for the next decade (Novick 1988: 210). One of the first and most important statements is Du Bois's "African Roots of War" (1915), which appeared in revised form as "Hands of Ethiopia" in *Darkwater* (1920) where he turns seriously to study of the world system. It appeared two years before Lenin's *Imperialism: the Highest Stage of Capitalism* (Lewis 1993: 503–504).

Du Bois ends his account with a prediction that if national elites continued to buy the allegiance of white working classes through exploitation of the periphery, a new more brutal War of the Color Line would follow. Many restatements of this theme by others would follow in the years to come.

Another institution founded at the same time as the *Journal of Race Development* reinforced these trends and laid the ground for what only later will come to be known as area and international studies centers and institutes. At Clark, Blakeslee began a regular series of summer conferences—seven were held between 1909 and 1920—focused on different world areas. The first dealt with Turkey and the Near East. In subsequent years they studied Latin America, the Far East, and problems generated by the war in Europe. Papers at the conferences were then published in the journal. After the war, the series resumed, first in Wiliamstown under the auspices of the newly created Institute of Politics at Williams College, and later at the University of Chicago, under the auspices of the Norman Wait Harris Memorial Foundation. Chicago's new Committee on International Relations, led by Quincy Wright, who also ran the foundation, would dominate the intellectual horizon more generally by the 1930s.

In New York, a mix of millionaire lawyers, bankers, including Morgan's Thomas Lamont, and professors who had served on Wilson's Inquiry founded the Council of Foreign Relations (CFR) in 1921 and began publication of the now famous quarterly journal *Foreign Affairs* in 1922. The trustees of the financially strapped Clark University sold the *Journal of International Relations* to the CFR. The links between the old and new journals were clear at first, as was originally intended by Archibald Cary Coolidge the new editor. Coolidge was Harvard's first professor of Russian history, a member of the Inquiry, and the mentor and close friend of Blakeslee. He lobbied for keeping the name to maintain the connection with "Blakeslee's magazine." When council leaders looked for a more sellable title, Coolidge came up with *American Quarterly Review*. Another Harvard man and founding member, the economics professor-turned-editor of the *New York Post*, Edwin Gay, said *American Review of Foreign Affairs* was better, which was ultimately shortened to *Foreign Affairs*. The question of the name aside, when it came time to develop a roster for the first issues, Coolidge turned to Blakeslee and others in the Cambridge-Worcester-Williamstown circuit, with Barnes writing the first book reviews, followed by a second Clark professor. Blakeslee joined the new editorial board, and another *Race Development* editor, W. E. B. Du Bois, published the first of several famous *Foreign Affairs* articles in 1925.[4]

The CFR itself became the vanguard of the Atlanticist or Anglo-Saxon current in American internationalism. Certainly, the outlook of this group resembled bondholders more than it did missionaries. Coolidge was frank about "the plutocrats" who steered it and who of course had millions of dollars more at stake in Europe than in the undeveloped areas, Mexico excepted.[5]

The CFR's private study groups were modeled in part on the Clark-Williamstown area studies and foreign policy conferences, although they were intended as well to recreate the intensive atmosphere of the Inquiry's work at Versailles. In the study groups, even more than in *Foreign Affairs*, "Europe, especially Germany, stood at the center of the Council's thinking during the twenties" (Schulzinger 1984: 22). Six of the council's original eight study groups dealt with consequences of World War I in Europe and a post-Versailles U.S. foreign policy. One dealt with the Far East and another with Latin America. None dealt with the European colonies or the mandates created at Versailles.

Virtually all post–World War II histories of IR begin the story at this point, believing *Foreign Affairs* to be the field's first journal and adopting the bankers' view of internationalism as the normative one. Thus, one data point anchors beliefs about Paris in 1919 as the galvanizing moment (rather than the gatherings of activists and scholars at the Lake Mohonk Conferences, near New Paltz, beginning in the 1880s, devoted at first to Indian policy and gradually expanding to include "Other Dependent People" of the United States, to the Pan-American Conferences, to the Berlin Conference, to the Universal Races Congress held in London in 1911). Development studies can be told as a story about models of European reconstruction exported to Latin America. Empire is made to disappear. And the central myth of a race-blind analytical tradition can continue to be propagated.

Given the divisions that erupted at Versailles, the fierce domestic struggles over participation in the League of Nations, the infamous Red and race scares at the war's end, and, above all, the weight of big finance in the new ventures, the shift from the missionary to the monied view of internationalism and, thus, away from race development in the first U.S. journal of international relations across the 1920s and '30s would seem to have been overdetermined. Such a shift did nothing to change the first paradigm of the new field-in-formation, which Woodrow Wilson himself advanced in the course of the peace conference. "We, Anglo-Saxons, have our peculiar contribution to make towards the good of humanity in accordance with our special talents. The League of Nations will, I confidently hope, be dominated by us Anglo-Saxons; it will be for the unquestionable benefit of the world" (Walworth 1986: 313). The bankers and others attended to the business of strengthening the bonds among the pan-Atlantic and -Pacific branches of the race through what they called interdependence.

Under Coolidge's direction, the revitalized journal advanced the intellectual project first mapped out in the campuses, clubs, and conference smokers along what we now think of as the Mass Pike and I95 corridors. Coolidge solicited most of the pieces for the journal. His student, the arch-racist Lothrop Stoddard, by then one of the most popular writers in the country, was too expensive for the financially shaky *Foreign Affairs*.[6] A young and unknown although prolific Harvard tutor such as Raymond Leslie Buell, teaching summer courses in IR in California, was much more eager to write for it, churning out pieces on oil interests and diplomacy and another one calling for civil rights for Japanese migrants in California, both of which were rejected.[7]

Before leaving Cambridge for Africa, Buell had tried one more time to sell Coolidge on a piece for *Foreign Affairs*. He proposed a piece analyzing the grave threat posed by growing numbers of white settlers in Kenya. He offered a critique of present British colonial policy and argued that the Conservative government was laying "the foundation in East Africa for the state of affairs which exists in South Africa today." But Coolidge turned him down once more, politely, arguing that it was not a topic of much interest "to the majority of our readers."[8]

Coolidge remained quite concerned with the international race issues of the moment, notably, Pan-Asianism, and he collaborated with Blakeslee's group in 1925 in organizing what became the Institute of Pacific Affairs, where he pressed for inclusion of Pacific-bordering Latin American countries against "the danger of a cat and dog fight between the Anglo-Saxon and the Mongolian."[9] Similarly, in 1927 he wanted council member and head of the American Geographical Society Isaiah Bowman (another member of the Inquiry), to write up a précis of the project he had launched with SSRC support on "Pioneer Belts," that is, on the vital significance of white settler movements in history.[10]

Coolidge's biographer insists that the ideas of Stoddard "and others like them" were "flatly rejected, by Coolidge" citing such evidence as the lack of correspondence between the two men and the absence in Coolidge's work of a concern with Anglo-Saxonism (Byrnes 1982: 75–86). Nonetheless, as I have shown, there had been contact between them. And since Coolidge was a student of the Slavic race he was not apt to have much to contribute to Anglo-Saxonism theory, but he knew well enough who he was and what he stood for. He held blacks to be an inferior race. He was convinced that "cross-breeding" of races was dangerous and advocated bans on Asian migration to the United States. Above all, he feared the likelihood of a long-term decline in the white race globally and the rise of colored races because of different rates of reproduction—which was *the* central theme in Stoddard's work. What distinguishes the two is Coolidge's rejection of the idea of an inevitable clash of civilizations. He believed that internationalism in the form of empire and expansionism worked against such an outcome.

PROGRESSIVIST CURRENTS

Progressives founded an alternative research and education organization to the CFR in New York in the 1920s, the Foreign Policy Association (FPA). Buell, the author of *International Relations*, moved to Manhattan after two years of field work in Africa (the first by a U.S. political scientist) to become research director in 1927. The FPA had grown out of a study group, the Committee on American Policy in International Relations, which began to meet in the summer of 1918. Charles Beard designed a course for them that focused on the nature and extent of future racial antagonisms, control of international waterways, the status of backward countries, control of natural resources, the place of nationality in world organizations, and, finally, the idea of a League of Nations.[11] By the mid-1920s a research department had been set up and the first of many local branch organizations were built, although we now know them as the World Affairs Councils.

One of the first projects funded by the FPA was a study of the "policy and operation of the League of Nations with respect to African peoples," which sent Alain Locke to Geneva in the summer of 1927. Locke was a forty-three-year-old professor of philosophy at Howard who had just published the remarkable *New Negro*, the book that named the "Harlem Renaissance" and situated this moment of racial awakening "on a national and perhaps even a world scale." He argued for comparing Harlem to "those nascent movements of folk-expression and self-determination which are playing a creative part in the world to-day. ... As in India, in China, in Egypt, Ireland, Russia, Bohemia, Palestine and Mexico, we are witnessing the resurgence of a people" (Locke 1992: xxvii). The *New Negro* ends with a revised version of "Worlds of Color," the essay that Du Bois had just published in *Foreign Affairs*. Essentially, Locke was pursuing the research program Du Bois lays out at the conclusion of the *New Negro*: The Labor Problem in the "tremendous and increasingly intricate world-embracing industrial machine that our civilization has built" and its relationship to the Color Problem. "But despite our concern and good will, is it not possible that in its consideration our research is not directed to the vital spots geographically?" (Locke 1992: 385).

Locke had proposed to go beyond the question of the political administration of the mandates to study the labor and education policies and their impact on native peoples. Locke argued for funding on the grounds that the results would be of particular interest to African Americans, and could serve as the basis for future FPA outreach efforts, because of "their relationship to the African peoples under mandate control and because of similarity of some of the problems to those of race relations in the US." Buell had met Locke, discussed the project with him, and loaned him sections of his soon-to-be-published two volumes on the mandate system in Africa. A year later, he would tell the FPA board that Locke's work was not fit for publication.[12] Did Buell know that Coolidge said the same about him?

The apogee of this progressivist and social gospel–inflected two decades in American international studies that William T. R. Fox and other cold war Whigs would later lament ("the inter-war period saw international government and various 'devil' theories of international relations—with munitions-makers, imperialists and capitalists variously cast as devils—flourish") is found

in the creation of the Institute of Pacific Relations. The IPR is actually the first
formal regional studies center in the United States. Businessmen, educators, and
disciples of the YMCA in Honolulu founded it in Hawaii in 1925. Led by
James Carter, it was set up to "study the conditions of the Pacific peoples" using
the "YMCA idea of bringing leaders of different racial communities together
for frank discussions of differences" (Thomas 1974: 3–4; Rosenberg 1982:
110; Hooper 1993). Membership was composed of various national councils
(United States, Canada, Australia, New Zealand, China, and Japan), which
partially supported the secretariat, and members convened in a biannual series
of conferences. The U.S. national council, the American Institute of Pacific
Relations, dominated the organization, and the secretariat was moved to New
York in 1930. Owen Lattimore at Johns Hopkins became editor of the institute's journal *Asian Affairs*, and the IPR grew into the preeminent research
organization on East Asia, supported by Blakeslee, Wright, and dozens of
other IR scholars.

The Social Science Research Council's first Advisory Committee on
International Relations was established in 1926, according to its first staff
member, James T. Shotwell, "in order to deal with the projects of research presented to it by the Institute of Pacific Relations. By reason of these requests, the
earliest program of the SSRC in this field had to do with relations with the
Orient."[13] Writing in *World Politics* in 1949, William T. R. Fox was either ignorant of the history or convinced that his understanding of the field was the only
true one because he claimed as a sign of its early "confused" state that the
SSRC's committee was funding research on land use patterns in the Far East."
(Fox 1968: 6). I would argue that we instead see the continuation of a clear and
by then twenty-year-old research program in race development.

The IPR model, an original form of the boundary-crossing Indian Ocean,
Pacific Rim, Atlantic World approach we saw take off in the 1990s, reflected
the intense interests in immigration issues, race conflicts, white settler movements, and so on through the interwar years. Shotwell, a professor of political
science at Columbia and a director of the Carnegie Endowment for International
Peace, had tried but failed to secure funding for a parallel Institute of Atlantic
Affairs (Josephson 1975: 188–91). The SSRC's IR committee secured some
resources in the 1930s for research on Latin America in support of institutions
such as the new Institute of Inter-American Affairs at the University of Florida,
but another early effort of the committee to organize an IPR clone for Central
and Eastern Europe also failed for lack of funding.

Although never discussed within this context, the creation in 1937 of the
International Committee on African Affairs (later the African Affairs Council)
was another effort at building an IPR-type institute, dedicated in this case
to the cause of decolonization and to educating the U.S. public on Africa.
Its founder, Max Yergan, had spent twenty years in the YMCA movement in
South Africa. The council brought together white progressives such as Buell and

Mary Van Kleeck, who headed the research arm of the Russell Sage Foundation, and black scholars and activists such as Ralph Bunche, Mordecai Johnson (president of Howard University), and, more controversially, Paul Robeson. The organization's rapidly evolving left-wing identity ("radical, black-led, and interracial") left Yergan searching in vain for established foundation support. Communists in the leadership ranks drove out people such as Buell and took the CAA down the road that led, as with the IPR, to government harrassment and collapse (Lynch 1978: 17; Von Eschen 1997).

During and just after World War II there were at least two more attempts to build IPR-like programs. The first, sponsored by the Princeton-based American Committee for International Studies, which also included Carter, the IPR head, began planning for a Conference on Atlantic Relations in 1941. The organizers also clashed over the design. Progressives such as Carter and Quincy Wright pressed for inclusion of representatives from the entire Atlantic world, including Brazil, the Caribbean, and Africa, but they also had a fallback position. Howard University's Ralph Bunche, the African American political scientist who had recent field work experience and expertise in colonial policies, could represent the Atlantic dependencies. They lost this battle, unfortunately. Raymond Leslie Buell, by then editor of *Fortune* magazine, continued to press for inclusion of African American intellectuals such as Bunche and his Howard colleague Rayford Logan in the wartime planning work of the committee.[14] He failed to move the Princeton group as well, and the "North Atlantic" became the organizing framework and took on the peculiar cast that we associate with the early cold war era.

Melville Herskovits's correspondence with Carnegie in the 1940s and Ford in the 1950s for a Black Atlantic-model of combined "African and Afro-American Studies" program at Northwestern University is a final example of the old progressivist current in American international race/relations/studies. The documents were unearthed in the 1990s by Jane Guyer, who, given the now familiar story about the founding of area studies after World War II and the relative insignificance of Africa to it, depicts Herskovits as an exception, "who did not support the area studies model" but instead was proposing a model that "reflected a disciplinary rather than a political division of the world" (Guyer 1998).

As we have seen, however, forty years earlier his teacher, Boas, had pioneered a new, interdisciplinary and quite explicitly political enterprise at the dawn of the twentieth century, to which Herskovits's thinking owed a great deal, obviously. International relations in America placed great emphasis originally on Africa and Asia as part of a "new" racial world order of increasing complexity, interaction, simultaneous fragmentation and integration, and above all interdependence. As Buell and others taught, complex interdependence had brought a host of new policy issues to the fore, for which the old, European-focused international legal theories and antiquo-historiography provided little guidance. These problems included drug trafficking, white slavery, the environment as a factor in future colonization projects, and miscegenation or, in other words, the "race question," as Lord Zimmern had put it in 1926.

CONCLUSION

Much remains to be done before we can claim to understand the history of international relations in America. There were two unstable boundary lines at play in the scholarship of the interwar era—between states and between races—but I have no good account yet of the way this is worked out. A few international relations scholars in the 1930s adopted the position that Myrdal would in 1944. They depicted racism as an atavistic, irrational prejudice found mainly in the traditions of lower-educated whites of the backward areas of the deep South, and, somewhat contradictorily, in the books on everyone's IR reading lists that represented the products of pseudoscientific apologists for hierarchy. A few others, beginning with Ralph Bunche, identified racism as a world capitalist class strategy of divide and rule. These liberal and Marxian counterarguments notwithstanding, racialism in theory and practice can be traced across the divide of the war.

Enough is known to be confident that practitioners are unreliable guides to the history of international relations, for a number of reasons. The one I want to highlight is the line they continue to draw that ostensibly defines a unique domain of expertise. Thus, where in the *Journal of Race Development/Journal of International Relations* one did not find articles on the Anglo-Saxon race and its branches, so in *World Politics* and every other international studies journal today one does not find articles on the domestic politics and culture of the United States. We sustain the fiction of occupying a position outside culture from which we observe the social world. Here the postcolonial studies critique matters a great deal. This blind spot in our definition of the field will be hard to overcome.

NOTES

Author's Note: This chapter is based on ongoing research in the private papers of scholars (Blakeslee, Buell, Corwin, Curti, Friedrich, Merriam, Reinsch, Wright) and institutions (Foreign Policy Association, Council on Foreign Relations) from about 1900–1960. I am grateful for criticisms or ideas suggested by Lee Baker, Tom Bierstecker, Cathy Boone, Fred Cooper, Bryan Coutain, Neta Crawford, Lee Ann Fujii, Avery Goldstein, Jane Gordon, Debi Harrold, Steve Heydemann John Ikenberry, John Isacoff, Janice Mattern, Anne Norton, Ido Oren, Paul Wapner, David Rousseau, Nicole Sackley, Brian Schmidt, Rogers Smith, Ed Webb, Wes Widmaier, and Kent Worcester. Four scholars, Kevin Gaines, Janette Greenwood, Vicky Hattam, and

Adolph Reed Jr., took on the added formal burden of reeducation. The American Political Science Association, Clark University's Provost's Office and Higgins School of the Humanities, and U. Penn's Christopher Browne Center for International Politics all provided research funds, for which I am grateful. A fellowship from the SSRC-MacArthur International Peace and Security Program bought me the time to begin this essay and finish its companion piece, "The Graceful and Generous Liberal Gesture."

   1.   Buell 1929. The volume was part of the prestigious American Political Science Series, edited by Edward Corwin (1878–1963), the constitutional law scholar hired by Woodrow Wilson at Princeton who assumed Wilson's chair, the McCormick Professor of Jurisprudence, in 1918. Buell (1896–1946) studied with Corwin, and taught at Occidental and Harvard. His textbook was one of approximately ten such works published in the period 1916–1925. Only one other was by an American, and Buell's is also the only one written from the emerging American social science perspective, "from the viewpoint of political science—to begin where international law leaves off. The hypothesis upon which I have proceeded is that a field of international relations exists which is almost as distinct from international law as the study of American government is from constitutional law" (vii). The text was also the only one to be reprinted in the decade. See Groom (1991: 80, 130).

   2.   See in particular Gunnell (1993: 9–13) and his student Schmidt (1998: 32–39). One might reconsider the adequacy of the "internalist" method, centrally concerned with recovering "older identities" (Schmidt 1998: 10) and yet unable to parse white supremacy in the extended disciplinary conversation among the leading theorists of the Herrenvolk democracy and Jim Crow empire.

   3.   The Institute for International Education commissioned a model syllabus that might encourage the creation of courses on international relations on more American college campuses. Moon worked in consultation with other Columbia faculty and Isaiah Bowman, director of the American Geographical Society. Three shorter and longer versions of the basic course of study were developed. The published syllabus includes lists of popular and academic texts, which provide a useful guide to the intellectual savior-faire of the time. I draw attention to the *Syllabus* in anticipation of the objection that Buell's text was possibly not representative of the ideas that actually formed the emerging core of the field.

   4.   For the history detailed here I have relied on the correspondence between Hamilton Fish Armstrong and Blakeslee, Box 8, and between Armstrong and Coolidge, Box 2, Hamilton Fish Armstrong Papers, 1893–1973, MCOO2, Seeley Mudd Library, Princeton University, Princeton, New Jersey. Armstrong, a journalist, was managing editor under Coolidge and, after the latter's death in 1928, *Foreign Affair's* editor for the next forty years.

   5.   For his description of the "plutocratic character" of the council see Coolidge to Armstrong, Sept 9, 1922, Box 17, Armstrong Papers.

   6.   "Lothrop Stoddard called in on me yesterday pretty well satisfied with the world in general and with his own fortunes in particular. He referred with good natured tolerance to Barnes's criticism on his book. He is going to Europe and is to write twelve articles for the *Saturday Evening Post* for which he will received $1,000 a piece. That

shows the financial competition that we are up against." Coolidge to Armstrong, Nov 2, 1922, Box 17, Armstrong Papers.

7.   See Coolidge to Armstrong, Dec 9 and 11, 1922, in Box 17, and June 13 and 14, 1923 in Box 18; and Buell to Coolidge, Nov 15, 1922 and April 12, 1923, in Box 21, Armstrong Papers. Armstrong complained that Buell was uncomfortable writing, and when Coolidge corrected him, since Buell had already published a book on the Washington Disarmament Conference (his dissertation) and another on Contemporary French Politics, the critique was changed to that he published too much. Nonetheless, I would guess that Buell's reading of the world, close to that of the *Nation* in the 1920s, was not welcomed at *FA* in this period.

8.   Buell to Coolidge, Sept 1, 1927, and Coolidge to Buell, Nov 4, 1927, Box 21, Armstrong Papers.

9.   Coolidge to Blakeslee, Jan 23, 1925, and Blakeslee to Coolidge, Dec 17, 1926, Box 21, Armstrong Papers.

10.   "A highly interesting as well as important subject. It also seems to me a many sided one, and as you are a many sided person, I am wondering whether you could not be persuaded to take one particular side for our benefit. ... Pioneer Belts have played a great role in history. ... Their role is not over today, as you can point out." Coolidge to Bowman, April 5, 1927, Armstrong Papers. See as well Bowman 1927.

11.   Edwin Bjorkman "The League of Free Nations Association of the United States," ms., FPA, Board Minutes and other Official Records of the Executive Committee, New York, Microfilm Reel 1, Foreign Policy Association Papers, Seeley Mudd Library, Princeton University, Princeton New Jersey.

12.   For Locke's proposal, see "Memorandum; Foreign Policy Association: Alain Locke re African Mandates Study Project" n.d. [1927]; for Buell's rejection of the final report, see Minutes of Meeting of Board of Directors, NY, Nov 14, 1928, p. 6, microfilm reel 1, FPA Papers.

13.   See "A Preliminary Draft of a Survey of the Study of International Relations in the United States," prepared in connection with the Program of Research in International Relations of the SSRC under the direction of Dr. James T. Shotwell, June 1933, p. 20, Box 133, Folder 7, Charles E. Merriam Papers, Regenstein Library, University of Chicago.

14.   "Confidentially, they feel somewhat offended that they have been overlooked. I believe they should be included in their own right; also because the Negro population of this country holds the political balance of power in many Northern states, and is now torn between traditional hostility against Britain and a growing fear of the consequences of Fascism to the American Negro. I certainly hope they can be included in any work of the American Coordinating Committee." Buell to Edward M. Earle, April 15, 1941, Box 2, Folder 5, Quincy Wright Papers.

References

Amin, Samir. 1977. *Imperialism and unequal development*. New York: Monthly Review Press.

Anonymous. 1869. Review of "Fragments of Political Science on Nationalism and Internationalism." *Revue de droit international et de legislation comparee* 1: 297.

Anonymous. 1943. The "New Deal" as a social philosophy (a comment on David Mitrany). *Nature* 3822: 20.

Ashworth, Lucian M. 1999. *Creating international studies: Angell, Mitrany, and the liberal tradition*. Aldershot: Ashgate.

———. 2002. Did the realist-idealist debate ever happen? A revisionist history of international relations. *International Relations* 16 (April): 33–51.

Baldwin, David A., ed. 1993. *Neorealism and neoliberalism: The contemporary debate*. New York: Columbia University Press.

Baldwin, David. 1995. Security studies and the end of the cold war. *World Politics* 48, no. 1: 117–41.

Band, D. C. 1980. The critical reception of English new-Hegelianism in Britain and America, 1914–1960. *Australian Journal of Politics and History* 26.

Banks, Michael. 1986. The international relations discipline: Asset or liability for conflict resolution? In *International conflict resolution: Theory and practice*, ed. E. Azar and John Burton, 5–27. Boulder: Lynne Reinner.

Barnes, H. E. 1921. Review of *Empire and Commerce in Africa*. *Journal of International Relations* (July).

Barron, T. J. 1977. Before the deluge: Leonard Woolf in Ceylon. *Journal of Imperial and Commonwealth History* vi: 47–63.

Bartelson, Jens. 1996. Short circuits: Society and tradition in international relations theory. *Review of International Studies* 4 (October): 339–60.

Beaumont, Gustave de, and Alexis de Tocqueville. 1833. *On the penitentiary system in the United States and its application in France.* Translated, with an introduction, notes and additions by Francis Lieber. Philadelphia: Carey, Lea and Blanchard.

Bederman, Gail. 1995. *Manliness and civilization: A cultural history of gender and race in the United States, 1880–1917.* Chicago: University of Chicago Press.

Bell, Duncan S. A. 2001. International relations: The dawn of a historiographical turn? *British Journal of Politics and International Relations* 3 (April): 115–26.

Bell, Quentin. 1995. *Elders and betters.* London: Pimlico.

Bender, Thomas, and Carl E. Schorske. 1998. *American academic culture in transformation: Fifty years, four disciplines.* Princeton: Princeton University Press.

Blakeslee, George Hubbard. 1910. Introduction. *Journal of Race Development* 1: 1–4.

Booth, Ken. 1991. Security in anarchy: Utopian realism in theory and practice. *International Affairs* 67 (3): 527–45.

Bosanquet, Bernard. 1958. *The philosophical theory of the state,* 8th ed. London: Macmillan.

Bowman, Isaiah. 1927. The pioneer fringe. *Foreign Affairs* 6: 49–66.

Brailsford, H. N. 1948. *The life-work of J. A. Hobson.* London: London School of Economics.

Brown, Chris. 1992. "Really existing liberalism" and international order. *Millennium* 21, no. 3: 313–28.

———. 2000. International political theory—A British social science? *British Journal of Politics and International Relations* 2 (April): 114–23.

Brysk, Alison, Craig Parsons, and Wayne Sandholtz. 2002. After empire: National identity and post-colonial families of nations. *European Journal of International Relations* 8, no. 2.

Buell, Raymond Leslie. 1928. *The native problem in africa.* Two volumes. New York: Macmillan.

———. 1929 [1925]. *International relations.* New York: Henry Holt.

Bull, Hedley, and Adam Watson eds. 1984. *The expansion of international society.* Oxford: Clarendon Press..

Bull, Hedley. 1966. The Grotian conception of international society. In *Diplomatic investigations,* ed. Herbert Butterfield and Martin Wight, 51–73. Cambridge: Harvard University Press.

———. 1977. *The anarchical society: A study of order in world politics.* London: Macmillan.

Bunche, Ralph. 1936. *A world view of race.* Washington, DC: The Associates in Negro Folk Education.

Burgess, John W. 1934. *The reminiscences of an American scholar.* New York: Columbia University Press.

Burns, Cecil. 1917. *The world of states.* London: Headley Bros.

Butler, Melissa. 1991. On Locke. In *Feminist interpretations and political theory,* ed. Mary Lyndon Shanley and Carole Pateman. University Park: Pennsylvania State University Press.

Byrnes, Robert F. 1982. *Awakening American education to the world: The role of Archibald Cary Coolidge, 1866–1928*. Notre Dame: University of Notre Dame Press.

Caird, Edward. 1997. Individualism and socialism. In *The British idealists*, ed. David Boucher, 173–94. Cambridge: Cambridge University Press.

Campbell, David. 1998 [1992]. *Writing security: United States foreign policy and the politics of identity*. Revised edition. Minneapolis: University of Minnesota Press.

Carr, E. H. 1945. *Nationalism and after*. London: Macmillan.

———. 1961. *What is history?* London: Macmillan.

———. 1964 [1939]. *The twenty years' crisis, 1919–1939: An introduction to the study of international relations*. New York: Harper and Row.

Cooper, Justin D. 1998. Science, politics, and conflict in the functional approach. In *New perspectives on international functionalism*, ed. David Long and Lucian Ashworth. Basingstoke: Macmillan.

Cox, Michael, ed. 2000. *E. H. Carr: A critical appraisal*. Houndmills: Palgrave.

Cox, Michael. 2001. Introduction. In *The twenty years' crisis, 1919–1939*, by E. H. Carr, ix–lxiii. Houndmills: Palgrave.

Crawford, Robert M. A., and Darryl S. L. Jarvis, eds. 2001. *International relations: Still An American social science? Toward diversity in international thought*. Albany: State University of New York Press.

Curti, Merle, and Vernon Carstensen. 1949. *The University of Wisconsin: A history, 1848–1925*, two volumes. Madison: University of Wisconsin Press.

Daily Mail. 1920. Review of *Empire and Commerce in Africa*. 16 January.

Darby, Philip, and A. J. Paolini. 1994. Bridging international relations and post colonialism. *Alternatives* 19 (Summer): 371–97.

Den Otter, Sandra. 1996. *British idealism and social explanation*. Oxford: Clarendon Press.

Deslandes, Paul. 1998. "The foreign element": Newcomers and the rhetoric of race, nation, and empire in "Oxbridge" undergraduate culture, 1850–1920. *Journal of British Studies* 37.

Dorfman, Joseph, and Rexford Guy Tugwell. 1938a. Francis Lieber: German scholar in America. *Columbia University Quarterly* 30 (September): 159–90.

———. 1938b. Francis Lieber: German scholar in America. *Columbia University Quarterly* 30 (December): 267–93.

Doty, Roxanne Lynn. 1993. The bounds of "Race" in international relations. *Millennium* 22: 443–63.

———. 1996. *Imperial encounters: The politics of representation in North-South relations*. Minneapolis: University of Minnesota Press.

Doyle, Michael. 1986. *Empires*. Ithaca: Cornell University Press.

Dryzek, John, and Stephen T. Leonard. 1988. History and discipline in political science. *American Political Science Review* 82: 1245–60.

Du Bois, W. E. B. 1915. The African roots of war. *Atlantic Monthly* 115: 707–14.

Dunne, Tim. 1993. Mythology or methodology? Traditions in international theory. *Review of International Studies* 19, no. 3: 305–18.

———. 1998. *Inventing international society: A history of the English school*. London: Macmillan.

Economist. 1920. Review of *Empire and Commerce in Africa*. 31 January.

Edel, Leon. 1981. *Bloomsbury: A house of lions*. London: Penguin Books.

Egerton, George. 1978. *Great Britain and the League of Nations*. Chapel Hill: North Carolina University Press.

Eisenstein, Zillah. 1981. *The radical future of liberal feminism*. New York: Longman.

Eldridge, C. C., ed. 1984. *British imperialism in the nineteenth century*. London: Macmillan.

"Empires, systems, and states: Great transformations in international politics," Special Issue of *Review of International Studies* 27 (2001).

Etherington, Norman. 1984. *Theories of imperialism: War, conquest, and capital*. Beckenham: Croom Helm.

European Press. 1920. Review of *Economic Imperialism*. 16 December.

Farr, James, John S. Dryzek, and Stephen T. Leonard, eds. 1995. *Political science in history: Research programs and political traditions*. Cambridge: Cambridge University Press.

Farr, James. 1995. From modern republic to administrative state: American political science in the nineteenth century. In *Regime and discipline: Democracy and the development of political science*, ed. David Easton, John Gunnell, and Michael Stein, 131–67. Ann Arbor: University of Michigan Press.

Feuer, Lewis S. 1989. *Imperialism and the anti-imperialist mind*. New Brunswick: Transaction Publishers.

Fieldhouse, D. K. 1961. "Imperialism": An historiographical revision. *Economic History Review* 14, no. 2: 187–209.

———. 1984. *Economics and empire 1830–1914*. London: Macmillan.

Fisher, H. A. L. 1940. *An unfinished autobiography*. Oxford: Oxford University Press.

Foner, Eric. 1972. *The Spanish-Cuban-American War and the birth of American imperialism*. New York: Monthly Review Press.

Foucault, Michel. 1984. Nietzsche, genealogy, history. In *The Foucault reader*, ed. Paul Rabinow. New York: Pantheon Books.

Fox, William T. R. 1968. *The American study of international relations*. Columbia: University of South Carolina Press.

Freeden, Michael. 1978. *The new liberalism*. Oxford: Oxford University Press.

Freeden, Michael, ed. 1988. *J. A. Hobson: A reader*. London: Unwin Hyman.

Freeman, Harrop A. 1948. International administrative law: A functional approach to peace. *The Yale Law Journal* 57, no. 6.

Freidel, Frank. 1943. Francis Lieber, Charles Sumner, and slavery. *Journal of Southern History* 9: 75–93.

———. 1947. *Francis Lieber: Nineteenth-century liberal.* Baton Rouge: Louisiana State University Press.

———. 1958. *The splendid little war.* Boston: Little, Brown.

Fritz, Jan-Stefan. 2000. Regime theory: A new theory of international institutions? PhD dissertation, London School of Economics.

Furner, Mary O. 1975. *Advocacy and objectivity: A crisis in the professionalization of American social science, 1865–1905.* Lexington: The University Press of Kentucky.

Galtung, Johan. 1971. A structural theory of imperialism. *Journal of Peace Research* 8: 81–117.

Gerstle, Gary. 2001. *American crucible: Race and nation in the twentieth century.* Princeton: Princeton University Press.

Gettell, Raymond Garfield. 1910. *Introduction to political science.* New York: Ginn and Co.

Gieryn, Thomas F. 1999. *The cultural boundaries of science: Credibility on the line.* Chicago: University of Chicago Press.

Gill, Stephen. 1990. *American hegemony and the trilateral commission.* Cambridge: Cambridge University Press.

Gilman, Daniel Coit. 1884. *Bluntschli, Lieber, and Laboulaye.* "Privately printed for a few friends in Baltimore."

Gilpin, Robert. 1981. *War and change in world politics.* Cambridge: Cambridge University Press.

Goldberg, Ellis, and Robert Vitalis. 2002. *The Arabian Peninsula: Crucible of globalization.* European University Institute. EUI Working Papers. RSC No. 2002/9. Mediterranean Program Series.

Goldmann, Kjell. 1996. International relations: An overview. In *A new handbook of political science,* ed. Robert E. Goodin and Hans-Dieter Klingemann, 401–27. Oxford: Oxford University Press.

Gong, Gerrit W. 1984. *The standard of "Civilization" in international society.* Oxford: Clarendon Press.

Goodnow, Frank J. 1906. Review of *Colonial Administration,* by Paul S. Reinsch. *Political Science Quarterly* 21: 135–38.

Greaves, H. R. G. 1931. *The League committees and world order: A study of the permanent expert committees of the League of Nations as an instrument of international government.* London: Oxford University Press.

Green, T. H. 1906. Liberal legislation and freedom of contract. In *The works of Thomas Hill Green,* vol.3, ed. R. L. Nettleship, 365–86. London: Longmans.

———. 1984. *Prolegomena to ethics,* ed. A. C. Bradley. Oxford: Clarendon Press.

Gunnell, John G. 1991. Disciplinary history: The case of political science. *Strategies: A Journal of Theory, Culture and Politics* 4, no. 5: 182–227.

———. 1993. *The descent of political theory: The genealogy of an American vocation.* Chicago: University of Chicago Press.

Guyer, Jane. 1998. Perspectives on the beginning. *PAS News and Events* 8: 2, 4.

Haas, Ernst B. 1975. On systems and international regimes. *World Politics* 29: 2.

Haddow, Anna. 1969. *Political science in American colleges and universities, 1636–1900.* New York: Octagon Books.

Haldar, Hiral. 1927. *Neo Hegelianism.* London: Heath Cranton.

Hammond, R. J. 1961. Economic imperialism: Sidelights on a stereotype. *Journal of Economic History* 22, no. 4: 582–98.

Hannaford, Ivan. 1996. *Race: The history of an idea in the West.* Baltimore: Johns Hopkins University Press.

Hardt, Michael, and Antonio Negri. 2000. *Empire.* Cambridge: Harvard University Press.

Haslam, Jonathan. 1999. *The vices of integrity: E. H. Carr, 1892–1982.* London: Verso.

Hattam, Victoria. 2000. *From "historic races" to ethnicity: Disarticulating race, nation, and culture.* Unpublished ms.

Healey, Denis. 2002. Interview with author. 9 March.

Hegel, G. W. F. 1967. *The philosophy of right,* trans. T. M. Knox. Oxford: Oxford University Press, 1967.

Hetherington, Penelope. 1978. *British paternalism and Africa, 1920–1940.* London: Frank Cass.

Hill, Norman L. 1931. *International administration.* London: McGraw-Hill.

Hindess, Barry. 2001. The liberal government of unfreedom. *Alternatives* 26, no. 2.

Hinsley, F. H. 1963. *Power and the pursuit of peace: Theory and practice in the history of relations of states.* Cambridge: Cambridge University Press.

Hobsbawm, Eric. 1987. *The age of empire, 1875–1914.* London: Weidenfeld and Nicolson.

Hobson, J. A. 1902. *Imperialism: A study.* London: James Nisbet.

———. 1902. The scientific basis of imperialism. *Political Science Quarterly* 17, no. 3.

———. 1909. *The crisis of liberalism.* London: P. S. King.

———. 1911. *Economic interpretation of investment.* London: Financial Review of Reviews.

———. 1915a. *A league of nations.* London: Union of Democratic Control.

———. 1915b. *Towards international government.* London: Allen and Unwin.

———. 1917. *Democracy after the war.* London: Allen and Unwin.

———. 1918. *Richard Cobden the international man.* London: Allen and Unwin.

———. 1930. *Rationalization and unemployment.* London: Allen and Unwin.

———. 1932. *The recording angel: A report from Earth.* London: Allen and Unwin.

———. 1919. *The new holy alliance.* London: Union of Democratic Control.

———. 1929. *Wealth and life.* London: Allen and Unwin.

———. 1965. *Imperialism: A study*. Ann Arbor: University of Michigan Press.

———. 1988. *Imperialism: A study*. Unwin.

Hoffmann, Stanley. 1977. An American social science: International relations. *Daedalus* 106: 41–60.

Holden, Gerald. 2002. Disciplinary history and IR discourse. *Review of International Studies* 28: 253–70.

Hollis, Martin, and Steve Smith. 1991. *Explaining and understanding international relations*. Oxford: Clarendon Press.

Hooper, Paul, ed. 1993. *Rediscovering the IPR: Proceedings of the First International Research Conference on the Institute of Pacific Relations*. Department of American Studies. Center for Arts and Humanities. Occasional Paper No. 2. University of Hawaii at Manoa.

Ignatieff, Michael. 2002. How to keep Afghanistan from falling apart: The case for a committed imperialism. *New York Times Magazine*, July 28, 26–31, 54–59.

International Commission on Intervention and State Sovereignty. 2001. *The Responsibility to Protect*. IDRC.

Ireland, Alleyne. 1899. *Tropical colonization: An introduction to the study of the subject*. New York: Macmillan.

———. 1906. On the need for a scientific study of colonial administration. *Proceedings of the American Political Science Association* 3: 210–21.

———. 1907. *Colonial administration in the Far East*. Boston: Houghton, Mifflin.

Iriye, Akira. 1997. The second clash: Huntington, Mahan, and civilization. *Harvard International Review* 19: 44–70.

Jacobson, Matthew Frye. 1998. *Whiteness of a different color: European immigrants and the alchemy of race*. Cambridge: Harvard University Press.

Jones, Charles. 1998. *E. H. Carr and international relations: A duty to lie*. Cambridge: Cambridge University Press.

Josephson, Harold. 1975. *James T. Shotwell and the rise of internationalism in America*. Rutherford: Fairleigh Dickinson University Press.

Kahler, Miles. 1997. Inventing international relations: International relations theory after 1945. In *New thinking in international relations theory*, ed. Michael Doyle and G. John Ikenberry, 20–53. Boulder: Westview Press.

Katzenstein, Peter J, Robert O. Keohane, and Stephen D. Krasner, eds. 1999. *Exploration and contestation in the study of world politics*. Cambridge: MIT Press.

Kegley, Charles W. Jr. 1993. The neoidealist moment in international studies? Realist myths and the new international realities. *International Studies Quarterly* 37, no. 2: 131–46.

Kendle, John. 1975. *The round table movement and imperial union*. Toronto: University of Toronto Press.

Kennedy, Paul. 1987. *The rise of Anglo-German antagonism: 1860–1914*. London: Ashfield Press.

Keohane, Robert O. 1989. *International institutions and state power: Essays in international relations theory*. Boulder: Westview Press.

———. 2002. Moral commitment and liberal approaches to world politics. In *The globalization of liberalism*, ed. Eivind Hovden and Edward Keene, 11–35. Houndmills: Palgrave.

Keppel, Ben. 1995. *The work of democracy: Ralph Bunche, Kenneth B. Clark, Lorraine Hansberry, and the cultural politics of race*. Cambridge: Harvard University Press.

Koebner, Richard, and Helmut Dan Schmidt. 1964. *Imperialism: The story and significance of a political word, 1840–1960*. Cambridge: Cambridge University Press.

Kramer, Paul. 1998. *The pragmatic empire: U.S. anthropology and colonial politics in the occupied Philippines, 1898–1916*. PhD dissertation. Princeton University.

Krasner, Stephen D., ed. 1983. *International regimes*. Ithaca: Cornell University Press.

Kuehl, Warren F., ed. 1983. *Biographical dictionary of internationalists*. Westport: Greenwood Press.

Kymlicka, Will. 1995. *Multicultural citizenship*. Oxford: Oxford University Press.

Labour Party. 1920. *The empire in Africa: Labour's policy*. London: Labour Party.

LaFeber, Walter. 1963. *The new empire: An interpretation of American expansion, 1860–1898*. Ithaca: Cornell University Press.

———. 1989. *The American age: United States foreign policy at home and abroad Since 1750*. New York: W.W. Norton.

———. 1995. The world and the United States. *American Historical Review* 100: 1020–21.

Lakoff, George, and Mark Johnson. 1980. *Metaphors we live by*. Chicago: University of Chicago Press.

Lakoff, George. 1987. *Women, fire, and dangerous things: What categories reveal about the mind*. Berkeley: University of California Press.

Lange, Christian L. 1919. *Histoire de l'internationalisme*, vol. 1–3. New York: G.P. Putnam's Sons.

Langer, W. L. 1935. *The diplomacy of imperialism: 1890–1902*. New York: Knopf.

Lasch, Christopher. 1958. The antiimperialists, the Philippines, and the inequality of man. *Journal of Southern History* 24: 319–31.

Latané, John H. 1932. *Development of the League of Nations idea: Documents and correspondence of Theodore Marburg*, vol. 1 and 2. New York: Macmillan.

Lauren, Paul Gorden. 1996 [1988]. *Power and prejudice: The politics and diplomacy of racial discrimination*. 2nd edition. Boulder: Westview.

Leacock, Stephen. 1906. *Elements of political science*. Boston: Houghton, Mifflin.

League of Nations Information Section. 1925. *Illustrated album of the League of Nations*. Geneva: League of Nations Press.

Lee, Francis. 1988. *Fabianism and colonialism: The life and political thought of Lord Sydney Olivier*. London: Defiant Books.

Lewis, David Levering. 1993. *W. E. B. Du Bois—Biography of a race, 1868–1919*. New York: Henry Holt.

Lieber, Francis. 1834. *Letters to a gentleman in Germany on a trip to Niagara*. Philadelphia: J. B. Lippincott. Published in London under the title of *The stranger in America*.

———. 1838. *Manual of political ethics*. Two Volumes. Boston: Charles C. Little and James Brown.

———. 1840. On international copyright: A letter to the Hon. William C. Preston. In *The miscellaneous writings of Francis Lieber*. Two Volumes. Volume II. 1880. *Contributions to political science*, 329–67. Philadelphia: J. B. Lippincott Company.

———. 1841. *Essays on property and labour, as connected with natural law and the constitution of society*. New York: Harper and Brothers.

———. 1845. The first constituents of civilization. In *The miscellaneous writings of Francis Lieber*. Two Volumes. Volume I. 1880. *Reminiscences, addresses, and essays*, 205–23. Philadelphia: J. B. Lippincott Company.

———. 1850. A paper on the vocal sounds of Laura Bridgman. In *Reminiscences, addresses, and essays*, 443–97. Philadelphia: J. B. Lippincott Company.

———. 1851. An address on secession. In *Contributions to political science*, 125–36. Philadelphia: J. B. Lippincott Company.

———. 1853. *On civil liberty and self-government*. Philadelphia: Lippincott, Grambo and Company.

———. 1858. History and political science necessary studies in free countries. In *Reminiscences, addresses, and essays*, 329–68. Philadelphia: J. B. Lippincott Company.

———. 1859. The ancient and the modern teacher of politics. In *Reminiscences, addresses, and essays*, 369–87. Philadelphia: J. B. Lippincott Company.

———. 1860–61. What is our Constitution—League, pact, or government? In *Contributions to political science*, 87–123. Philadelphia: J. B. Lippincott Company.

———. 1864. Washington and Napoleon. In *Reminiscences, addresses, and essays*, 413–41. Philadelphia: J. B. Lippincott Company.

———. 1868. Fragments of political science on nationalism and internationalism. In *Contributions to political science*, 221–43. Philadelphia: J. B. Lippincott Company.

———. 1869. Notes on fallacies of American protectionists. In *Contributions to political science*, 389–459. Philadelphia: J. B. Lippincott Company.

———. 1871a. On the idea of the "Latin Race" and its real value in international law. In *Contributions to political science*, 306–10. Philadelphia: J. B. Lippincott Company.

———. 1871b. "De l'unite des measures et etalons dans ses rapports avec le droit des gens et avec le droit et les rapports prives de nation a nation." *Revue de droit international et de legislation comparee* 2: 651–58.

———. 1872. Suggestions on the sale of arms by the U.S. government during the Franco-Prussian War. In *Contributions to political science*, 310–22. Philadelphia: J. B. Lippincott Company.

———. 1885. *Miscellaneous writings*, vol. II. Philadelphia: J. B. Lippincott and Co.

Lijphart, Arend. 1974. International relations theory: Great debates and lesser debates. *International Social Science Journal* 26: 11–21.

Lind, Michael. 1995. *The next American nation: The new nationalism and the fourth American Revolution.* New York: Free Press.

Linklater, Andrew. 1998. *The transformation of political community.* Cambridge: Polity Press.

Lippmann, Walter. 1915. *The stakes of diplomacy.* New York: Henry Holt.

Little, Richard. 1996. The growing relevance of pluralism? In *International theory: Positivism and beyond,* ed., Steve Smith, Ken Booth, and Marysia Zalewski, 66–86. Cambridge: Cambridge University Press.

Lloyd, Lorna. 1995. Philip Noel-Baker and Peace Through Law. In *Thinkers of the twenty years' crisis: Inter-war idealism reassessed,* ed. David Long and Peter Wilson, 25–57. Oxford: Clarendon Press.

Locke, Alain, ed. 1992 [1925]. *The new negro.* New York: Atheneum.

Long, David. 1991. J. A. Hobson and idealism in international relations. *Review of International Studies* 17, no. 3: 285–304.

———. 1996a. *Towards a new liberal internationalism: The international theory of J. A. Hobson.* Cambridge: Cambridge University Press.

———. 1996b. Liberalism and paternalism: J. S. Mill and J. A. Hobson on the relationship of liberal and non-liberal peoples. Paper presented at the ISA-JAIR Convention, Chiba, Japan.

Long, David, and Peter Wilson, eds. 1995. *Thinkers of the twenty years' crisis: Inter-war idealism reassessed.* Oxford: Clarendon Press.

Love, Eric Tyrone Lowrey. 1997. *Race over empire: Racism and United States imperialism, 1865–1900.* PhD dissertation. Princeton University.

Low, D. A. 1991. *Eclipse of empire.* Cambridge: Cambridge University Press.

Luard, Evan. 1983. Functionalism revisited: The UN family in the 1980s. *International Affairs* 59, no. 4.

Luedeking, Leila and Michael Edmonds. 1992. *Leonard Woolf: A bibliography.* Winchester: St Paul's Bibliographies.

Lynch, Hollis R. 1978. *Black American radicals and the liberation of Africa: The Council on African Affairs, 1937–1955.* Africana Studies and Research Center. Monograph Series No. 5. Cornell University.

Magdoff, Harry. 1969. *The age of imperialism: The economics of U.S. foreign policy.* New York: Monthly Review Press.

Maghroori, Ray. 1982. Introduction: Major debates in international relations. In *Globalism versus realism: International relations' third debate,* ed. Ray Maghroori and Bennet Ramberg, 9–22. Boulder: Westview Press.

Mallaby, Stephen. 2002. The reluctant imperialist: Terrorism, failed states, and the Case for American imperialism. *Foreign Affairs* 80, no. 2: 2–7.

Manchester Guardian. 1920. Review of *Empire and Commerce in Africa.* 27 January.

Manning, C. A. W. 1975. *The nature of international society.* London: Macmillan in Association with the London School of Economics and Political Science.

Markwell, D. J. 1986. Sir Alfred Zimmern revisited: Fifty years on. *Review of International Studies* 12: 279–92.

Martin, Geoffrey J. 1973. *Ellsworth Huntington: His life and thought.* Hamden, CT: Archon Books.

May, Ernest. 1961. *Imperial democracy: The emergence of America as a great power.* New York: Harcourt Brace.

McCormick, Thomas J. 1989. *America's half-century: United States foreign policy in the cold war.* Baltimore: Johns Hopkins University Press.

Mehta, Uday Singh. 1999. *Liberalism and empire: A study in nineteenth-century British liberal thought.* Chicago: University of Chicago Press.

Merriam, Charles. 1921. The present state of the study of politics. *American Political Science Review* 15: 173–85.

Misra, Maria. 2002. Heart of smugness. *Guardian Weekly*, August 1–7.

Mitrany, David. 1941. Some postulates which an international order should satisfy. *Essays on international government.* Mitrany Archives, February 1941.

———. 1945. Problems of international administration. *Essays on international government.* Mitrany Archives.

———. 1946. *A working peace system: An argument for the functional development of international organization.* London: National Peace Council.

———. 1966. *A working peace system.* Chicago: Quandrangle.

———. 1970. The United Nations in historical perspective. *International Relations* 3, no. 10.

———. 1975. *The functional theory of politics.* London: Martin Robertson.

———. no date. Mitrany Archives, the British Library of Political and Economic Science, London School of Economics.

Moon, Parker T. 1925. *Syllabus on international relations.* New York: Macmillan.

———. 1926. *Imperialism and world politics.* New York: Macmillan.

Morel, E. D. 1920. Review of *Empire and Commerce in Africa. Daily Herald*, 4 February.

Morgenthau, Hans. 1946. *Scientific man vs. power politics.* Chicago: University of Chicago Press.

———. 1948. *Politics among nations: The struggle for power and peace.* New York: Alfred A. Knopf.

Morris, Henry C. 1904. Discussion. *Proceedings of the American Political Science Association* 1: 139–42.

Morrison, Toni. 1992. *Playing in the dark: Whiteness and the literary imagination.* New York: Random House.

———. 1996. Unspeakable things unspoken: The Afro-American presences in American literature. In *Criticism and the color line: Desegregating American literary studies*, ed. Henry B. Wonham. New Brunswick: Rutgers University Press.

Moses, Bernard. 1906. The control of the dependencies inhabited by the less developed races. In *Congress of arts and sciences*, vol. 7., ed. Howard J. Rogers, 387–98. Boston: Houghton, Mifflin.

Muirhead, John. 1900. The family. In *Ethical democracy: Essays in social dynamics*, ed. Stanton Coit. London: Grant Richards.

Murphy, Craig N. 1994. *International organization and industrial change: Global governance since 1850*. Oxford: Oxford University Press.

———. 1996. Seeing women, recognizing gender, recasting international relations. *International Organization* 50, no. 3.

Murray Butler, Nicholas. 1913. *The international mind: An argument for the juridical settlements of international disputes*. New York: Charles Scribner's Sons.

Murray, Gilbert. Bodl. MS. Gilbert Murray (500), fol. 184.

Nation. 1920. Review of *Empire and Commerce in Africa*. 6 March.

———. 1921. Review of *Economic Imperialism*. 1 January.

Navari, Cornelia. 1989. The great illusion revisited: The international theory of Norman Angell. *Review of International Studies* 15: 341–58.

———. 1995. David Mitrany and international functionalism. In *Thinkers of the twenty years' crisis*, ed. David Long and Peter Wilson, 214–46. Oxford: Clarendon Press.

New Leader. 1928. Review of *Imperialism and Civilization*. 16 May.

New Statesman. 1920. The ethics of imperialism (review of *Empire and Commerce in Africa*). 19 June.

———. 1921. Review of *Economic Imperialism*. 15 January.

Ng, Franklin. 1994. Knowledge for empire: Academics and universities in the service of imperialism. In *On cultural ground: Essays in international history*, ed. Robert David Johnson. Chicago: Imprint Publications.

Noel-Baker, Philip. 1969. Mr Leonard Woolf: Vision of international cooperation. *Times*, 21 August.

Novick, Peter. 1988. *That noble dream: The objectivity question and the American historical profession*. Cambridge: Cambridge University Press.

Offer, Anver. 1993. The British Empire, 1870–1914: A waste of money? *Economic History Review* 46, no. 2: 215–38.

Ogg, Frederic A. 1917. News and notes. *American Political Science Review* 11: 373.

Olson, William C., and A. J. R. Groom. 1991. *International relations then and now: Origins and trends in interpretation*. London: HarperCollins.

Olson, William, and Nicholas Onuf. 1985. The growth of a discipline reviewed. In *International relations: British and American perspectives*, ed. Steve Smith, 1–28. New York: Blackwell.

Onuf, Nicholas. 2002. Institutions, intentions, and international relations. *Review of International Studies* 28 (April): 211–28.

Oren, Ido. 2000. Uncritical portrayals of Fascist Italy and of Iberic-Latin dictatorships in American political science. *Comparative Studies in Society and History* 42: 87–118.

Osgood, Herbert L. 1903. Review of *The Administration of Dependencies: A Study of the Evolution of the Federal Empire*, by Alpheus H. Snow. *Political Science Quarterly* 18: 141–43.

Osiander, Andreas. 1998. Rereading early twentieth-century IR theory: Idealism revisited. *International Studies Quarterly* 42: 409–32.

Painter, Nell Irvin. 1987. *Standing at Armageddon: The United States 1877–1919*. New York: W. W. Norton and Company.

Palmer, Norman D. 1980. The study of international relations in the United States. *International Studies Quarterly* 24, no. 3: 343–64.

Patterson, Thomas. ed. 1973. *American imperialism and anti-imperialism*. New York: Crowell.

Perry, Thomas Sergeant, ed. 1882. *The life and letters of Francis Lieber*. Boston: James R. Osgood and Company.

Pettman, Jan Jindy. 1998. Nationalism and after. *Review of International Studies* 24: 149–64.

Pimlott, Ben, ed. 1984. *Fabian essays in socialist thought*. London: Heinemann.

Plummer, Brenda. 1982. The Afro-American response to the occupation of Haiti. *Phylon* 43: 125–43.

Potter, Pitman. 1923. Political science in the international field. *American Political Science Review* 17: 381–91.

———. 1928. *An introduction to the study of international organization*. New York: Century.

———. 1945. Origin of the term international organization. *American Journal of International Law* 39, no. 4.

Pugach, Noel H. 1970. *Paul S. Reinsch: Open door diplomat in action*. Millwood, NY: KTO Press.

Pugh, Patricia. 1984. *Educate, agitate, organise: 100 years of Fabian Socialism*. London: Methuen.

Quigley, Carroll. 1981. *The Anglo-American establishment: From Rhodes to Clivenden*. New York: Books in Focus.

Reinsch, Paul S. 1900. The political spirit of the last half century. *The Conservative Review* 4, no. 2.

———. 1900. *World politics at the end of the nineteenth century as influenced by the Oriental situation*. New York: Macmillan.

———. 1902. *Colonial government*. New York: Macmillan.

———. 1903. Review of *Imperialism: A Study*, by J. A. Hobson. *Political Science Quarterly* 18: 531–33.

———. 1904a. Colonial autonomy, with special reference to the government of the Philippine Islands. *Proceedings of the American Political Science Association* 1: 116–39.

———. 1904b. The American Political Science Association. *Iowa Journal of History and Politics* 2: 155–61.

———. 1905. *Colonial administration*. New York: Macmillan.

———. 1906. The problems of colonial administration. In *Congress of arts and sciences*, vol. 7, ed. Howard J. Rodgers, 399–416. Boston: Houghton, Mifflin.

———. 1907. International unions and their administration. *American Journal of International Law* 1 (July): 579–623.

———. 1909. International administrative law and national sovereignty. *American Journal of International Law* 3 (January): 1–45.

———. 1911. *Public international unions their work and organization: A study in international administrative law*. Boston: Ginn and Co.

———. 1922. *Secret diplomacy: How far can it be eliminated?* London: George Allen and Unwin.

Righter, Rosemary. 1995. *Utopia lost: The United Nations and world order*. New York: Twentieth Century Fund Press.

Ritchie, David. 1891. *Darwinism and politics*. London: Swan Sonnechshein and Co.

———. 1916. *Natural rights: A criticism of some political and ethical conceptions*, 3rd ed. London: George Allen and Unwin Ltd.

Robbins, Peter. 1982. *The British Hegelians*. London: Garland Publishing Inc.

Robinson, R. E., and J. A. Gallagher. 1953. The imperialism of free trade. *Economic History Review* 6, no. 1: 1–15.

———. 1961. *Africa and the Victorians: The official mind of imperialism*. London: Macmillan.

Robson, C. B. 1946. Francis Lieber's nationalism. *Journal of Politics* 8: 57–73.

Rogin, Michael. 1987. *Ronald Reagan, the movie, and other episodes in political demonology*. Berkeley: University of California Press.

Rosenau, James. 1973. *International studies and the social sciences*. Beverly Hills: Sage.

Rosenberg, Emily S. 1982. *Spreading the American dream: American economic and cultural expansion 1890–1945*. New York: Hill and Wang.

Rosow, Stephen J. 1990. Forms of internationalization: Representations of Western culture on a global scale. *Alternatives* 15, no. 3.

Ross, Dorothy. 1972. *G. Stanley Hall: The psychologist as prophet*. Chicago: University of Chicago Press.

———. 1991. *The origins of American social science*. Cambridge: Cambridge University Press.

Rostow, W. W. 1960. *The stages of economic growth: A non-communist manifesto.* Cambridge: Cambridge University Press.

Ruggie, John G. 1975. International responses to technology: Concepts and trends. *International Organization* 29, no. 3.

Said, Edward. 1978. *Orientalism.* New York: Pantheon.

Sayre, Frances B. 1919. *Experiments in international administration.* New York: Harper and Brothers.

Schmidt, Brian C. 1994. The historiography of academic international relations. *Review of International Studies* 20: 349–67.

———. 1998a. Lessons from the past: Reassessing the interwar disciplinary history of international relations. *International Studies Quarterly* 42, no. 3: 433–59.

———. 1998b. *The political discourse of anarchy: A disciplinary history of international relations.* Albany: State University of New York Press.

———. 2002a. Anarchy, world politics, and the birth of a discipline: American international relations, pluralist theory, and the myth of interwar idealism. *International Relations* 16 (April): 9–31.

———. 2002b. On the history and historiography of international relations. In *Handbook of international relations,* ed. Walter Carlsnaes, Thomas Risse, and Beth A. Simmons, 3–22. London: Sage Publications.

Schmidt, Hans. 1995 [1971]. *The United States occupation of Haiti 1915–1934.* New Brunswick: Rutgers University Press.

Schulzinger, Robert. 1984. *The wise men of foreign affairs: The history of the Council on Foreign Relations.* New York: Columbia University Press.

Schuman, Frederick L. 1937 [1933]. *International politics: An introduction to the western state system.* 2nd edition. New York: McGraw-Hill.

Sears, Louis. 1928. The human side of Francis Lieber. *South Atlantic Quarterly* 27: 42–61.

Shimazu, Naoko. 1998. *Japan, race, and equality: The racial equality proposal of 1919.* London: Routledge.

Siddiqi, Javed. 1995. *World health and world politics.* London: Hurst.

Skinner, Quentin. 1969. Meaning and understanding in the history of ideas. *History and Theory* 8, no. 1: 3–53.

Smith, Rogers. 1997. *Civic ideals: Conflicting visions of citizenship in U.S. history.* New Haven: Yale University Press.

Smith, Steve. 1992. The forty years' detour: The resurgence of normative theory in international relations. *Millennium: Journal of International Studies* 21: 489–506.

———. 1995. The self-images of a discipline: A genealogy of international relations theory. In *International relations theory today,* ed. Ken Booth and Steve Smith, 1–37. University Park: Pennsylvania State University Press.

———. 2000. The discipline of international relations: Still an American social science. *British Journal of Politics and International Relations* 2, no. 3: 374–402.

Snow, Alpheus Henry. 1902. *The administration of dependencies: A study of the evolution of the federal empire, with special reference to American colonial problems.* New York: G. P. Putnam's Sons.

———. 1908. Neutralization versus imperialism. *American Journal of International Law* 2 (July): 562–90.

Spater, George, and Ian Parsons. 1977. *A marriage of true minds: An intimate portrait of Leonard and Virginia Woolf.* London: Jonathan Cape and the Hogarth Press.

Spotts, Frederic. 1990. *Letters of Leonard Woolf.* London: Weidenfeld and Nicolson.

Stapleton, Julia. 1994. *Englishness and the study of politics: The social and political thought of Ernest Barker.* Cambridge: Cambridge University Press.

Suganami, Hidemi.1989. *Domestic analogy and world order proposals.* Cambridge: Cambridge University Press.

Sutcliffe, Bob. 2001. *Imperialism after imperialism.* London: I. B. Tauris.

Tamir, Yael. 1993. *Liberal nationalism.* Princeton: Princeton University Press.

Taylor, A. J. P. 1985. *The troublemakers: Dissent over foreign policy, 1792–1939.* Harmondsworth: Penguin Books.

Taylor, Charles. 1975. *Hegel.* Cambridge: Cambridge University Press.

ter Meulen, Jakob. 1917, 1929, 1940. *Der Gedanke der Internationalen Organisation in Seiner Entwicklung: 1300–1800, 1789–1870, and 1867–1889*, Volumes 1–3. Den Haag: Martinus Nijhoff.

Theis, Cameron G. 2002. Progress, history, and identity in international relations theory: The case of the idealist-realist debate. *European Journal of International Relations* 8, no. 2: 147–85.

Thomas, John. 1974. *The Institute of Pacific Relations: Asian scholars and American politics.* Seattle: University of Washington Press.

Times Literary Supplement. 1920. Review of *Empire and Commerce in Africa.* 9 February.

Todorov, Tzvetan. 1984. *The conquest of America: The question of the other.* New York: HarperPerennial.

Townshend, Jules. 1988. Introduction to Hobson's *Imperialism.* London: Unwin.

———. 1990. *J. A. Hobson.* Manchester: Manchester University Press.

Toynbee, Arnold. 1915. *Nationality and the war.* London: J. M. Dent and Sons.

———. 1967. *Acquaintances.* Oxford: Oxford University Press.

Trubowitz, Peter. 1998. *Defining the national interest: Conflict and change in American foreign policy.* Chicago: University of Chicago Press.

Union of Democratic Control. 1920a. Review of Empire and Commerce in Africa. *Common Sense*, 31 January.

———. 1920b. Review of *Empire and Commerce in Africa. Common Sense*, 27 March.

Vasquez, John A. 1998. *The power of power politics: From classical realism to neotraditionalism.* Cambridge: Cambridge University Press.

Vincent, Andrew, and Raymond Plant. 1984. *Philosophy, politics, and citizenship.* London: Basil Blackwell.

Vitalis, Robert. 2000. The graceful and generous liberal gesture: Making racism invisible in American international relations. *Millennium: Journal of International Studies* 29, no. 3: 331–356.

Von Eschen, Penny. 1997. *Race against empire: Black Americans and anticolonialism, 1937–1957.* Ithaca: Cornell University Press.

Waever, Ole. 1998. The sociology of a not so international discipline: American and European developments in international relations. *International Organization* 52: 687–727.

Walker, Rob. 1993. *Inside/outside: International relations as political theory.* Cambridge: Cambridge University Press.

Waltz, Kenneth N. 1959. *Man, the state, and war: A theoretical analysis.* New York: Columbia University Press.

———. 1979. *Theory of international politics.* New York: Random House.

Walworth, Arthur. 1986. *Wilson and his peacemakers: American diplomacy at the Paris peace conference, 1919.* New York: W. W. Norton.

Wellek, Rene W. 1931. *Immanuel Kant in England: 1793–1838.* Princeton: Princeton University Press.

Weston, Rubin Frances. 1972. *Racism in U.S. imperialism: The influence of racial assumptions on american foreign policy, 1893–1946.* Columbia: University of South Carolina Press.

Wheeler, Nick. 1992. Pluralist or solidarist conceptions of international society: Bull and Vincent on humanitarian intervention. *Millennium* 21: 463–87.

Wiener, Joel, ed. 1972. *Great Britain: Foreign policy and the span of empire, 1689–1971— A documentary history.* Four Volumes. New York: Chelsea House Publishers.

Wight, Martin. 1946. The realist's utopia. *Observer.* 21 July.

———. 1991. *International theory: The three traditions,* ed. Gabriele Wight and Brian Porter. Leicester: Leicester University Press.

Wilde, Jaap H. de. 1991. *Saved from oblivion: Interdependence theory in the first half of the 20th century.* Aldershot: Dartmouth Publishing Co.

Williams, William Appleman. 1969. *The roots of the modern American empire.* New York: Random House.

———. 1972. *The tragedy of American diplomacy,* New Edition. New York: W. W. Norton.

Wilson, Peter. 1995. Leonard Woolf and international government. In *Thinkers of the twenty years' crisis: Inter-war idealism reassessed,* ed. David Long and Peter Wilson, 122–60. Oxford: Clarendon Press.

———. 1996. The New Europe debate in wartime Britain. In *Visions of European unity,* ed. Philomena Murray and Paul Rich. London: Westview Press.

———. 1997. The international theory of Leonard Woolf: An exposition, analysis, and assessment in the light of his reputation as a utopian. PhD dissertation, University of London.

———. 1998. The myth of the "first great debate." *Review of International Studies* 24: 1–15.

———. 2000. Carr and his early critics: Responses to *The Twenty Years' Crisis, 1939–46*. In *E. H. Carr: A critical appraisal*, ed. Michael Cox, 165–97. London: Palgrave.

———. 2003. *The international thought of Leonard Woolf: A study in twentieth century idealism*. New York: Palgrave.

Wilson, Woodrow. 1887. The study of administration. *Political Science Quarterly* 2: 202–17.

Wood, Alan. 1990. *Hegel's ethical thought*. Cambridge: Cambridge University Press.

Woolf, Leonard. 1916. *International government*. London: George Allen and Unwin.

———. 1917. *The framework of a lasting peace*. London: George Allen and Unwin.

———. 1919. The league and the tropics. *The Covenant* 1, no. 1: 28–32.

———. 1920a. *Empire and commerce in Africa: A study of economic imperialism*. London: Labour Party Research Department and George Allen and Unwin.

———. 1920b. *Economic imperialism*. London: Swarthmore Press.

———. 1920c. *Mandates and empire*. London: League of Nations Union.

———. 1924. *Stories from the East*. London: Hogarth Press.

———. 1928. *Imperialism and civilization*. London: Hogarth Press.

———. 1940. *The war for peace*. London: Routledge.

———. 1943. A challenge to all of us: Two views on the responsibilities of colonial empire. *Listener*, 12 August 1943, 179–80.

———. 1960. *Sowing: An autobiography of the years 1880–1904*. London: Hogarth Press.

———. 1961. *Growing: An autobiography of the years 1904–1911*. London: Hogarth Press.

———. 1964. *Beginning again: An autobiography of the years 1911 to 1918*. London: Hogarth Press.

———. 1967. *Downhill all the way: An autobiography of the Years 1919–1939*. London: Hogarth Press.

———. 1969. *The journey not the arrival matters: An autobiography of the years 1939 to 1969*. London: Hogarth Press.

———. 1981 [1913]. *The village in the jungle*. Oxford: Oxford University Press.

Wright, Quincy. 1930. *Mandates under the League of Nations*. Chicago: University of Chicago Press.

———. 1952. Realism and idealism in international politics. *World Politics* 5: 116–28.

———. 1955. *The study of international relations*. New York: Appleton-Century-Crofts.

Zakaria, Fareed. 1998. *From wealth to power: The unusual origins of America's world role*. Princeton: Princeton University Press.

Zilliacus, Konni. 1946. *Mirror of the past: A history of secret diplomacy*. New York: Current Books.

Zimmern, Alfred. 1913. The ethics of empire. *The Round Table*. June.

———. 1916. Progress in industry. In *Progress and history*, ed. Francis Sydney. New York: Books for Libraries Press.

———. 1916b. Progress in government. In *Progress and history*, ed. Francis Sydney. New York: Books for Libraries Press.

———. 1917. *Some ethical aspects of international relations*. Oxford: Oxford University Press.

———. 1918. *Nationality and government*. New York: Robert M. McBride.

———. 1921. Political thought. In *The legacy of Greece*, ed. R. W. Livingstone. Oxford: Clarendon Press.

———. 1923. Nationalism and internationalism. *Foreign Affairs* 1: 115–26.

———. 1926. *The third British empire: Being a course of lectures delivered at Columbia University, New York*. London: Oxford University Press.

———. 1926a. The new international outlook: Two lectures at the Fenton Foundation of the University of Buffalo, Delivered in November. *The University of Buffalo Studies* 5, no. 1.

———. 1926b. The development of the international mind. In *Problems of peace: Lectures delivered at the Geneva Institute of International Relations*. Oxford: Oxford University Press.

———. 1927. *Learning and leadership: A study of the needs and possibilities of international intellectual co-operation*. Geneva: Intellectual Co-operation Section, League of Nations Press.

———. 1928a. Introduction. In *The war and democracy*, ed. R. W. Seton Watson, J. Dover Wilson, Alfred E. Zimmern, and Arthur Greenwood. London: Macmillan.

———. 1928b. German culture and the British Commonwealth. In *The war and democracy*, ed. R. W. Seton Watson, J. Dover Wilson, Alfred E. Zimmern, and Arthur Greenwood. London: Macmillan.

———. 1929. Nationalism and internationalism. In *The prospects of democracy*. London: Chatto and Windus.

———. 1931. *The study of International relations, An inaugural lecture, delivered before the University of Oxford, on 20 Feb., 1931*. Oxford: Oxford University Press.

———. 1936. *The League of Nations and the rule of law, 1918–1935*. London: Macmillan.

———. 1936. *The League of Nations and the rule of law*. London: Macmillan.

Zinn, Howard. 1980. *A people's history of the United States*. New York: Harper and Row.

Ziring, Lawrence. 1992. *The Middle East: A political dictionary*. Santa Barbara, CA: ABC-CLIO.

Contributors

David Clinton is Associate Professor in the Department of Political Science at Tulane University. He is the author of *The Two Faces of National Interest* (LSU Press, 1994) and *Tocqueville, Lieber, Bagehot: Liberalism Confronts the World* (Palgrave, 2003). He has published widely in journals such as *The Review of International Studies*, *The Review of Politics*, and *Presidential Studies Quarterly*.

Jan-Stefan Fritz is Scientific Officer in the International Bureau of the German Federal Ministry of Education and Research. He completed his PhD at the London School of Economics. He is the co-editor of *Value Pluralism, Normative Theory and International Relations* (MacMillan Press, 2000).

David Long is Associate Professor in the Norman Paterson School of International Affairs, Carleton University. He is the author of *Towards a New Liberal Internationalism: The International Theory of J. A. Hobson* (Cambridge, 1996), co-editor with Peter Wilson of *Thinkers of the Twenty Years' Crisis: Inter-War Idealism Reassessed* (Oxford University Press, 1995), and co-editor with Lucian Ashworth, *New Perspectives on International Functionalism* (MacMillan, 1999).

Jeanne Morefield is Assistant Professor of Politics at Whitman College. She is the author of *"Covenants Without Swords": Liberalism, Internationalism, and the Crisis of Community in the Political Theories of Alfred Zimmern and Gilbert Murray* (Princeton University Press, forthcoming).

Brian C. Schmidt is Assistant Professor of Political Science at Carleton University. He is the author of *The Political Discourse of Anarchy: A Disciplinary History of International Relations* (SUNY Press, 1998). He has published widely in journals such as *International Studies Quarterly*, *Review of International Studies*, and *Millennium*.

Robert Vitalis is Associate Professor of Political Science and Director of the Middle East Center, University of Pennsylvania. He is the author of *When Capitalists Collide: Business Conflict and the End of Empire in Egypt* (University of California Press, 1995) and editor with Madawi Al-Rasheed of *Counter Narratives: History, Society, and Politics in Saudi Arabia and Yemen* (Palgrave, forthcoming). He has published numerous articles in journals such as *Diplomatic History*, *International Journal of Middle East Studies*, *Arab Studies*, and *Millennium*.

Peter Wilson is Senior Lecturer in International Relations at the London School of Economics. He has published articles and book chapters on the history of international theory, especially on the interwar period. He is the author of *The International Theory of Leonard Woolfe* and co-author with Spyros Economides, *The Politics of International Economic Relations* (I. B. Tauris, 2001), and co-editor with David Long, *Thinkers of the Twenty Years' Crisis* (Oxford, 1995).

SUNY series in Global Politics

James N. Rosenau, Editor

LIST OF TITLES

American Patriotism in a Global Society—Betty Jean Craige

The Political Discourse of Anarchy: A Disciplinary History of International Relations—Brian C. Schmidt

From Pirates to Drug Lords: The Post—Cold War Caribbean Security Environment—Michael C. Desch, Jorge I. Dominguez, and Andres Serbin (eds.)

Collective Conflict Management and Changing World Politics—Joseph Lepgold and Thomas G. Weiss (eds.)

Zones of Peace in the Third World: South America and West Africa in Comparative Perspective—Arie M. Kacowicz

Private Authority and International Affairs—A. Claire Cutler, Virginia Haufler, and Tony Porter (eds.)

Harmonizing Europe: Nation-States within the Common Market—Francesco G. Duina

Economic Interdependence in Ukrainian-Russian Relations—Paul J. D'Anieri

Leapfrogging Development? The Political Economy of Telecommunications Restructuring—J. P. Singh

States, Firms, and Power: Successful Sanctions in United States Foreign Policy—George E. Shambaugh

Approaches to Global Governance Theory—Martin Hewson and Timothy J. Sinclair (eds.)

After Authority: War, Peace, and Global Politics in the Twenty-First Century—Ronnie D. Lipschutz

Pondering Postinternationalism: A Paradigm for the Twenty-First Century?—Heidi H. Hobbs (ed.)

Beyond Boundaries? Disciplines, Paradigms, and Theoretical Integration in International Studies—Rudra Sil and Eileen M. Doherty (eds.)

Why Movements Matter: The West German Peace Movement and U.S. Arms Control Policy—Steve Breyman

International Relations—Still an American Social Science? Toward Diversity in International Thought—Robert M. A. Crawford and Darryl S. L. Jarvis (eds.)

Which Lessons Matter? American Foreign Policy Decision Making in the Middle East, 1979–1987—Christopher Hemmer (ed.)

Hierarchy Amidst Anarchy: Transaction Costs and Institutional Choice—Katja Weber

Counter-Hegemony and Foreign Policy: The Dialectics of Marginalized and Global Forces in Jamaica—Randolph B. Persaud

Global Limits: Immanuel Kant, International Relations, and Critique of World Politics—Mark F. N. Franke

Power and Ideas: North-South Politics of Intellectual Property and Antitrust—Susan K. Sell

Money and Power in Europe: The Political Economy of European Monetary Cooperation—Matthias Kaelberer

Agency and Ethics: The Politics of Military Intervention—Anthony F. Lang Jr.

Life After the Soviet Union: The Newly Independent Republics of the Transcaucasus and Central Asia—Nozar Alaolmolki

Theories of International Cooperation and the Primacy of Anarchy: Explaining U. S. International Monetary Policy-Making After Bretton Woods—Jennifer Sterling-Folker

Information Technologies and Global Politics: The Changing Scope of Power and Governance—James N. Rosenau and J. P. Singh (eds.)

Technology, Democracy, and Development: International Conflict and Cooperation in the Information Age—Juliann Emmons Allison (ed.)

The Arab-Israeli Conflict Transformed: Fifty Years of Interstate and Ethnic Crises—Hemda Ben-Yehuda and Shmuel Sandler

Systems of Violence: The Political Economy of War and Peace in Colombia—Nazih Richani

Debating the Global Financial Architecture—Leslie Elliot Armijo

Political Space: Frontiers of Change and Governance in a Globalizing World—Yale Ferguson and R. J. Barry Jones (eds.)

Crisis Theory and World Order: Heideggerian Reflections—Norman K. Swazo

Political Identity and Social Change: The Remaking of the South African Social Order—Jamie Frueh

Social Construction and the Logic of Money: Financial Predominance and International Economic Leadership—J. Samuel Barkin

What Moves Man: The Realist Theory of International Relations and Its Judgment of Human Nature—Annette Freyberg-Inan

Democratizing Global Politics: Discourse Norms, International Regimes, and Political Community—Rodger A. Payne and Nayef H. Samhat

Collective Preventative Diplomacy: A Study of International Management—Barry H. Steiner

International Relations Under Risk: Framing State Choice—Jeffrey D. Berejikian

Globalization and the Environment: Greening Global Political Economy—Gabriela Kutting

Imperialism and Nationalism in the Discipline of International Relations—David Long and Brian C. Schmidt (eds.)

Index

Aberystwyth, University of Wales, 6,
   17, 94, 164
Africa, 65, 72–73, 82, 125–127,
   129–130, 138–140, 161–162,
   177–178
American Political Science Association,
   14, 16, 43, 46, 51, 59, 163, 171
Angell, Norman, 54
Ashworth, Lucian, 4–5

Bell, Duncan, 7
Berlin Conference, 25
Bismarck, 125–126
Buell, Raymond Leslie, 15, 20,
   159–162, 166, 171, 174–176, 178
Bull, Hedley, 41
Bunche, Ralph, 161, 178
Burgess, John, 46, 161, 167

Carr, E.H., 6, 10, 21n. 2, 47, 93, 110,
   119, 136
Chamberlain, Joseph, 124, 126
Chicago, University of, 166, 173
China, 17, 28, 51–52, 54, 56–57, 67,
   91n. 10, 131
civilization: Hobson on, 76–80, 82–86;
   Lieber on, 28, 36–39, 40–41;
   Reinsch on, 46, 49, 52–54, 56, 58, 62
Cobden, Richard, 74–75

Columbia University, 23, 46
colonial administration,
   55–56, 58–64
colonial government, 16–17
colonialism, 12, 43, 52, 56–57; and
   Hobson, 74–76
commonwealth, 18, 36, 39, 95–96,
   106–113
Coolidge, Archibald Cary, 173–175
cooperative internationalism, 19,
   141–142, 144, 155
cosmopolitanism, 11, 18, 48, 75
Council on Foreign Relations,
   173–174
Cuba, 32, 58, 61

development, 60–61, 79–81, 86, 89
disciplinary history, 1–6, 24, 44–47,
   118–120
Doty, Roxanne Lynn, 49, 160
Du Bois, W.E.B., 6, 14, 20, 168–169,
   171–173

education, 63, 77, 84–86, 88
Ely, Richard, 50, 61
empire, 2, 11–13, 54, 72, 82, 95, 98,
   160, 163, 165–167
English School, 10, 41, 44
expansionism, 55–56, 62, 94

Fabian paternalism, 18, 76, 139–140
Foreign Affairs, 20, 173–175
Foreign Policy Association, 175–176
Fox, William T.R., 176–177
free trade, 37, 41, 57, 74, 81
functionalism, 5, 19, 67, 146, 154,
    157n. 3

Germany, 31, 50, 98
Geneva Institute of International
    Affairs, 14, 94
Goldmann, Kjell, 3, 7
Green, T.H., 94, 96, 101, 105–107
Groom, A.J.R., 9, 52
Grotius, Hugo, 38, 41, 53
Gunnell, John G., 8, 180n. 2

Hardt and Negri's *Empire*, 2, 12–13
Hegel, 53, 94, 98
Hindess, Barry, 12–13, 72
historiography, *see* disciplinary history
Hobson, J.A., 14–15, 19; and anti-
    imperialism, 17, 73–76, 142–43; and
    discipline of IR, 6; on imperialism,
    71–90; on liberalism, 72–75, 77–78,
    88, 90n.; on liberal internationalism,
    73–4; on nations and nationalism,
    75, 77–79, 86; and paternalism, 17,
    72–3, 84–90; Reinsch review of, 55;
    and science, 147–48. *See also* civiliza-
    tion; international government
Hoffmann, Stanley, 163

idealism, 3–6, 14–15, 136–137. *See also*
    idealist-realist debate; utopianism
idealist-realist debate, 1–5, 9, 15, 19, 47
imperialism, 1–2, 9–15, 25–32, 48,
    53–58, 71–90, 123–124, 160
Institute of Pacific Relations, 177–178
institutionalism, 10, 14, 48, 66, 69
interdependence, 29, 36–37, 40, 48,
    65–67, 79–80, 153
international administration, 150–152
international government, 80–84, 101,
    153–155
International Labour Office, 67

international law, 40–41, 53
international organization, 17, 34, 41,
    48, 66–67, 81–84, 87, 141, 145. *See
    also* public international unions
internationalism, 1–2, 9–15, 19, 48,
    64–68, 73–75
interwar period, 3–4, 14–15
Ireland, Alleyne, 59–60, 166

Journal of Race Development, 6, 20, 161,
    163, 171–173

Kahler, Miles, 4
Kant, Immanuel, 8, 35–36, 53
Koebner, Richard, 12
Kymlicka, Will, 112–113

League of Nations, 13, 17, 68, 80, 82,
    87, 93, 100–101, 104, 109–110, 174
liberal internationalism, 5, 13, 73–74,
    81, 89–90
liberalism, 12; and Hobson, 71–75, 77,
    78, 90n. 1; and Lieber, 40; and
    Reinsch, 50, 54; and Zimmern, 18, 93,
    96–99
Lieber, Francis 15–16, 23–42, 52; back-
    ground, 23–24; on commonwealth,
    36, 39; on imperialism, 25–32, 39; on
    internationalism, 33–39; on nations
    and nationalism, 16, 24, 29–32,
    34–35, 40; on organic theory of the
    state, 26–7, 32, 35; and race,
    27–30, 38
Lippmann, Walter, 54
Lugard, Sir Frederick, 125–126

Machiavelli, 8, 9, 47–48, 53
Marxism, 11, 21n. 4
Mehta, Uday Singh, 12–13, 72, 95
Mexican War, 31, 40
Mill, J.S., 73–75, 87–88, 90n. 1, 95
Mitrany, David, 19, 67, 154; on inter-
    national administration, 151–153;
    and cooperation, 148–149; role of
    technical experts, 146
Moon, Parker T., 14, 15, 20, 166–167

Morgenthau, Hans J., 10, 17, 47, 150
Morrison, Toni, 163–164
Muirhead, Henry, 96–97

NAACP, 168
nationalism: Hobson on 75–79; and
imperialism, 20, 48, 52–6, 65; and
internationalism, 53, 65, 68; Lieber
on, 24, 29–34; Reinsch on, 48,
52–53; Zimmern on, 93, 104,
107–08
Nietzsche, 53–54
nonintervention, 74, 80–81

Olson, William C., 9, 52
Open Door Policy, 54, 57
Oxford University, 100; liberalism at,
96–98
organicism, 77, 98, 101. *See also* the
state
paternalism: Hobson on 17, 71–75;
Reinsch on 44; Woolf on 18, 140;
Zimmern on 95, 98, 105

Philippines, 58, 62–64
political science, 3, 14–15; and Lieber
23, 29; and Reinsch 43, 46, 50–51,
59–61, 67
postcolonialism, 11, 12–13, 21n. 4, 72
public international unions, 5, 17, 44,
48, 66–67, 151

race, 5, 20, 46, 160–161, 167; Lieber on
27–30, 38; Reinsch on 55, 64
realism, 5, 10–11, 41, 47–48
regimes, international, 14, 19, 40, 44,
48, 66, 156
Reinsch, Paul S., 16–17; background,
49–51, 161; on colonial administration, 43–44, 49, 51, 55–6, 58–64; and
disciplinary history, 44–49; and idealism and realism, 47, 65–67; on
imperialism, 16, 48, 53–58; on internationalism, 19, 48, 64–68, 148; on
nationalism, 16, 48, 52–53; and
political science, 43, 50–51, 59–61,

67; on role of technical experts,
145–46. *See also* civilization; race
Rosenau, James, 164
Ross, Dorothy, 165–166, 171
Round Table Society, 94, 105–106, 110
Royal Institute of International
Affairs, 94
Ruggie, John, 156

Schuman, Frederick, 162
science, 19, 29, 83, 141–144, 149–150,
162–163; and technology, 33, 36, 66,
78–79
Shotwell, James T., 177
slavery, 27–28, 31
Smith, Steve, 3, 48
state, the, 10–12, 18, 25–32, 94, 122–123
Social Darwinism, 76, 84, 147, 167
sovereignty, 66–67, 95
Spanish American War, 43, 58, 69n. 10

Tamir, Yael, 112–113
Thucydides, 8–9
tradition, 8–9
Toynbee, Arnold, 94, 96

United Nations, 11–12, 80
utilitarianism, 77, 79

Waever, Ole, 7–8
Walker, Rob, 8
Waltz, Kenneth N., 10, 71
Whig history, 162–163
Wight, Martin, 41, 44
Williams, William Appleman, 57
Wilson, Woodrow, 17, 24, 51, 61, 67,
150, 174
World Trade Organization, 41
Woolf, Leonard, background, 117,
121–122; and causes of economic
imperialism, 122–128; and conse-
quences of economic imperialism,
128–132; on interdependence 153;
on international administration, 151;
on international government, 155.
See also Fabian paternalism; idealism.

World Politics, 172
Wright, Quincy, 47, 173

Zimmern, Alfred, 12–13, 17–18, 164,
    168; on commonwealth, 18, 95–96,
106–113; on internationalism,
100–104, 112–113; on liberalism,
98–99; on nationalism, 93, 104,
107–108. *See also* commonwealth;
liberalism; nationalism.